Basketball
Officials Guidebook
Volume III

NFHS Mechanics 2003-05
For a Crew of Two Officials

by Bill Topp, Editor, *Referee* Magazine
and Keith Zirbel, Assistant Editor, *Referee* Magazine

BASKETBALL OFFICIALS GUIDEBOOK
Volume III
NFHS Mechanics 2003-05
For a Crew of Two Officials

by Bill Topp, Editor, *Referee* magazine
and Keith Zirbel, Assistant Editor, *Referee* magazine

Graphics and layout by Matt Bowen, Graphic Designer, *Referee* magazine

Copyright © 2003 by Referee Enterprises, Inc., P.O. Box 161, Franksville, Wis. 53126.
First printing 1997
Second printing 1998
Third printing 2001
Fourth printing 2003

Printed in the United States of America

ISBN 1-58208-042-9

Table of Contents

Acknowledgments

Special thanks to Matt Bowen, *Referee* publication design manager, for his efforts and talents. The visual effects that set this book apart are the result of his dedication, hard work and ability. Keith Zirbel, *Referee* assistant editor, also deserves credit for the updates in this book.

The following people provided invaluable input and editing prowess into the first edition, which is carried through to this updated version: John Katzler, Mt. Prospect, Ill., longtime high school and college official and *Referee* "By the Rules" columnist; Steven Ellinger, Houston, Texas, veteran prep and NCAA official and *Referee* contributor; and Dave Libbey, El Cajon, Calif., NCAA men's Division I Final Four veteran. Their commentary and attention to detail made this book much better.

Bill Topp
Editor
Referee magazine

Introduction

Educating basketball referees has changed a lot in the past two decades. In the 1980s the association training officer stood at the front of the room and read the rulebook to the aspiring officials. Boring!

But with new technology and new graphics, *Referee* is able to bring you something much more exciting than a dull recitation of the rules. We are particularly proud of this book because it is the only one we know of that focuses exclusively on the mechanics you need to whistle a better game.

Every two years, the NFHS publishes changes to their mechanics manual. *Referee* and the NFHS are working together closely to make sure you have current, detailed information.

Thus, in this *Volume III*, we decided to focus entirely on high school officials, where two-person mechanics is still the norm. That focus means more detail. There are no more comparisons to NCAA mechanics in this book because, simply put, there aren't many officials out there using two-person NCAA mechanics anymore.

The end result means this book is more in-tune with what the NFHS — and ultimately your state association and assigners — want done.

We hope you learn as much reading it as we did writing it. Drop me a note and let me know what you think — btopp@referee.com.

Bill Topp
Editor
Referee magazine

Chapter 1

NFHS Mechanics Changes

NFHS mechanic changes through 2003-05

The following are changes to the high school official's manual for a crew of two officials. Since the NFHS publishes the official's manuals every two seasons, these changes apply to the 2003-04 and 2004-05 seasons.

1. Kicking signal
A new signal for the violation of a kicked ball was added to the signal chart. The addition of the signal allows officials to better communicate with players, coaches, team benches and the scorer's table. The new mechanic to signal the violation is a straight leg, kicking motion forward about one foot.

For more information, see "Kick signal" p. 49.

2. Non-calling official informs coach
When a player fouls out, the non-calling official notifies the head coach, the player and then starts the 30-second substitution interval. Previously, the calling official handled those duties.

For more information, see "Reporting Disqualifications" p. 282.

3. Halftime Positions
Now at halftime, the officials are positioned halfway between the farthest point of the center circle and the sideline opposite the scorer's table.

For more information, see "Court positioning: halftime" p. 109.

4. Timeout Positions
The timeout positions for officials for 60- and 30-second timeouts have changed. The administering official will stand on the block nearest the throw-in spot opposite the team benches during 60-second timeouts and intermissions between quarters and stand at the top of the near three-point arc during 30-second timeouts. The non-administering official is at the same location on the other end of the court.

For more information, see "Court positioning: NFHS 60-second timeout" p. 110 and "Court positioning: NFHS 30-second timeout" p. 111.

5. Bird Dog Optional
The "bird dog" foul signal (point to the fouler) need only be used for clarification.

For more information, see "Signaling at the spot" p. 39.

6. Ball-side primary changed
The coverage area for the ball-side lead is now extended to the area between the three-point arc and the closest lane line, below the free-throw line extended. Prior to that change, the lead only had coverage up to the lane line — basically "in the paint" but not beyond it — which impacted who had coverage when post players were just outside the lane. Now, the lead is clearly responsible when ball-side.

For more information, see "Court coverage: basic frontcourt responsibilities" p. 73.

NFHS mechanics changes through 2001-03

A look back

The following is a look back at some changes to the high school official's manual for a crew of two officials. Since the NFHS publishes the official's manuals every two seasons, these changes began with the 2001-02 seasons. Only those changes that are still applicable are noted.

1. Signals
Two new signals were added to the signals chart.

a. 60-second timeout. (Note: The NFHS changed the term "full" timeout to "60-second" timeout to help differentiate between that and a 30-second timeout.) When indicating a 60-second timeout, the reporting official shall place the fingertips of both hands together in front of the chest and spread the hands outward past shoulder width, extending both arms parallel to the floor with palms extending and facing the scorer's table.

b. Start the clock. The committee also approved a "start the clock" signal. The signal is used by the reporting official to the timer to indicate when a timeout period should start and when the 30-second substitution limit should start following notification of a player's disqualification (for example, a player's fifth foul). To use the signal, point your index finger out at the timer and say, "Please start the 30-second clock."

For more information, see "Signal chart," p. 48.

2. Coverage areas changed
The committee made slight adjustments to the coverage areas for officials using two-person crews. The trail official's primary coverage area is extended to include the area between the three-point arc and the nearest free throw lane line, below the free-throw line extended, when the ball is in that area.

Previously, the lead official was responsible for on-ball coverage across the lane and beyond the lead's far lane line up to the three-point arc when the ball was below the free-throw line extended. That meant the lead was looking across the lane — and likely through the bodies of lane congestion — to cover an area beyond the far lane line.

For more information, see "Court coverage: basic frontcourt responsibilities," p. 73.

3. "First horn"
At the warning signal to end a timeout (60-second or 30-second), the officials will take a step or two toward the team huddle and notify the coaches (bench personnel) by raising an index finger and saying, "First horn." The officials then move toward their proper positions to resume play. That procedural change is designed to get the ball back in play more quickly following a timeout.

For more information, see "Signal chart," p. 48.

Chapter 2

Definition of Terms

Definition of terms

The following terms are used throughout the book. Although many of the terms will seem self-explanatory, a brief review will insure complete understanding.

Backside — Refers to the area in the lane when a player moves away from the lead into the lane.

Balance the floor — Refers to the positions of both the lead and the trail. When the floor is balanced, the officials are near their respective sidelines. That is the normal set position in two-person mechanics. The floor becomes unbalanced when the lead moves ball side.

Ball side — See "Visual definition," p. 17.

CCA — Collegiate Commissioners' Association. The CCA produces the official basketball manual for the NCAA.

Close down — Refers to the movement by the lead along the endline from the sideline toward the near lane line.

Dead-ball officiating — Activity during the time immediately after the ball becomes dead. Good dead-ball officials don't stop officiating when the ball is dead. They continue to watch the players and prevent problems.

Drop pass — A drop pass is thrown from a perimeter player to a post player, usually from the three-point arc area to the low block area. It is a high arcing pass that is usually thrown over a defender fronting the post (sometimes referred to as a "dump" pass).

Free-throw line extended — An imaginary line drawn from the free-throw line out to the sidelines. The area around the free-throw line extended is a significant guideline for two-person officiating coverage and movements.

Freeze your eyes, not your feet — Refers to the responsibility and technique for the non-calling official when a foul is called. *Freeze your eyes* means it's your responsibility to watch all the players during the dead ball while your partner reports the foul (the eyes actually should scan the player area, so they're not actually "frozen" on one player). *Not your feet* means you can begin moving to your new position and prepare players for the ensuing play while watching them carefully.

Fronting the post — A defensive technique designed to prohibit passes into the low block area. The defensive player is positioned directly in front of the post player between the perimeter player with the ball and the basket.

Inside-out look — See "Visual definition," p. 19.

Lane line — Refers to the free-throw lane lines perpendicular to the endline which intersect the free-throw line and the endline and run parallel to the sideline. During free throws, players are lined up in lane spaces along the lane line.

Lead — The lead official in a halfcourt setting is normally positioned outside the endline and is primarily responsible for play under the basket and in the lane area. See "Visual definition," p. 17.

Lead moving to trail — Refers to the movements and changed positions of the lead during a transition play. For example, when a play moves from one end of the court to the other, the lead moves from that position to the trail position at the other end of the court. See "Visual definition," p. 17.

Low block — The area along the free-throw lane line closest to the basket but not in the lane. It is usually marked on the court with a solid square or "block."

NFHS — Short for the National Federation of State High School Associations. The NFHS is the governing body for high school athletics and produces the official basketball manual for the NFHS. The NFHS manual is used throughout high school basketball and is referred to often in this book.

New lead — Refers to the official's new position during transition. The trail becomes the "new lead" when moving to the other end of the court in transition. See "Visual definition," p. 17.

New trail — Refers to the official's new position during transition. The lead becomes the "new trail" when moving to the other end of the court in transition. See "Visual definition," p. 17.

Opposite — The side of the court opposite the table side. See "Visual definition," p. 17.

Perimeter area — The perimeter area is the area in a halfcourt setting away from the basket nearer the three-point arc.

Perimeter player — Perimeter players, usually small forwards and guards, move around the perimeter to establish position. Perimeter players are usually good shooters and are effective drop passers.

Player designations — For the case studies, player designations are assigned. ① is the point guard, usually a smaller player who handles the ball, is a good passer and plays primarily on the perimeter. ② is another guard, usually a smaller player who also handles the ball, is a good shooter and plays primarily on the perimeter. ③ is a small forward, usually an average sized player who penetrates and shoots well and plays mostly on the perimeter. ④ is a power forward, usually a large player who posts up on the low block and is a good rebounder. ⑤ is a center, usually the largest player on the court who posts up on the low block and is a good rebounder.

Post area — The post area is around the low block and in the bottom half of the lane nearest the basket.

Post player — Post players, usually centers and forwards, position themselves in the post area. Offensive players try to "post up" defensive players in the post area to receive passes from the perimeter.

Preventive officiating — Refers to actions by officials who prevent problems from occurring by talking to players and coaches. Preventive officiating is often related to dead-ball officiating.

Referee the defense — A strategy and philosophy that has the official focusing on the defensive player's movements to correctly judge contact situations.

Screen — A legal action by a player who delays or prevents an opponent from reaching a desired position (also referred to as a "pick").

Selling the call — Placing emphasis on a call with louder voice and whistle, and slightly more demonstrative signals. Selling only occurs on close calls and should be used sparingly. It is designed to help the call gain acceptance and show the official's decisiveness.

Skip pass — A pass thrown across the perimeter from one side of the court to the other. The pass usually starts from one free-throw-line-extended area to the other free-throw-line-extended area, "skipping" a player positioned near the top of the key.

Spacing — See "Visual definitions," p. 20-21.

Stay deep — Refers to an official's position on the court away from the play, usually the trail in a halfcourt setting. When the trail stays deep, the trail stays out of the passing lanes and avoids interfering with the play.

Straightlining — See "Visual definition," p. 22.

Strong side — When coaches describe plays, the strong side is the side of the court where the ball is. However, in this book, the strong side refers to the side of the court that the lead is positioned on.

Sweep the floor — Refers to looking over the entire court (players, bench areas, scorer's table, partner) before administering a throw-in or a free-throw.

Swing pass — A swing pass is a pass from one side of the court to the other. Most times, a swing pass involves three players moving the ball from one free-throw-line-extended area to the top of the key to the other free-throw-line-extended area.

Table side — The side of the court on which the scorer's and timer's table is located. See "Visual definition," p. 17.

Top of the key — The top of the key is the area near the top of the free-throw circle.

Trail — In a halfcourt setting the trail official is positioned near the sideline opposite the lead and is responsible for perimeter play, including the outer part of the frontcourt. The trail is also primarily responsible for the backcourt. See "Visual definition," p. 17.

Trail moving to lead —Refers to the movements and changed positions of the trail during a transition play. For example, when a play moves from one end of the court to the other, the trail moves from that position to the lead position at the other end of the court. See "Visual definition," p. 17.

Weak side — When coaches describe plays, the weak side is the side of the court opposite the ball. However, in this book, the weak side refers to the side of the court opposite the lead.

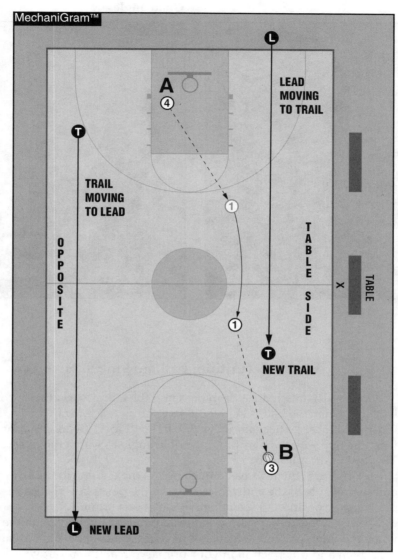

Visual definition: definition of terms

As with anyone learning new terms — the jargon — there might be some confusion. *Referee* wants to clear up any possible confusion by graphically showing you how the terms relate as the ball transitions down the floor.

When the ball is in position marked by "A," both the lead official (off the court at the top of the MechaniGram) and trail official have balanced the court — one is table side and one is opposite.

As the shot goes up and the other team gets the rebound and passes or dribbles down the court, those same officials keep those same relative names — trail moving to lead and lead moving to trail. Table side and opposite do not change.

With the ball settled in the other halfcourt (the ball has moved to the position marked by "B"), the officials switch their positions relative to the teams — the official who was the trail is now the "new lead" and the official who was the lead is now the "new trail."

The exact moment that you no longer think of yourself as "new trail" and begin to think of yourself as simply trail is open to personal feel. Perhaps after a pass or two by the offensive team is good timing.

Bad angle

Good angle

Visual definition: ball side mechanics

The lead must anticipate a drop pass into the low post on the opposite lane line when the ball is below the free-throw line extended (see "Lead must use ball side mechanics," p. 85). In PlayPic A, the lead is near the lane line opposite the play. It is a terrible angle to watch the post play. The lead is straightlined.

In PlayPic B, the lead has moved across the endline to the lane line on the trail side of the court to clearly see the post play. The lead is in a much better position to see potential violations or fouls.

Keep your head and shoulders turned toward the players in the lane when moving. Remember, you still have responsibilities for watching the screen and other action in your primary area. If you put your head down and sprint across the lane to the new spot you will miss off-ball contact. Move with dispatch, but move under control and with your eyes on your primary off-ball area. If the ball moves out of the post area, simply move back to your original position to balance the floor with the trail.

The lead moves for two reasons: The lead is in a better position to see the play clearly (if the lead stayed on the off-ball side, the lead would be looking through bodies and guessing) and the lead is closer to the play, which helps sell the call or no-call. Perception is important and if you look like you're closer to the play and in good position, your ruling has a better chance of being accepted.

From this set up

Use this movement

Avoid this movement

Visual definition: 'inside-out' look

The trail must avoid straightlining on a shot attempt from the wing. A simple one- or two-step adjustment *toward the center of the court* gives you the proper angle.

In PlayPic A, the trail is straightlined on the play and must move to see potential contact on or by the shooter. In PlayPic B, the trail moves one or two steps toward the center of the court. From there, the trail has a great look at the defensive player lunging at the shooter.

You must fight the urge to run around the entire play toward your sideline, using six steps or more and wasting precious time. By the time you run around the play, the offensive player could take a shot (was the shooter's foot on or behind the three-point arc?), violate or have been fouled, and you may not have seen it (PlayPics C, D, E, F).

After adjusting one or two steps toward the center of the court to improve your angle, watch the rest of the shooting action from there, including the follow-through and landing after a jump shot. After you've taken care of that responsibility, you can start moving toward your sideline and endline, working for your next good angle on rebounding action.

Too close

Good spacing

Too close

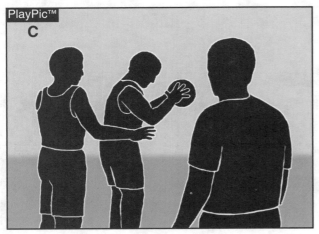

Good spacing

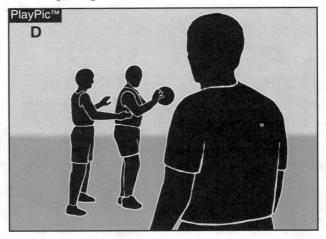

Visual definition: spacing for the lead

Lead officials need to back off the endline to give proper visual perception. You must create "spacing" on each play that is near the endline. Spacing is the distance between you and the play. If you're too close or too far, you can't see the play clearly.

When you get too close to a play, your view of the play is distorted. Your depth perception is off and your field of vision is narrow.

In most small gyms, the lead's spacing ability is limited. When a wall is close behind you, back up as far as you can without leaning up against the wall. If you still feel there's not enough room, adjust toward the sideline to create more spacing. You might be giving up a great angle, but you're seeing the whole play better.

What's the right distance off the endline for the lead?

It depends on your field of vision needs on a particular play. If the play is directly in front of you and you are on-ball, move about five-10 feet off the endline. If the players are away from you and you're off-ball, position yourself about two to five feet off the endline. Rarely should the lead be directly on the endline to view a play. Ultimately, you want to be close enough to give the perception you can see the play from where you are and far enough to keep the proper perspective.

In PlayPic A, the lead is too close. In PlayPic B, the lead creates proper spacing by backing up. PlayPics C and D show a similar play with the lead's view. In PlayPic C, the lead is too close. In PlayPic D, the lead creates proper spacing by backing up.

Too close

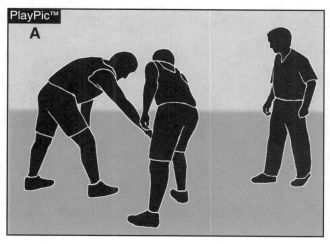

Good spacing

Too close

Good spacing

Visual definition: spacing for the trail

Officiating with a crew of two officials requires a lot of movement. That movement offers better court coverage, but sometimes the movements of the official and the players cause the official to be too close to the action.

"Spacing" is the distance between you and the play. If you're too close or too far, you can't see the play clearly.

When you get too close to a play, your view of the play is distorted. Your depth perception is off and your field of vision is narrow. It's kind of like reading this book when it's two inches from your nose vs. at normal reading length. You can see it a lot better when it's further away from your face. The same principles hold true on the court. Also, if you're too close, you're more likely to get in the way by colliding with players or being in passing lanes. You risk impacting the play or causing injuries to the players and yourself.

If you're too far, you're not in position to see the play. This time it's like reading a book that is across the room.

Even if you could see the play clearly, you're not going to be able to convince anyone you did see the play right when you're so far away. The perception is that you were too far away to see it.

What's the right distance for the trail? It depends on where the play is. If the play is in the immediate area, position yourself around 10-15 feet from the play. If the play is closer to the far sideline, 20-25 feet, depending on defensive pressure. With more pressure, 15-20 feet. Those distances are only guidelines. Ultimately, you want to be close enough to give the perception you can see the play from where you are and far enough to keep the proper perspective and stay out of the way.

In PlayPic A, the trail is too close. In PlayPic B, the trail creates proper spacing by backing up. PlayPics C and D show a similar play with the trail's view. In PlayPic C, the trail is too close. In PlayPic D, the trail creates proper spacing by backing up.

Straightlined

Good angle

Straightlined

Good angle

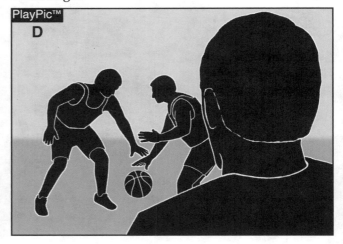

Visual definition: straightlining

"Straightlining" occurs when your view of a play is obstructed by the players themselves. In effect, you are in a straight line with the players and have no angle to see between them.

A one- or two-step move left or right eliminates straightlining. Keep your head up and continually watch the play when moving.

The most common straightlining concerns:

1. Offensive player with the ball with defensive pressure. You must avoid straightlining so that you can see between the players and correctly judge the play. Did the defender slap the dribbler's arm? Did the offensive player push off on the drive? Did the defender establish legal guarding position?

2. Low post play. To correctly officiate action around the low blocks — on-ball or off-ball — you must avoid

straightlining. Coupled with proper spacing, you can judge whether or not the offensive player pushed off to receive the drop pass, the defender pushed the offensive post player in the lower back or if the offensive player hooked the defender on the spin move to the basket.

3. Screens. Get good angles to see screens. Avoid straightlining and you'll see if the screen was legally set, if the defender fouled while pushing through the screen or if the screener fouled by extended a leg, hip or elbow.

Those decisions and others are nearly impossible if you're straightlined.

In PlayPic A, the trail is straightlined. In PlayPic B, the trail moves one or two steps to get a better angle. PlayPics C and D show a similar play with the official's view. In PlayPic C, the official is straightlined. In PlayPic D, the official has a better angle.

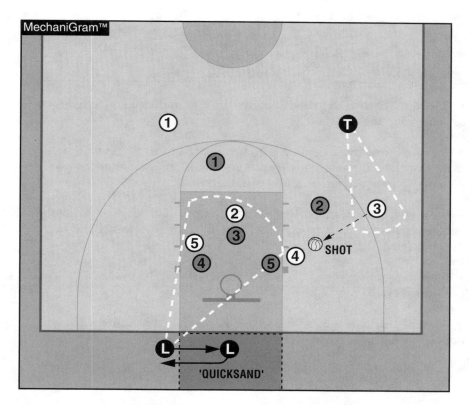

Visual definition: avoid 'quicksand'

"Quicksand" is a danger area for the lead. Quicksand is the area directly underneath the basket. Never position yourself directly under the basket because you can't see much of anything from there. You're straightlined on most rebounding angles. You might as well fall into the quicksand and let your partner call the whole floor!

The lead can get caught in the quicksand when moving ball side as a player takes a shot. The lead moves ball side anticipating a drop pass into the post. Sometimes what we anticipate doesn't happen. A shot is quickly taken while the lead is moving ball side. Now the lead must get out of the quicksand and establish good rebounding angles.

When caught in the quicksand, the lead has two choices: continue through the lane area and get ball side or go back where the lead came from and balance the floor. In most situations, opt for backing up and balancing the floor. But, if you're almost through the lane already when the shot is taken, continue through the lane for a ball side look. Why? Fewer steps forward as opposed to many steps backward.

In the MechaniGram, the lead begins moving ball side to watch low post action. When the lead is halfway through the lane, ③ shoots. If the lead stayed put, the lead is straightlined on all rebounding angles and gets caught in the quicksand. Instead, after ③ takes the shot, the lead decides to balance the floor. The lead is again in good position to watch rebounding action.

How does the lead know a shot is being attempted if the lead is looking off-ball? Read the off-ball players' movements. *Do not watch the shooter and ignore off-ball coverage.*

Off-ball players in the lane area will begin to obtain rebound positioning when a shot is airborne. Look for players watching the flight of the ball. Watch for offensive players moving to rebound spots in anticipation of a miss. Look for defensive players boxing out offensive rebounders. There are plenty of off-ball clues that let you know a shot is on the way.

Definitions

- The normal halfcourt set position for the lead and trail is referred to as "balancing the floor."

- The free-throw line extended is an imaginary line drawn from the free-throw line out to the sidelines. It is a significant guideline for two-person officiating coverage and movements.

- The lead official in a halfcourt setting is normally positioned along the endline and is primarily responsible for play under the basket and in the lane area.

- The strong side refers to the side of the court that the lead is positioned on.

- The trail official in a halfcourt setting is positioned near the sideline opposite the lead and is responsible for perimeter play.

- The weak side refers to the side of the court opposite the lead.

Quiz

Without referring back, you should be able to answer the following true-false questions.

1. Referee the defense is a strategy and philosophy that has the official focusing on the defensive player's movements to correctly judge contact situations.

2. You should sell every call so every call is accepted.

3. The lead moving ball side improves angles on low post play.

4. The "inside-out" look means the trail takes one or two steps toward the center of the court to improve the angle instead of running around the play toward the sideline.

5. Whether the lead or trail, proper spacing is essential to see plays correctly.

1 - True, 2 - False, 3 - True, 4 - True, 5 - True

Chapter 3

Philosophy

Officiating philosophy

"Referee the defense but think like the offense."

While no single sentence can really summarize basketball officiating, that one gives you the framework for success. To do that effectively, you've got some homework to do.

The greatest single thing you can do to help improve your officiating is gain a better understanding of the game itself. Anticipation is critical in officiating. You give yourself a much better chance of getting in proper position and making the correct call if you anticipate what is going to happen. That doesn't mean anticipate *the call*, a major error. It means knowing what's likely to happen and adjusting accordingly. The only way you can get better at anticipating is by becoming a student of the game.

To elevate your officiating, you must learn about offensive and defensive strategies. If you know what each team is trying to do (well beyond "score more points than the other team"), your game awareness, communication, court coverage and judgment will improve.

This book places a great deal of emphasis on recognizing plays and adjusting accordingly. In order to "referee the defense and think like the offense," you must first understand each element of the sentence.

Referee the defense

When officiating a game, you must recognize, understand and react to what the defense is doing. Defensive coverages often dictate offensive plays; they also greatly impact your court coverage. Watch where defenders are positioned on the court and what they're doing from those positions. Are they in a man-to-man? A zone? What type? By recognizing the defense, you can adjust your coverage and positioning accordingly.

Referee the defense also means primarily watching the defender movements. You must watch the defense before judging whether the offensive player or defensive player committed a foul. The best example is the legal guarding rule. Say a player dribbles into a defender and significant contact occurs. If you watched the dribbler, you don't know if the defender established legal guarding position. Who committed the foul? If you correctly watched the defender, you know if the defender established legal guarding position. You can now call that play correctly. The simple philosophy is a crucial part of good judgment.

Obviously, referee the defense doesn't mean you can watch only the defender. You must also watch the offensive player for violations and fouls. By maintaining good angles and establishing proper spacing, you can watch both players. Refereeing the defense is more of an attitude than a visual command.

Think like the offense

Good students of the game usually make good referees. Why? The have learned as players to recognize defenses and they know what to do to beat those defenses. Good officials do the same thing. Once you've learned to recognize defenses and understand defensive tendencies, you must think about what the offense is likely to do and adjust accordingly. Gaining that knowledge allows you to anticipate correctly and move to get proper angles and spacing.

The more you know about the game, the less chance you have of getting surprised. Studying the rules and mechanics isn't enough. A complete official knows what's going on from the players', coaches' and officials' perspectives.

This book emphasizes offensive plays that combat defensive strategies. It will help you understand what players are trying to do so you can be prepared on the court to make the proper coverage adjustments.

Trust

When it comes down to it, trust is a vital element in officiating. You must trust yourself and the knowledge you've obtained to see you through game situations. You must also trust your partner not only to handle situations properly, but to implement proper court coverage.

You must develop trust with your partner to establish good on-ball, off-ball coverage. In almost every instance, only one official should be watching the player with the ball. The other official must watch players off-ball. Think about it: Usually there are only a couple of players around the ball. That leaves the majority of the players in other areas. If both officials were glued to the ball, the majority of the players would be unattended. That's when problems occur, like rough play or trash-talking. If one official is on-ball and the other is off-ball, all the players are watched and the game stays under control.

You must trust your partner to handle things correctly when on-ball so you can watch off-ball and vice versa. Referees have a tendency to want to watch the ball even when they're not supposed to. Maybe that stems from watching games on TV, which always focuses on the ball. Maybe it comes from the belief that more exciting things happen with the ball. Whatever the reason, you must trust your partner to handle it. If you don't, off-ball coverage is non-existent and the game suffers.

Two officials who trust each other in handling situations and court coverage responsibilities form the building blocks to successful officiating. Fight the urge to watch the ball all the time. Trust your partner to handle it. Your game will stay under control, your judgment will improve and you will become a better partner and a better official.

Communication
Effective communication rounds out the successful official. It makes sense: If you've got a lot of knowledge and make good decisions but can't effectively communicate with others, no one can tell that you've got a lot of knowledge and make good decisions. Good communicators make good officials.

Communication goes well beyond words. It includes body language and signals. There is a great deal of emphasis on proper, clear signals throughout this book. Why? Signals are our language. They're our way of telling others what's going on. Bad signals mean poor communication. Good signals show decisiveness, clearly indicate what's going on and even help calls become accepted.

Learn how to referee the defense, think like the offense, trust yourself and your partner, and communicate effectively. You'll find yourself improving every time you step onto the court.

Basketball fundamentals
To succeed in any profession, you must be aware of the basic ground rules. Basketball officiating is no different. Extracted from the *NFHS Basketball Rules Book* and *NFHS Basketball Officials Manual*, here are some fundamental principles to guide your philosophy.

1. While the ball remains live, a loose ball always remains in control of the team whose player last had control, unless it is a try or tap for goal.

2. Neither a team nor any player is in control during a dead ball, jump ball or throw-in, or when the ball is in flight during a try or tap for goal.

3. A goal is made when a live ball enters the basket from above and remains in or passes through, unless canceled by a throw-in violation or a player-control foul.

4. The jump ball, the throw-in and the free throw are the only methods of getting a dead ball live.

5. Neither the dribble nor traveling rule operates during the jump ball, throw-in or free throw.

6. It is not possible for a player to travel during a dribble.

7. The only infractions for which points are awarded are goaltending by the defense or basket interference at the opponent's basket.

8. There are three types of violations and each has its own penalty.

9. A ball in flight has the same relationship to frontcourt or backcourt, or inbounds or out of bounds, as when it last touched a person or the floor.

10. Personal fouls always involve illegal contact and occur during a live ball, except a common foul by an airborne shooter.

11. The penalty for a single flagrant personal or flagrant technical foul is two free throws and disqualification plus awarding the ball to the opponents for a throw-in.

12. Penalties for fouls are administered in the order that the fouls occurred.

13. A live ball foul by the offense (team in control or last in control if the ball is loose) or the expiration of time for a quarter or extra period, causes the ball to become dead immediately, unless the ball is in flight during a try or tap for goal. The ball also becomes dead when a player-control foul occurs.

14. Any free-throw violation by the offense causes the ball to become dead immediately.

15. A double personal foul involves only personal fouls and only two opponents; no free throws are awarded and the ball is put in play by the team entitled to the throw-in under the alternating-possession procedure. A double technical foul involves only technical fouls and only two opponents; no free throws are awarded, and the ball is put in play by the team entitled to the throw-in at the division line opposite the table under the alternating-possession procedure.

16. The official's whistle seldom causes the ball to become dead (it is already dead).

17. "Continuous motion" applies both to tries and taps for field goals and free throws, but it has no significance unless there is a foul by the defense during the interval which begins when the habitual trying or tapping movement starts and ends when the ball is clearly in flight.

18. Whether the clock is running or is stopped has no influence on the counting of a goal.

19. A ball that touches the front face or edges of the backboard is treated the same as touching the floor inbounds, except that, when the ball touches the thrower's backboard, it does not constitute a part of a dribble.

20. If the ball goes through the basket before or after a player-control foul, the goal shall not be counted.

Court coverage philosophy for a crew of two officials

Movement and compromise are the characteristics of two-person officiating. Ten players are moving around a closed court, competing for space and positions; two officials must utilize hustle, angles, distance and planned compromises to observe and control the action.

Hustle

Hustle is an overused word today. Everyone knows it's needed to succeed, but what does it really mean when relating it to two-person officiating? Think of it this way: NCAA conferences (from all Division I to most Division III conferences), plus the NBA use three officials per game. Even some high school conferences and state tournaments are now using three officials. Why? Because of the speed, size, quickness and the physical nature of games at those levels, three officials can better control a game than two officials. That extra set of eyes and ears prevents many problems. Plus, athletic budgets allow it at those levels, something that would be difficult at the lower levels.

The game control expectations are no different with two officials, yet there's one less person to help control the game. Significant movement by both officials is critical for proper court coverage. Hustle gives you a chance. In essence, two officials must work hard enough to cover the entire court that is better covered by three officials at higher levels. That equates to more running and a well-placed concern for angles.

Movements

Both officials must work hard at understanding, then obtaining, proper angles. Your line of sight must provide you with an opportunity to view a developing play or part of a play. You must be able to see completely through the play, which means your vision must be unobstructed by the players directly involved in the play and others near the play.

Basketball is a game of nearly continual motion. An official's angle and distance adjustments are constant as play is in motion. A step or two in the right direction may open up a whole new viewing experience, free from obstruction; a step in the wrong direction will screen you from the critical game action.

With two officials, the trail must move off (away from) the sideline for proper court coverage. Far too often officials who can't (or won't) run well stay on the sideline. They're afraid of getting in the way and aren't confident they can move quickly enough to avoid passing lanes and get good angles. The game suffers because court coverage suffers. A good trail official moves off the near sideline when the ball is nearer the far sideline; it's the best way to get good angles and proper distance from the play.

Why such an emphasis on trail movement? That allows the lead to watch players off-ball, the critical component to combating physical play. Rough play was a point of emphasis throughout the last decade. When the trail moves off the sideline to cover plays, the lead can focus on the lane area, where most rough play occurs.

The lead also moves along the endline to improve angles. There's usually at least four and sometimes six or eight players in the lane area battling for position. Lead movement is critical to watching low-post action. It's paramount to game control.

Proper movements on rebounding action are also important. Because there are only two officials, there's a tendency to think about moving to the other end of the court when a shot goes up to avoid getting beat downcourt. If either official ignores rebounding action, physical play develops and game control suffers. Both officials must move to get good angles on rebounding action.

Compromises

Two officials can't see everything. If they could, you'd see two officials in the Final Four and the NBA Finals. Though all areas of officiating are important, conscious sacrifices must be made to ensure game control and quality off-ball officiating.

Because of the necessary emphasis on off-ball coverage, some boundary line coverage is compromised. It's simply a tradeoff. You're focusing on great off-ball coverage and giving up a bit of sideline coverage in some areas. You're playing the percentages because you're more likely to have rough play than you are to have close sideline violations that aren't obvious. Later in this book, you'll learn about what compromises to make and when.

A complete understanding of court coverage

Proper coverage is enhanced by good eye contact and a "feel" for where your partner is looking. You must learn about all aspects of two-person officiating to know who is covering what. Once you've mastered that, practical on-court application develops through partner communication, including eye contact and understanding. At the risk of being obvious, you've got to know exactly what both you and your partner are expected to do in specific situations — then effectively communicate with your partner — to truly master two-person officiating. When you understand why angles and distance are important and how and when to obtain them, you'll find yourself in great position throughout each game.

Chapter 4

Basketball Basics

Basketball basics

Good officials project professionalism on and off the court. Among the areas where you can stand out:

Accepting games
Before even getting on the court, you've obviously got to get assigned games. There are many different assigning methods that vary from state to state, level to level and association to association.

Learn what the process is from other local officials and association leaders. Then, follow the system. Do not compromise your principles to get games. In some areas, it's wrong to contact coaches directly for games. If that's the case, don't do it. You'd be sacrificing your integrity just for an assignment. It's not worth it.

In other areas, officials must get games from coaches or athletic directors. While that practice often gives the appearance of favoritism and impropriety, follow the procedures that are accepted and don't deviate. Be careful.

Once you've figured out the procedure and accepted an assignment, keep it. Few things upset assignors more than turned back games. Obviously emergencies do happen, but they should be few in number. Officials who continually have problems making assignments eventually don't get called.

It's tempting to turn back a game when a better one comes along. Some assignors allow turn-backs if the official has a chance to move up a level, for example from a JV game to varsity. Others frown upon it no matter what. If you know you can't turn a game back without upsetting someone, don't do it.

If you've got a better opportunity that moves you up a level and your assignor is open minded, be upfront about it. Don't commit to the new game until you've talked to the assignor for the game you've already got.

If you get caught being dishonest about assignments, you're going to burn the bridge on both ends. The assignor you lied to won't call. The assignor you lied for won't call because that assignor is smart enough to know that if you did it to someone else to move up, you'll do it again! You gain more credibility by keeping the assignment you've got. After all, if you're worthy of a chance to move up, other assignments will come your way.

When you receive a contract in the mail, return it in a timely fashion. Think of your officiating as a business. As the business owner, realize how important contracts are to your business. If they are returned late or incomplete your business will suffer because you're less likely to get other contracts. Get the contract back in the mail as soon as you get it.

Conditioning
Basketball officiating requires you to be in good physical condition. Consider taking a physical examination before each season. *Stay* in shape rather than *get* in shape. Being physically fit is a lifestyle. If you never get out of shape it won't be such a chore getting ready for the season.

Arriving to game site
Arrive at the game site well in advance of the scheduled start time. Allow enough time to get stuck in traffic and still make it in plenty of time.

The proper amount of time varies by level and by local practice. General rule: Arrive at least 60 minutes before tipoff.

Allow enough time to stretch out, get dressed, have a pregame with your partner and conduct pregame duties without rushing.

When arriving at the game site, park in a well lit area and, if possible, near an exit not used by most fans. If possible, park with open space in front of and behind your car to ensure no one can box you in after the game and cause problems. Put all valuables (like a briefcase, clothes, etc.) in your trunk so there's less of a reason to break into your car.

If possible, drive with your partner. That gives you time for idle chit-chat and possibly a pregame conference on the way to the game.

Dress
At most levels, officials have private locker rooms. When that's the case, do not go to the game dressed in any part of your uniform. It just looks unprofessional. Make a good first impression on game management by arriving nicely dressed.

Carry your uniform in a garment bag or gym bag. The bag should be nice looking (no frayed edges, etc.) and be entirely black. Some associations have their group's logo or the official's name embroidered on the bag. That's acceptable if that's what the group in the area is doing. If no one else in the area is doing it, don't do it just to stand out.

Many officials at the upper levels use all black, wheeled, airline-travel type luggage. They keep your clothes clean and pressed and, because of the wheels, are easy to transport.

Your uniform should be clean and well kept. Included:

Jacket
Black preferred; navy blue accepted in some areas. They are worn before the game during pregame warmups. Both officials should wear the same color or not wear them at all. Association patches are allowed if it's accepted in the area. Check with other officials to make sure you're buying the right style and color.

Shirt
Standard black and white vertical stripes are worn. The shirt must be short sleeve with black cuffs. V-neck is preferred. The officials should match styles. If you wear a v-neck with an undershirt, be sure the undershirt is also v-neck and does not stick out of the "v" near the neck. An undershirt should be plain white or black. White tends to work better; black underneath the white stripes tends to make them look gray. The undershirt should not have any letters or pictures that could be seen through your striped shirt. Your shirt should always be tucked in. Hint: Use a rubber belt or garters to keep your shirt neatly tucked into your pants.

Pants
All black pants with normal lower leg cut; no flares and no pleats. Beltless pants are considered more professional than belt-looped pants. If you wear a belt, it must be black with a non-descript buckle.

Shoes
Entirely black shoes are most acceptable, however, some state associations allow black with minimal white markings (like shoe logos). Black laces are always worn.

Socks
All black.

Whistle
Black lanyard with all-black plastic whistle. Metal whistles (even with rubber caps) are outdated and appear unprofessional. Carry a spare in your pants pocket.

Meeting with game management
Upon arrival at the game site, inform someone from game management that you have arrived. At the youth level, the game manager is likely a league supervisor. In high school, it's probably the host athletic director or representative. Letting them know you're there immediately means they don't have to wonder and worry if the officials arrived.

The game manager likely will show you to your locker room. With the game manager:

- Confirm tipoff time.
- Ask if there's going to be an extended halftime for parent's night, special presentations, etc. If there is, make sure the game manager informs both teams before the game.
- Find out where the game manager will be located during the game. You may need to find the game manager quickly during the game to take care of crowd control or other administrative duties.
- Find out who is going to escort you and your partner to your locker room at halftime and immediately after the game. Make sure your locker room is locked after you leave and someone is there to open it when needed. It's very upsetting when you want to get into your locker room at halftime or after the game and no one is there to open the door.

By taking care of duties with game management before the game, you won't have to worry about those details during the game.

After the game
If facilities are available, shower and change back into the same clothes you arrived in. Don't leave with your uniform on. You want to leave with a professional appearance, just like you arrived.

Leave the game site with your partner. There's safety in numbers. In cold weather climates, make sure both cars start properly before leaving. If you and your partner are going to stop for a bite to eat, consider stopping out of the town you just officiated in. You don't want to be a local celebrity or a target.

Communicating with the governing body
If conduct or game reports are necessary, they should be sent promptly to the proper authorities. Send all reports within 24 hours of the game.

If there was a problem during the game that warrants a report to your supervisor, consider calling the supervisor as soon as possible before mailing the report. Supervisors usually like to hear about problems first from the officials so they don't get surprised when the angry coach or administrator calls.

Report all items that are supposed to be reported. Most governing bodies require all disqualifications to be reported. If you don't report yours, the governing body can't discipline the offender. You may think the ejection was "minor" and doesn't warrant suspension, etc. *That's not your call!* Report all disqualifications (if required) and let the governing bodies make their decisions. Sometimes, officials don't report because they think they're doing the offender a favor. What if the offender has been disqualified four or five times throughout the season but only one has been reported? The authorities won't be aware of the continuing problem and can't take care of business. You are hurting yourself and other officials by not reporting properly.

Frequent study
Learning is an on-going process. A complete knowledge of the rules and mechanics is essential. Study the rules year round, with special emphasis on new rules at the beginning of the season. Test taking and small group discussion are effective educational tools.

Players' welfare
Officials should constantly be alert to the possibility of player injury. Injured players should be attended to as outlined in the rules. In all situations, the welfare of an injured player has the highest priority.

Courtesy
Politeness is the lubricant for good human relations. Sometimes officials are afraid that politeness implies softness or "politicking." That is far from the truth. A polite person can be very strict and exacting. Cheerfulness and optimism tend to bring out the same qualities in players.

Good officials are courteous, but avoid "visiting" with players during the game. Carelessly placing an arm on players' shoulders or around their waist tends to destroy respect. A player should be addressed by number rather than by name. In addressing the captain of a team, do so by title.

Loafing in the coaches' offices or carrying on long conversations with them before, during or after the game may give the appearance of favoritism. If conditions warrant a conference, both coaches should be involved. The quickest way to lose respect of coaches and players is to get the reputation of being a horse trader. All actions should reflect strict and total impartiality.

Loyalty
Loyalty to fellow officials implies an active, intelligent desire to carry out the intent of the rules by a well-coordinated team. Each official must be willing to share the responsibility and must avoid attempts to shift the blame. There should be no press or radio interview about a game worked by any official and never any criticism of a fellow official.

Anticipating problems
Officials must anticipate when trouble is brewing. The presence of an official in whom the players have confidence will prevent most of those situations. Being in a position to observe any questionable contact will go a long way toward preventing such contact. When a player attempts to bait an opponent, it is a circumstance that requires immediate attention before it gets out of hand. In some borderline cases, the official can get best results by calling the matter to the attention of the team captain so that the captain can handle the unnatural conduct. Captains should be made to understand that they can stop the problem without penalty. The only way the official can stop it is to penalize.

Courage
A courageous official will be quick to call violations or fouls when they occur. Do that consistently without regard to the score, position on the floor, whom it may hurt or how it may affect future relations with the school or coach. Regardless of pressure from fans, coaches or players, the official must go "straight down the middle" and have the courage to call them as they occur. Your honesty must be above reproach or you would not be an official in the first place. It takes real courage to resist pressure and intimidation. To a large extent, the personal reputation of an official is built on courage.

Chapter 5

The Pregame

Pregame conferences

The great importance placed on the pregame conference with officiating partners has made the concept almost cliché. Nearly everyone in officiating — camp directors, clinicians, book authors, columnists, veteran officials — all say a pregame conference is a significant ingredient of success. They're all right: If you can talk about it before it happens on the floor, you're better prepared to deal with it.

There are as many different pregame conferences as there are officials. There is no magic formula for a "successful" pregame conference. There are a number of topics, however, that should be included:

Teambuilding
Ask about your partner's family. Check up on recent assignments with fellow officials. Create a pleasant working atmosphere with your partner. Judge your partner's temperament — tough day at the office, feeling great about life in general, eager for a good contest? All too often, crews stop right at this point and don't get into the serious business of conducting a pregame. Proceed!

Rule changes/major differences
Cover recent rule changes, especially at the beginning of the season when the rules and interpretations may still be a bit unclear. Cover major rule differences when you work different levels of play — for example, going from small college games to high school or grade school to recreation ball.

There are a number of mechanics changes, signal changes and court-coverage changes. Be sure to go over them.

Pregame responsibilities
Decide when you and your partner are taking the floor, when you're checking the scorebook, when you're meeting coaches and captains, etc. By talking about those things before the game, you and your partner can look smooth doing it on the floor.

Table duties
Talk about how you will approach the table personnel. Perhaps one partner has worked in this gym recently and knows the table crew is experienced and proficient. Perhaps you're calling a conference championship match in front of a packed gym, so you will have to rely on hand signals exclusively — the table won't hear you over the crowd.

Jump ball
Discuss who is going to toss the ball, the philosophies on "calling it back," and the proper coverage of all initial plays.

Court coverage
This is probably the most time-consuming portion; it is also the most important. Discuss floor coverage as a trail official and a lead official. Diagram, if necessary, proper off-ball coverage to ensure control of the game. Talk about what to do in the event of a press, special defense, etc.

Making the call
Go over proper signals, eye contact and dead-ball officiating. Is the lead watching the players as the trail reports a foul to the scorer? What are you going to do if you have a double-whistle?

Free-throw responsibilities
Discuss accepted mechanics and signals. Plus, decide how you're going to get the correct shooter to the free-throw line.

Throw-ins
Eye contact is a must before placing the ball at the disposal of the thrower. Talk about balancing court coverage and areas of responsibility.

Timing counts
Are you aware there are seven different timing counts that are important to officials during a contest? It should be no surprise that three seconds, five seconds, 10 seconds, 30 seconds, one minute, three minutes and 10 minutes all play a vital role in the rules.

Particularly with five-second closely guarded counts, which may continue even after a player leaves an official's area of primary responsibility, know how your partner prefers to handle those counts. Talk about your philosophy on each of the possible timing infractions.

Technical fouls
Who's going to administer? Do those circumstances ever change? Where is the non-administering official going to stand?

Timeout responsibilities
Who's reporting the timeout to the scorer's table? It should be the official who calls the timeout, given the

recent mechanics change. Where are the officials positioned during the timeout?

Substitutions

How will you handle substitutions? On page 100, *Referee* presents the reasons for why you might consider an alternative to standard mechanics. If you are going to use that deviation, both partners better know about it ahead of time and agree to use it.

Goaltending and basket interference

In games where the players are likely to be "above the rim," discuss the nuances and differences of each rule.

Fighting

Fighting happens so seldom, many officials are confused about what to do in the aftermath. Spending a moment on that vital topic during pregame allows you to go through a "What if ..." and collect your thoughts before you are surprised on the court. Talk about what happens to those who participate. Mention what to do about players who leave the bench to participate. Don't mess up the restart after double technical fouls.

Bench decorum

This is a key element, often overlooked in pregame conferences. It is especially important if you're working with someone you're largely unfamiliar with. Make sure that the officials involved have roughly the same idea about what conduct is out of line and what isn't.

Injured players

Go over certain liability concerns, then decide what action should be taken if a player becomes injured.

Halftime

Are you going to let the coaches and teams leave the floor before heading off yourselves? Also, someone needs to make sure the officials are properly notified of the time on the clock so they can return in time. Who is it?

Shot at the buzzer

Make certain both officials know who has what responsibility for last-second shots. There's not much worse than two officials making opposite calls on a shot at the buzzer.

Leaving the floor

Is eye contact with your partner necessary before you leave the floor? What about the scorer? Should you leave as soon as possible after the final horn?

Game expectations

If you know of some team history that may affect the game, discuss it. For example, if the two teams were involved in a fight the last time they met, you may want to talk about those ramifications on the game and the players' and coaches' attitudes.

Take the time to discuss the above mentioned items (and others that apply) and you won't have to guess what your partner is doing, you'll know.

Pregame Outline

A. Pregame floor duties
   1. Position during warmup
   2. Count players
   3. Check equipment, including uniforms

B. Table duties
   1. Referee
      a. Fix table problems early, before 10-minute mark
      b. Establish rapport with table personnel
      c. Check scorebook for correct number of players and duplicate names, numbers
      d. Check clock
      e. Check alternating-possession (A/P) arrow
      f. Ask scorer to help hold substitutes for official's beckon
      g. Inform table personnel of pertinent rule changes, timing concerns, etc.
   2. Umpire
      a. Watch both teams

C. Captains' and coaches' meeting
   1. Ask players for questions
   2. All players will exhibit good sportsmanship throughout the contest
   3. Keep it brief

D. Return to pregame floor duty position
   1. Watch players
   2. Relax and begin final mental preparations

E. Jump ball
   1. Position, mechanics
   2. Trail checks the arrow

F. Court coverage
   1. Lead position
      a. Move outside endline for angles
      b. Stay with the shooter if in your area
   2. Trail position
      a. Must get off sideline when ball is on opposite side
      b. Penetrate toward endline on a try
      c. Stay with the shooter if in your area
   3. Adjust to defensive pressure
      a. Halfcourt pressure
      b. Fullcourt pressure
   4. Off-ball coverage

G. Throw-ins
   1. Eye contact
   2. Check table and benches
   3. Step away from thrower
   4. Bounce pass

H. Foul call
   1. Use advantage/disadvantage principles in contact situations. See the entire play.
   2. Mechanics: Calling official
      a. Proper signals
      b. Pointing to player
      c. Signaling at the spot
      d. Throw-in spot or free throws? Your partner must know!
      e. Reporting to table
         1. Stationary in reporting area

2. Eye contact with scorer
        3. Clear signals
    3. Mechanics: Non-calling official
        a. Dead-ball officiating
        b. Ball enters basket: Help if necessary — "The ball went in."
        c. Align players for throw-in or free throws
    4. Double whistles
I. Free-throw administration
J. Timing counts, timeouts
K. Substitutions, disqualifications — take your time administering
L. Key rules
    1. Lengthen coaching box and "X" for substitutes
    2. Several new signals approved
    3. Team may run endline after violation or foul after made goal
    4. Three points for thrown ball from outside arc
M. Points of emphasis
    1. Stop rough post play
    2. Handchecking
    3. Track closely guarded
    4. Free-throw disconcertion
    5. Uniforms and jewelry
    6. Bench decorum
N. Bench decorum
O. Last-second shot
    1. Special timing rules
    2. Remind each other of duties oncourt if situation permits
P. Establish tempo — let the game come to you

Halftime
A. Check A/P arrow before leaving floor
B. Relax
C. Discuss concerns/problems
D. Adjustments, if necessary
    1. Court coverage
    2. Philosophy: Are the points of emphasis under control?
E. Review overtime procedure
F. Remind each other of the things done well in first half
G. Return to floor
    1. Watch players
    2. Just before throw-in, check with table personnel for questions/concerns

Postgame
A. Leave floor together
B. Relax
C. Review game
    1. Points of emphasis?
    2. Tempo?
    3. Bench decorum?
    4. Strange plays, rulings?
D. Solicit constructive criticism — "What could I have done better?"
E. Leave facility together — there's safety in numbers

Chapter 6

Philosophy of Signals

Philosophy of signals

Clear and concise communication is a necessary ingredient for any successful person, regardless of the profession. The same is true for officials. When people hear the word "communication," most think of how a person speaks to an individual or group. A sometimes overlooked yet critically important communication method is body language.

In many ways, an official's body language is just as important as any verbal communication. Just like profanity to a player or coach can get an official in trouble, poor body language can escalate a negative situation. Conversely, positive body language can help ease and control a potential conflict.

Think about this: Why do we bother to give signals? It's because we need to tell others (players, coaches, fans, etc.) what happened on the court and it's impossible to yell loud enough for everyone to hear. Sounds condescendingly simple, but keeping that basic principle in mind will make you more aware of what signals you use and how you give them.

Signaling at the spot

When you call a foul or violation, your body language sends a message to everyone watching. Raise your fisted (for a foul) or open (for a violation) hand high and straight above your head as you blow the whistle to stop the clock. A bent arm looks weak and shows people you're unsure of your call.

If calling a foul, use the raised fist signal. If clarification is needed to identify the fouler, calmly extend the other hand, fingers straight and aligned, palm down toward the fouling player's midsection. Keep the point out of a player's face (that appears confrontational) and off the floor. Pointing down to a player's feet is confusing to your partner; you're possibly pointing to a spot for a throw-in.

Next, verbalize what you've called while giving the preliminary signal at the spot.

Selling a call is like raising your voice. Sometimes it is necessary and effective. Do it too often and people get angry or turned off. Sell a call only when necessary. Obvious calls need good signals too, but close calls need a little extra emphasis to communicate to everyone clearly. Don't over-sell; you don't want to embarrass a player or make it appear that you're caught up in the emotions of the game.

Before leaving for the reporting area, verbalize what you've got with your partner. Visually show the number of free throws to be attempted, if applicable. Signal the spot of the throw-in, if appropriate.

Follow the prescribed signals in the manuals. It's important because people have come to accept and understand them. Again, think about signals as words. If two English-speaking people were talking and one briefly switched to a foreign language, confusion would set in. The same is true for signals. By using your own, unauthorized signals, you're speaking a "foreign" language and confusion reigns.

There are, however, some commonly accepted signals that are not included in the manual. Listed as "additional signals" in the "Signals chart," consider using them if your governing bodies allow.

Signaling to the scorer's table

Equally important is your presentation to the scorer's table. That's one of the few times where all eyes in the gym are focused on you.

Come to a complete stop at the reporting area. Make eye contact with the scorer. Slowly state the color of the shirt and the fouler's number. Signal the number with one hand as you say the words. Hold your hand at about chin height and off to the side of your face; if your hand is in front of your face, the scorer sees skin (fingers) with a skin (face) background and it's difficult to see.

Make sure your palm always faces the scorer; don't spin your hand when using double digits. Also, don't repeat the numbers because it adds confusion: "The foul is on blue twenty-four, two, four" is puzzling. Give the signal indicating the nature of the foul to the scorer without verbalizing it. Finally, point to the throw-in spot if appropriate (see "Reporting fouls," p. 66).

Slow down and think about your signals as a language. If you "speak" slowly and clearly and use the right "words," the correct message and tone will get across.

Signals chart

Stop clock or do not start clock

One of two preliminary signals used to stop play, this signal is given simultaneously as you blow your whistle. In this case, because the palm is open, another signal for a violation will follow.

The following signal is given after a short delay. There are two, distinct signals — one to stop play, one to signal the nature of the violation.

This signal is also used to continue a stoppage in play, i.e., substitutes are coming into the game.

Stop clock for foul

One of two preliminary signals used to stop play, this signal is given simultaneously as you blow your whistle. In this case, because the palm is closed into a fist, another signal for a foul will follow.

The following signal is given after a short delay. There are two, distinct signals — one to stop play, one to signal the nature of the foul.

Stop clock for jump ball

Three-second violation

Stop clock for radio/TV timeout (point toward table)

(Clarification only)

Stop clock for foul, then point to offender
There are two, distinct signals when signaling a foul. The first is the fist raised above the head. The second is the point to the offender, which need only be used for clarification of who the foul was on. There is a slight delay between the two signals. That delay allows you an extra split second when making decisions regarding the foul.

(Clarification only)

Technical foul
Show the fist-over-head signal before the technical foul
signal; only use it to stop the clock if it's running.

(Clarification only)

Blocking

(Clarification only)

Holding

(Clarification only)

Pushing or charging

(Clarification only)

Intentional foul

(Clarification only)

Double foul

(Clarification only)

Handchecking

(Clarification only)

Illegal use of hands

Player-control foul

Three-point field goal attempt; three-point field goal successful

Traveling

Illegal dribble

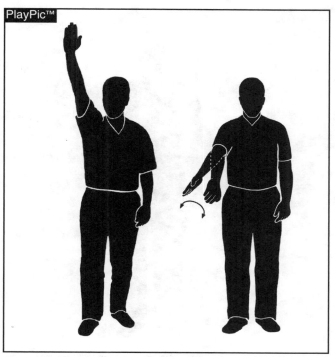

Over and back or carrying the ball

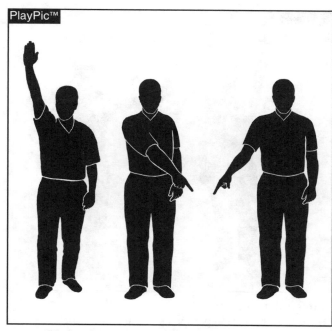

Designated spot throw-in violation

When a thrower-in moves beyond the prescribed limits on a designated spot throw-in, use this signal. Many officials incorrectly use the traveling signal. That is confusing because there is no pivot foot on a designated spot throw-in. Plus, by rule, it is not a traveling violation.

Five-second violation

10-second violation

Directional signal

The two signals are separate. Do not use the "stop the clock" signal and the directional signal at the same time. Use the same arm for both signals. You can use either arm; the arm you use depends on the direction of the ensuing play. Use the arm that keeps your torso and head facing the players. Do not turn your back to the players when you signal a direction.

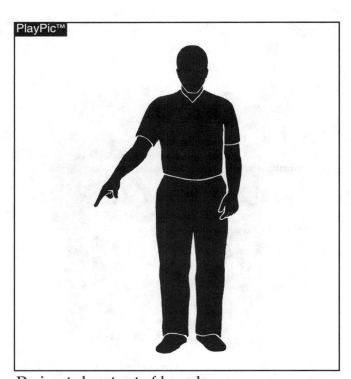

Designated spot out-of-bounds

In most cases, this signal immediately follows the directional signal.

No score

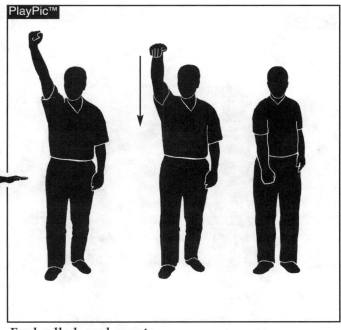

Foul called; goal counts

Use the "goal counts" signal (without fist overhead) as the first signal to the scorer if a foul is called and a goal is scored. Also, use the "goal counts" signal (without fist overhead) to count a goal at the end of a period.

Awarded goal: Basket interference or goaltending
Show the number of points awarded by using the
appropriate number of fingers.

Two free throws
If one free throw, use one finger. If three free throws, use
three fingers.

Bonus free throw

Free-throw violation by opponent

30-second timeout
Players on both teams remain standing. Cheerleaders remain off the floor

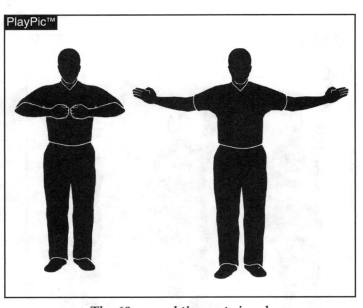

The 60-second timeout signal
The 60-second timeout signal indicates that a granted timeout is a regular length timeout and not a 30-second timeout. Start with your hands together in front of your chest then pull your arms apart to the side. By stretching your arms out, you are indicating the timeout is "stretched" to a full timeout.

"First horn"

First horn
Take a step or two toward the team bench and give the signal. Make sure someone on the bench (assistant coach, trainer, non-uniformed player) sees the signal. Make eye contact with that person.

C signal
When the coach is the one requesting the timeout, make a "C" with your hand as you report to the table.

Start clock

"Start the clock"

Start clock
Use this signal to direct the official timer to start a separate clock for timeouts or to replace a disqualified player.

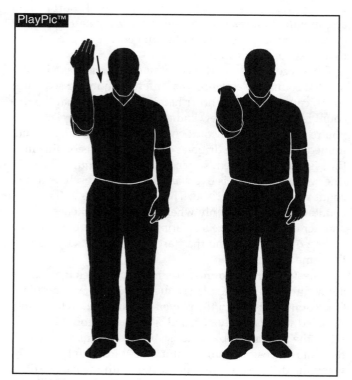

Beckon substitute
Substitutes must have reported to the official scorer ("X" on the floor) and await the beckoning motion.

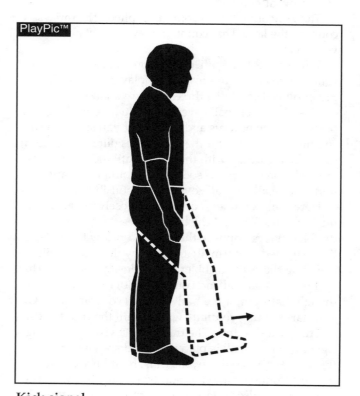

Kick signal
To signal a kicking violation, use a straight leg, kicking motion forward about one foot.

Counting

The arm swing while visibly counting is from the waist and below the shoulders, out to the side.

When do you count? Specific times require the visible count:

• When the ball is at the disposal of a thrower for a throw-in.

• When a backcourt count applies.

• When a closely guarded count applies.

• When the ball is at the disposal of the shooter during a free-throw attempt.

The only other time a count is applied: The three-second count in the lane. That count, however, is *not* a visible or verbal count.

Who counts? The official with on-ball responsibility counts when the count involves a player with the ball. Either official can call a three-second violation.

On-ball and off-ball coverages switch depending on the position of the officials and the ball. If you started a count, continue with it even if the ball moves out of your normal coverage area. Stay with the count until the count ends or the violation occurs. As soon as the count ends, apply normal on-ball, off-ball coverage responsibilities.

Here's an example: A dribbler is closely guarded near the top of the key and the trail applies the count. The dribbler moves opposite the trail and below the free-throw line extended — normally covered by the lead. While dribbling there, the dribbler is still closely guarded. The trail remains on-ball and continue with the count, even though that's out of the trail's normal coverage area. Once you start a count, continue with it until the count ends.

Free-throw counts. The trail gives a visible counting signal when the ball is placed at the disposal of a free thrower. For a free throw, the trail should use the arm furthest from the basket to not distract the thrower. The count should also be less demonstrative than a normal count (only a wrist flick is really necessary) so it does not distract the shooter or draw attention to the official.

Non-verbal. In all counting situations the counts are non-verbal, meaning only the hand signal is used; no voice. A verbal count gives an offensive player an unfair advantage by letting the player know there's about to be a violation. The player can react to the official's voice because rarely does the player see the arm motion; the player is more apt to look to dribble, pass or shoot and not watch the official.

Switching hands. There's no specific preference for which hand to start a count with. Use which ever is most comfortable. As the trail when applying a backcourt count and moving in transition, consider using the hand that is closer to the scorer's table and team benches to give them a clear view of your count.

Once a count has started, continue with the same hand for that counting sequence. If a different counting sequence starts, count with your other hand. That shows that the first count is over and the new count began. For example, if you're applying a backcourt count with your left hand and immediately after the dribbler crosses the division line in time is closely guarded, stop counting with your left hand (the backcourt count is over) and begin the closely guarded count with your right hand. That shows there's a new count. Change hands only when one count switches to another quickly. If there's an appreciable delay between the ending of one count and the start of another, it's OK to use the same hand.

Closely guarded counts. You may have to change hands a few times during the play sequence. Here's an example: One count starts when the player with the ball (who hasn't dribbled yet) is closely guarded. The second count begins when the player dribbles and is still closely guarded; use the hand opposite the first count. The third count begins when the dribble ends and the player with the ball is still closely guarded; use the hand you used when you began the first count. Switching hands ensures everyone knows a new count began.

Signal Sequence – Timeout

Signals tend to be a part of a flow — much like separate words in a conversation. If you jumble your "words," you can't be understood. To help you understand how a series of signals interrelates, let's look at the coach of team A calling a 30-second timeout after a made basket by B4.

At the spot, as soon as the referee notices the coach's request

After the referee has moved to the reporting area and addresses the table

After the first warning buzzer to resume play, and some preventive officiating reminders

Additional signals

These signals are not approved but are commonly used in games.

Last shot

Use this signal to remind your partner that time remaining in the period is winding down. The raised finger stands for "likely one shot remaining" or simulates pointing up to a clock. Some officials tap their wrist in front of their bodies, as if to tap a watch. The raised finger signal is better because it is in the air and easier to see than the tapped wrist. Hold the signal in the air until your partner recognizes it by mirroring the signal or acknowledging it in some way.

Stop sign

The stop sign has two uses: stopping substitutes from entering the game too quickly and letting a coach or player know you've taken enough heat. For handling a confrontation, use the stop sign *sparingly*. It is simply a signal that demonstrates, "Coach, I've listened to enough." If you use it sparingly, the offender and others will know the offender has been warned. Then if the offender acts up again and is whistled for a technical foul you have visual proof (possibly on videotape) that the offender was warned.

The tip signal

When a ball that is in team possession is knocked from the frontcourt into the backcourt by a defender, the tip signal can communicate exactly what you saw. Sometimes a defender's touch of the ball is so slight that few people realize the defense caused the ball to go into the backcourt, eliminating the possibility of a backcourt violation. When an offensive player is the first to touch the ball in the backcourt, the cry "over-and-back!" echoes from players, coaches and fans, though no violation occurred.

To help sell the call and let everyone know the defense caused the ball to go into the backcourt, use the tip signal and point to the defender that tipped the ball into the backcourt. Those that see your signal will know a defender hit the ball into the backcourt and you're less likely to get complaints from players, coaches and fans.

Do not break the plane

As a preventive officiating tool, move your arm up and down over the boundary line while telling the defensive player to remain behind the boundary, "Number 12, don't break the plane during the throw-in."

Additional signals
These signals are not approved but are commonly used in games.

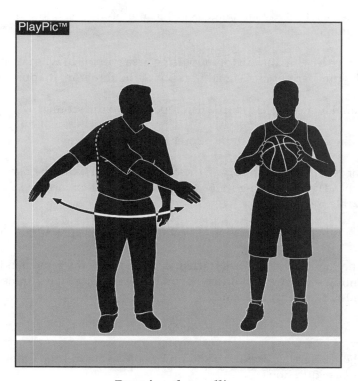

Running the endline

After a made basket when the ball is not immediately put into play, the new offensive team has the right to run the endline. Examples of that may be after a player drives the lane for a layup but is slightly injured due to incidental contact or a called timeout. The team is also entitled to also run the endline after a violation or foul after a made goal.

After the delay, you and your partner both count the number of players on the court, make eye contact, sound your whistle and hand or bounce pass the ball to the thrower-in. But, if you take one extra action, you will reduce any confusion or mistaken rights due that player. If you move your arm parallel to the endline in a full sweeping motion (like a pendulum), you are telling everyone the player has the right to run the full endline. Some officials also talk directly to the thrower-in, saying something like, "You can run it, if you wish." Then, step away from the player with the ball, opening up some space in case the player chooses to run in your direction.

Signals

- An official's body language is just as important as any verbal communication.

- Before leaving for the foul reporting area, verbalize what you've got with your partner and signal the spot of the throw-in, if appropriate.

- Come to a complete stop when reporting to the scorer.

- Make eye contact with the scorer before signaling.

- For NFHS games, stopping the clock for a foul (with the fist overhead) and pointing to the fouler for clarification are two distinct, separate movements.

- The NFHS manual says to signal all fouls at the spot of the foul.

- Once a visible count has started, continue with the same hand for that counting sequence. If a different counting sequence starts immediately, count with your other hand.

Quiz

Without referring back, you should be able to answer the following true-false questions.

1. The handchecking signal is an approved signal.

2. You should use the "traveling" signal when a designated-spot throw-in violation occurs.

3. The "over and back" or "carrying the ball" signal is not an approved signal.

4. The arm swing for a visible count is from the waist and below the shoulders, out to the side.

1 - True, 2 - False, 3 - False , 4 - True

Chapter 7

Foul Signaling Sequence

Foul signaling sequence

The order of your signals is just as important as the clarity of your signals. Again using the language parallel, think of signal sequence as words in a sentence. The singular words, "Sequence important the is the of signals," makes little sense when thought of as individual words, but "The sequence of the signals is important," uses the same words and is easy to understand.

The key to quality signaling is remembering that it is a sequence of fluid movements. Take your time. Signals executed with separate and distinct motions ensure clarity; jumbled quickly together and the messages are lost.

- Verbalize the fouling player's team color and number.
- If clarification is needed, point to the fouling player. Point at the player's midsection.
- Signal all fouls at the spot.
- Always point to the ensuing throw-in spot or indicate the number of free throws.
- If the foul results in free throws, indicate the foul is a shooting foul by showing the number of free throws above your head. Simultaneously tell your partner the player attempting the free throws and the number of free throws that will follow.

Under the NFHS code:

- If you are going to count the goal, count the goal immediately at the spot.
- If you are not going to count the goal and the ball has entered the basket, wave it off immediately at the spot.
- An off-ball foul on an offensive player called by either the lead or trail usually requires an extra bit of selling.
- The trail must help the lead when the lead doesn't see a ball enter the basket, using the phrase, "The ball went in."
- During the signaling sequence, keep your head up to watch for additional player activity and ensure good dead-ball officiating.
- Do not leave the area to report the foul to the scorer until the players appear calm and you're sure your partner is watching the dead-ball action.

By following those principles and using the correct, accepted signals you will effectively communicate your decisions to all involved.

Option 1

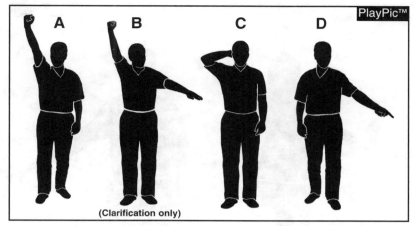

(Clarification only)

Option 2

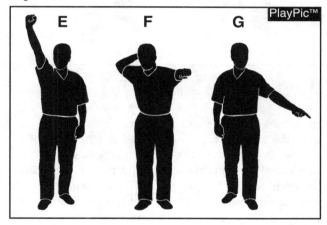

Option 3

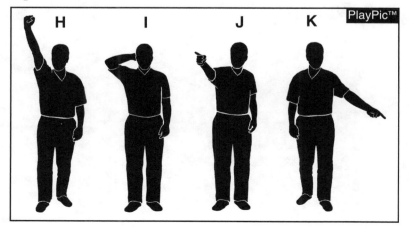

Player-control foul

There are three commonly accepted player-control foul signal sequences.

The first option is reserved for plays that don't need extra selling.

1. Hold your fist above your head (PlayPic A). Simultaneously blow your whistle. Advance on the foul, if necessary.

2. For clarification, point to the fouler (PlayPic B).

3. Using the same hand, move it from a fist above your head to cupping the back of your head (PlayPic C). Verbalize the fouling player's team color and number.

4. Point to the throw-in spot (PlayPic D). Simultaneously tell your partner that a throw-in is to follow.

Sell it. If a player-control foul needs some extra selling, there are two options (PlayPics A and D remain the same). Neither option is NFHS-approved, but is commonly accepted.

Using the same hand, move it from a fist above your head to cupping the back of your head. Simultaneously point (or punch a fist) down court, signaling the charging foul and the direction of the ensuing play (PlayPic F). If necessary, simultaneously yell "offense" to indicate the player-control foul. Do not point to the fouler. Verbalize the fouling player's team color and number.

Second selling option. Using the same hand, move it from a fist above your head to cupping the back of your head (PlayPic I).

Using the same hand, point down court, signaling the direction of the ensuing play (PlayPic J). If necessary, simultaneously yell "offense" to indicate the player-control foul. Do not point to the fouler. Verbalize the fouling player's team color and number.

During the signaling sequence, keep your head up to watch for additional player activity and ensure good dead-ball officiating.

Do not leave the area to report the foul to the scorer until the players appear calm and you're sure your partner is watching the dead-ball action. If there was significant contact on the foul and players ended up on the floor, remain in the area until the players have returned to their feet. When there's significant contact, be especially wary of angry players before leaving to report.

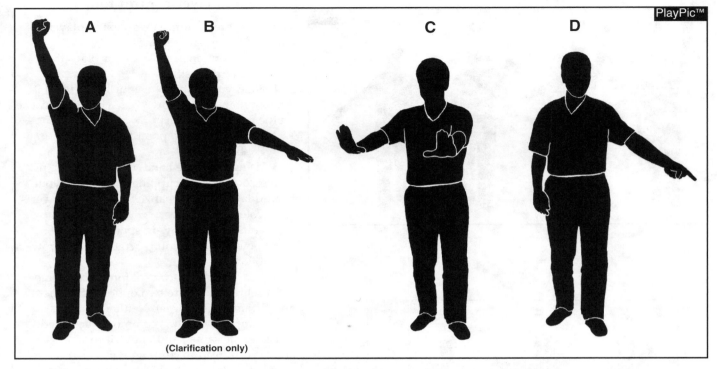

(Clarification only)

Foul called; throw-in

Distinct, separate movements are important when signaling a foul at the spot.

1. Hold your fist above your head (PlayPic A). Simultaneously blow your whistle. Advance on the foul, if necessary.

2. For clarification, raise your opposite arm and point to the fouler with open palm facing the floor (PlayPic B). Point at the player's midsection. Verbalize the fouling player's team color and number.

3. Signal the foul (PlayPic C). The NFHS manual says to signal all fouls.

4. Point to the throw-in spot (PlayPic D). Simultaneously tell your partner that a throw-in is to follow.

During the signaling sequence, keep your head up to watch for additional player activity and ensure good dead-ball officiating.

Do not leave the area to report the foul to the scorer until the players appear calm and you're sure your partner is watching the dead-ball action. If there was significant contact on the foul and players ended up on the floor, remain in the area until the players have returned to their feet. When there's significant contact, be especially wary of angry players before leaving to report.

Once the players in the area appear calm, circle around the players to the foul reporting area (see "Foul reporting area," p. 67).

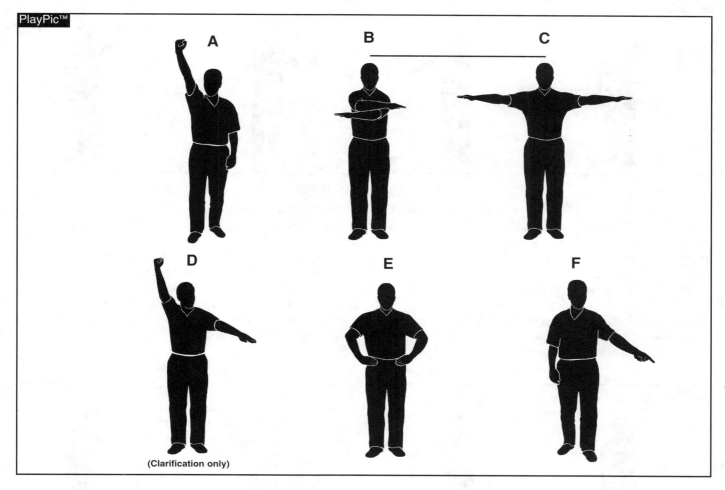

(Clarification only)

Foul called; no goal

When a foul is called, a shot is taken and the ball passes through the basket, and the official does *not* count the goal, there is a specific signal sequence. Distinct, separate movements are important when signaling.

1. Hold your fist above your head (PlayPic A). Simultaneously blow your whistle. Advance on the foul, if necessary.

2. If the ball has already entered the basket, immediately wave it off (PlayPics B and C). Simultaneously verbalize, "no shot." If the ball enters the basket later in your reporting sequence, wave it off immediately after signaling the foul.

3. For clarification, hold your fist above your head and raise your opposite arm and point to the fouler with open palm facing the floor (PlayPic D). Point at the player's midsection. Verbalize the fouling player's team color and number.

4. Signal the foul (PlayPic E). Signal all fouls.

5. Point to the throw-in spot (PlayPic F).

Simultaneously tell your partner that a throw-in is to follow.

During the signaling sequence, keep your head up to watch for additional player activity and ensure good dead-ball officiating.

Do not leave the area to report the foul to the scorer until the players appear calm and you're sure your partner is watching the dead-ball action. If there was significant contact on the foul and players ended up on the floor, remain in the area until the players have returned to their feet. When there's significant contact, be especially wary of angry players before leaving to report.

Once the players in the area appear calm, circle around the players to the foul reporting area (see "Foul reporting area," p. 67). Use the "cancel the goal" signal as your first signal to the scorer (see "Foul reporting sequence," p. 69).

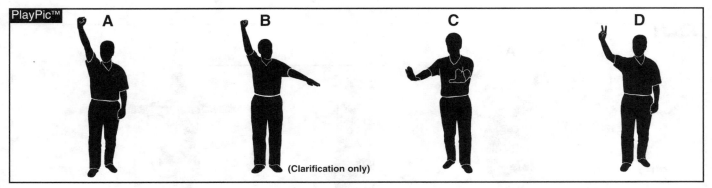

Shooting foul (option 1)

The sequence to signal a shooting foul at the spot is a matter of personal style and preference. No matter what sequence you use, the basic signaling principles still apply. Distinct, separate movements are important when signaling a foul at the spot.

The most common sequence:

1. Hold your fist above your head (PlayPic A). Simultaneously blow your whistle. Advance on the foul, if necessary.

2. For clarification, point to the fouler with open palm facing the floor (PlayPic B). Point at the player's midsection. Verbalize the fouling player's team color and number.

3. Signal the foul (PlayPic C). Signal all fouls.

4. Indicate the foul is a shooting foul by showing the number of free throws above your head (PlayPic D). Simultaneously tell your partner the player attempting the free throws and the number of free throws that follow. For example, "Number twenty-four, two shots."

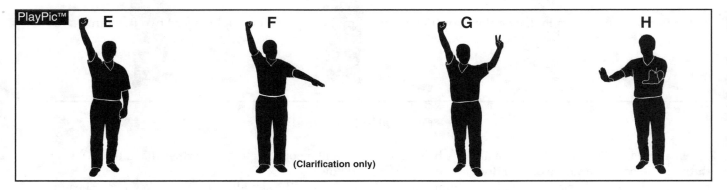

Shooting foul (option 2)

Another sequence option:

1. Same as above (PlayPic E).

2. Same as above (PlayPic F).

3. With your fist still above your head, raise your other hand above your head and indicate the number of free throws to be attempted (PlayPic G).

4. Signal the type of foul (PlayPic H). Simultaneously tell your partner the player attempting the free throws and the number of free throws that follow. For example, "Number twenty-four, two shots."

Signaling the number of shots before the type of foul helps sell the fact that free throws are to be attempted. *Referee* recommendation: Use the first foul-calling sequence above for most shooting fouls; use this second foul-calling sequence if you need to sell the fact that the player was fouled in the act of shooting.

As the calling official during the signaling sequence, keep your head up to watch for additional player activity and ensure good dead-ball officiating.

An excellent mechanic for the non-calling official: After being told by your partner who is shooting the free throw(s) and how many are to be attempted, point to the shooter and repeat the shooter and number of shots. For example, point toward number 24 and say, "Twenty-four, two shots." That way, if you've got the wrong information, the calling official can correct it right away. Plus, the point indicates to all watching that you've got the correct shooter shooting the free throws.

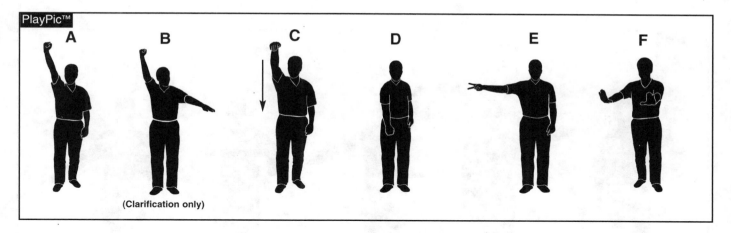

(Clarification only)

Shooting foul; goal is scored

The sequence to signal a shooting foul plus a scored goal at the spot helps sell the call. Distinct, separate movements are important when signaling a foul at the spot.

1. Hold your fist above your head (PlayPic A). Simultaneously blow your whistle. Advance on the foul, if necessary.

2. For clarification, raise your opposite arm and point to the fouler with open palm facing the floor (PlayPic B). Point at the player's midsection. Verbalize the fouling player's team color and number. Glance up to the basket to see if the ball passed through for a goal or, if you had

to focus on the players involved in hard physical contact, get the needed help from your partner (see "Trail helps on made basket," p. 63).

3. If the ball passed through, count the goal immediately using the appropriate signal (PlayPics C and D).

4. Signal the number of free throws to be awarded, using one or two fingers (PlayPic E). In the rare case of a multiple foul, you might award two free throws.

5. Signal the foul (PlayPic F). Simultaneously tell your partner the number of the player attempting the free throw.

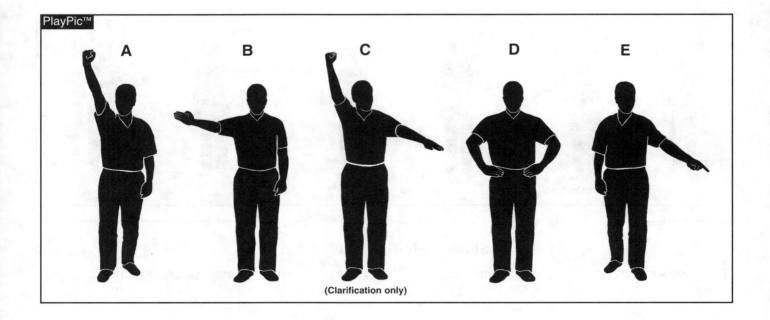

Offensive off-ball foul

An off-ball foul on an offensive player called by either the lead or trail usually requires an extra bit of selling. Though not the approved NFHS signal sequence, inserting a directional point early in the foul signaling sequence helps. Distinct, separate movements are important when signaling an off-ball foul.

1. Hold your fist above your head (PlayPic A). Simultaneously blow your whistle. Advance on the foul, if necessary.

2. Point down court, signaling the direction of the ensuing play (PlayPic B). If necessary, simultaneously yell, "Offense!" to indicate the foul was on the offensive player. Though not the approved sequence, that lets everyone know immediately that you've got a foul on an offensive player.

3. For clarification, hold your fist above your head and raise your opposite arm and point to the fouler with open palm facing the floor (PlayPic C). Point at the player's midsection. Verbalize the fouling player's team color and number.

4. Signal the foul (PlayPic D). Signal all fouls.

5. Point to the throw-in spot (PlayPic E). Simultaneously tell your partner that a throw-in is to follow.

During the signaling sequence, keep your head up to watch for additional player activity and ensure good dead-ball officiating.

Do not leave the area to report the foul to the scorer until the player's appear calm and you're sure your partner is watching the dead-ball action. If there was significant contact on the foul and players ended up on the floor, remain in the area until the players have returned to their feet. When there's significant contact, be especially wary of angry players before leaving to report.

Once the players in the area appear calm, circle around the players to the foul reporting area (see "Foul reporting area," p. 67).

If free throws are the result of the foul, be sure the calling official and the non-calling official get the correct shooter. Many times, the non-calling official can help sort that out. Communication between both partners is essential.

An excellent mechanic for the non-calling official: After being told by your partner who is shooting the free throw(s) and how many are to be attempted, point to the shooter and repeat the shooter and number of shots. For example, point toward number 24 and say, "Twenty-four, one-and-one." That way, if you've got the wrong information, the calling official can correct it right away. Plus, the point indicates to all watching that you've got the correct shooter shooting the free throw(s).

Trail helps on made basket

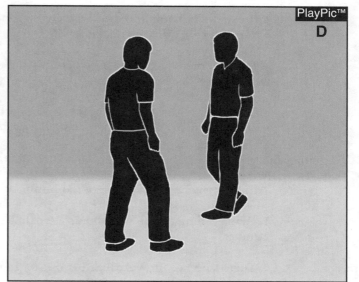

The lead sometimes doesn't see the ball enter the basket when calling a foul. When that happens, the trail must help.

In PlayPic A, the lead signals to stop the clock for the defensive pushing foul. The offensive player is fouled in the act of shooting. In PlayPic B, the lead, for clarification, extends the opposite arm and points toward the fouler. The shooter continues with the shot and makes it. The trail notices the lead didn't signal the made basket immediately (see "Shooting foul; goal scored," p. 61).

In PlayPic C, the lead signals the type of foul. In PlayPic D, the trail hustles over to the lead to let the lead know the ball entered the basket. When helping, use the phrase, "The ball went in." The lead now must make a decision to count or cancel the score. That's the lead's decision only (saying something like, "It's good" takes the judgment away from the lead when it might in fact *not* be good because the foul was not in the act of shooting).

In PlayPic E, the lead immediately signals to count (or cancel) the goal at the spot. The trail watches the players, ensuring good dead-ball officiating.

The first signal to the scorer is either to count or cancel the goal.

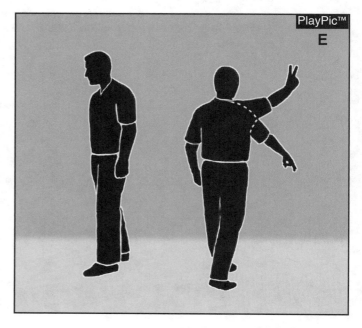

Review

Foul Signaling Sequence

• The order of your signals is just as important as the clarity of your signals.

• Signal all fouls at the spot.

• If clarification is needed, point to the fouling player. Point at the player's midsection.

• Always point to the ensuing throw-in spot or indicate the number of free throws.

• If you count a goal when calling a foul, count the goal immediately at the spot.

• If you are not going to count the goal when calling a foul and the ball enters the basket, wave it off immediately at the spot.

• The trail must help the lead when the lead doesn't see a ball enter the basket, using the phrase, "The ball went in."

• Do not leave the area to report the foul to the scorer until the players appear calm and you're sure your partner is watching the dead-ball action.

Quiz

Without referring back, you should be able to answer the following true-false questions.

1. When calling a foul, you should verbalize the fouling player's team color and number.

2. There's no need to verbalize to your partner the number of the player to attempt free throws.

3. When helping your partner on a made basket, you should say, "Count the basket" because the ball went in.

1 - True, 2 - False, 3 - False

Chapter 8

Reporting Fouls

Reporting fouls

Just like your signaling sequence at the spot of the foul, your signals and sequence at the table speak a language. Using signals to report to the scorer is just like talking to the scorer, only you're using signals instead of words.

The first step in quality communication with the scorer is making sure the scorer is watching. That sounds simple enough, but too often scorers are looking down at the scorebook and referees start signaling before the scorer is watching. If one of the two communicators is not ready to communicate, the message is lost. You run the risk of having to report twice because the scorer didn't see you or, worse, a mistake being made in the book. Stand at your reporting area until you've made eye contact with the scorer, then slowly give your signals.

There are three major reporting problems: Moving while signaling, getting too close to the scorer's table and not giving the signals on a clear background. If you never come to a complete stop in the reporting area and are constantly moving, it's difficult for the scorer to see correctly. Stop before doing anything else.

There is no need to go all the way over to the scorer's table. That area is a danger zone for officials because coaches are nearby. If you've just called a foul, that player's coach will often want to discuss and/or complain about it. If you're over by the table, you're giving the coach an easier chance to voice displeasure and start a negative conversation. One of your duties while reporting is watching both benches for bench decorum and oncoming substitutes. If you're too close to the table, you lose that perspective.

Lastly, if you're giving your signals on an unclear background, there is a chance of confusion. If your fingers are directly in front of your face, the scorer sees a flesh-on-flesh contrast and may miss a finger, resulting in incorrect information being entered in the book. Give your signals off to the side of your body.

There are some consistent principles when reporting:
- Come to a complete stop at the reporting area.
- Make eye contact with the scorer.
- Slowly state the fouler's team color and number.
- Signal the fouler's numbers with one hand and simultaneously say the numbers.
- Hold your hand at about chin height and off to the side of your head.
- Make sure your palm always faces the scorer; don't spin your hand when using double digits.
- Give the same foul signal that you gave at the spot of the foul to the scorer.

- Indicate the number of free throws or point to the throw-in spot as appropriate.
- Do not let substitutes enter the court or grant a timeout until all signals are complete.

Partner. The non-reporting official also has specific duties during the dead ball. Keep all players within your field of vision. Penetrate toward the crowd slightly — maybe just a step or two depending on where the players are — and stop. You are now the eyes and ears of two officials as your partner reports to the table. During this dead-ball time, you can prevent extracurricular or illegal activities from brewing into bigger problems. Use your voice to let players know you're in the area. Your mere presence may stop a problem.

Ball. Do not worry about the basketball. Many times the ball will bounce away from the area. *It is not your responsibility to chase it!* Going after the ball leaves players unattended.

If the players appear calm, begin moving toward the throw-in spot or begin preparing players for free throws. Move slowly and with your head up, watching the players as you move toward the spot. Use your voice to tell the players what's next. If the players are ready for the next play, the ball will get back in play quickly and smoothly.

The dead-ball time after a foul is critical for both officials. The calling official must communicate clearly to the scorer's table. The non-calling official must watch all players and prepare them for ensuing action. Take your time, yet get the ball back in play as quickly as possible without sacrificing quality communication and dead-ball officiating.

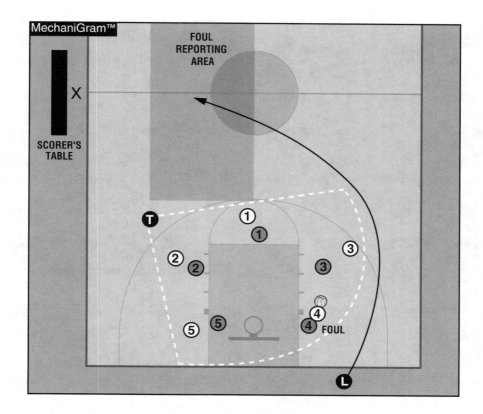

Foul reporting area

Being a good dead-ball official means a variety of things, including watching players and reporting and signaling effectively during a dead ball. When a foul is called, you must fight the instinct to mentally relax because you think the action has stopped. Playing action may have stopped, but your dead-ball duties and responsibilities have just begun. The impact of your dead-ball officiating will affect live ball game action.

In the MechaniGram, the lead official has called a foul on the defender in the low post. At that time, the lead must do a number of things:

1. Delay momentarily after signaling the foul at the spot to ensure there is no continuing action or trash-talk among the players.

2. Do not worry about the basketball. Many times the ball will bounce away from the area. *It is not your responsibility to chase it!* Going after the ball leaves players unattended.

3. Once the immediate area appears calm, the lead clears all the players by running around them toward the reporting area. Do not run through a crowd because then players are behind you and you lose sight of them. That's when problems occur. Plus, by running around the crowd, you're ensuring your safety and their safety; you don't want any accidental bumps or trips to hurt anyone.

4. Stop and square up to the scorer's table in the reporting area. Make eye contact with the scorer before communicating and do not get too close to the table. If you run too close to the table, you're losing sight of bench conduct and you're giving the coaches an easier chance to voice displeasure with the call.

5. Give clear, crisp signals. Make sure most everyone sees what you called.

The trail also has specific duties during the dead ball:

1. Keep all players within your field of vision. Penetrate toward the crowd slightly — maybe just a step or two depending on where the players are — and stop. You are the eyes and ears of two officials as your partner reports to the table. During this dead-ball time, you can prevent many extracurricular illegal activities from brewing into bigger problems. Use your voice to let players know you're in the area. Your mere presence may stop a problem.

2. Again, do not worry about the basketball. Going after the ball leaves players unattended.

3. If the players appear calm, begin moving toward the throw-in spot or begin preparing players for free throws. Move slowly and with your head up, watching the players as you move toward the spot. Use your voice to tell the players what's next. By having the players ready for the next play, the ball will get back in play quickly and smoothly (see "Switching on fouls," p. 171).

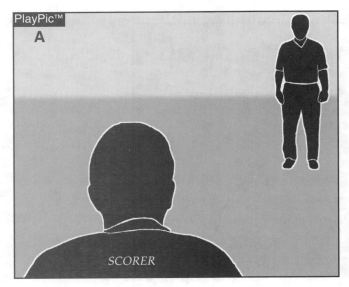

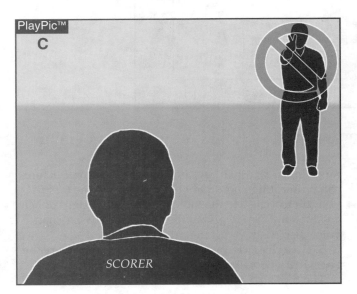

Reporting numbers

Few things are more irritating to officials than problems at the scorer's table. It's easy to blame scorebook problems on the scorer, but first you've got to look at yourself. You can make your job easier.

When reporting a foul to the scorer, square up to the table with your feet comfortably apart, well away from the table, somewhere between the center restraining circle and the sideline and *stop* (PlayPic A).

Stopping is the key. For a scorer, walking through your signals is like trying to read a billboard while flying by it at 90 miles an hour. The more movement, the more likely the scorer will not see everything correctly.

After making eye contact with the scorer, give your signals at about chin height and away from your body

(PlayPic B). When doing so, do not "push" the numbers toward the scorer, pumping your arm forward. Keep your hand away from your face. Skin (hand) on skin (face as the background) is hard to see (PlayPic C).

Slowly raise your fingers with the appropriate number. When giving a number combination — like "number 22" — give a distinct pause between numbers so the scorer doesn't get confused. Do *not* spin your hand (PlayPic D) when giving the second number. That quick turn can cause confusion.

Slow down. There's no reason to speed through reporting; the game can't restart without you! By doing the right things, you're making the scorer's job easier; that makes *yours* easier.

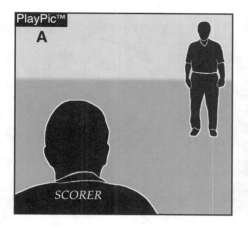

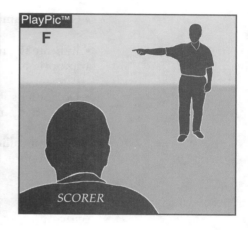

Foul reporting sequence

There's a specific sequence of signals when reporting a foul to the scorer. Using the same sequence reduces confusion for the scorer.

1. Do not let substitutes enter or grant a timeout until after reporting is complete.

2. After moving to the reporting area (see "Foul reporting area," p. 67), *stop* and square up to the scorer (see "Reporting numbers," p. 68). Stopping is critical. If you're moving while reporting, you increase the chances of the scorer missing something.

3. After stopping, make eye contact with the scorer (PlayPic A). Wait if you have to! It doesn't make sense to report when the scorer's not watching; you'll probably have to do it again.

4. If a goal was scored and a player was fouled in the act of shooting, signal to the scorer that the goal counts before any other signal (see "Signals chart," p. 46). Also, if you signaled a canceled goal at the spot of the foul (for example, the foul did not occur in the act of shooting), use the "no goal" signal before any other signal (see "Signals chart," p. 46 and "Trail helps on made basket," p. 63).

5. Verbalize the team color of the player that fouled. Some codes ask the reporting official to point to the offending player's bench while verbalizing the team color. The arguments for: It helps the scorer quickly locate the fouler's team in the scorebook. Plus, it's easier to see than to hear in noisy gyms. The arguments against: It is not an approved signal. Plus, no one uses it in major

college games and if those scorers can figure it out with 20,000 screaming fans, it shouldn't be a problem with 200 people at a high school game. If your association mandates pointing to the bench, do it. If not, don't.

6. Use your dominant hand to signal the number(s) of the player that fouled (PlayPic B). Most officials use their right hand, but there's nothing wrong with lefties using their left hand. Verbalize the numbers at the same time. When verbalizing a two-digit number, say the full number, not the two parts. For example, a foul on number 24 should be said, "Blue, twenty-four" not "blue, two-four." The "two-four" reference can be confusing to the scorer (see "Reporting numbers," p. 68).

7. Signal the type of foul (PlayPic C). Use the same signal that you gave at the spot of the foul (see "Foul signaling sequence," p. 56). If you use different signals, it opens you up for criticism; it appears you don't know what you called. Do not verbalize the foul signal. Verbalizing usually starts a potentially unpleasant dialogue with a coach who takes exception to the call. For example, if you say, "Blue, twenty four, with a push." The coach will more often take exception to "the push" by saying something like, "That wasn't a push!" than if you simply signaled it.

8. Signal what comes next, a one-and-one (PlayPic D), one, two or three free throws (PlayPic E) or the throw-in spot (PlayPic F).

9. Beckon substitutes or grant a timeout as necessary.

10. Move to the appropriate spot for ensuing action.

Reporting Fouls

• Make eye contact with the scorer before reporting.

• Come to a complete stop before reporting; movement causes confusion.

• Slowly state the fouling player's team color and jersey number.

• Signal the fouler's numbers with one hand and simultaneously verbalize the number.

• Hold your hand at about chin height and off to the side of your head.

• Give the same foul signal you gave at the spot to the scorer.

• Indicate the number of free throws or point to the throw-in spot as appropriate.

• Do not let substitutes enter the court or grant a timeout until all signals are complete.

• The non-calling official must watch all players while the calling official reports to the scorer.

Quiz

Without referring back, you should be able to answer the following true-false questions.

1. It's OK to use both hands when reporting numbers to the scorer, just like the NBA refs do.

2. The non-calling official's first responsibility is the chase the basketball.

3. The non-calling official may prepare players for the ensuing play while the calling official reports to the scorer.

4. You must get the ball back in play as quickly as possible without sacrificing quality signals or good dead-ball officiating.

5. On every foul, the calling official should go all the way over to the scorer's table to report the foul to be sure that scorer heard everything correctly.

1 - False, 2 - False, 3 - True, 4 - True, 5 - False

Chapter 9

Court Coverage

Court coverage

With a crew of two officials, court coverage is about significant movement — especially by the trail — and making conscious, intelligent sacrifices. The trail must move off the sideline for proper court coverage. That allows the lead to watch players off-ball, the critical component to controlling physical play.

In all cases, only one official watches the player with the ball. By maintaining proper spacing and angles, that on-ball official can also see some off-ball players within the immediate area. Usually, however, the on-ball official is watching the offensive player with the ball, plus the defender guarding. If both officials were watching the player with the ball, that leaves up to eight other players unattended, where the off-ball push, elbow or punch goes unnoticed. The off-ball official must watch those players carefully at all times.

Because of the necessary emphasis on off-ball coverage, some boundary line coverage is sacrificed. It's simply a tradeoff. You're focusing on great off-ball coverage and giving up a bit of sideline coverage in some areas. You're playing the percentages because you're more likely to have rough play than you are to have sideline violations that aren't obvious.

Coverage areas shift depending on where the ball is. If you started a play on-ball, you switch to off-ball coverage when the ball leaves your coverage area and you're certain your partner is watching on-ball. Your coverage switches back to on-ball if the ball returns to your coverage area. Those on-ball, off-ball, on-ball (or any variation thereof) switches occur on most plays. By studying the ensuing PlayPics and MechaniGrams and explanations, you'll learn who's got what and know when coverage switches occur.

Generally, in a halfcourt setting:

• The trail's on-ball responsibilities include the area above the free-throw line extended opposite the trail to the division line and from the free-throw lane line to the sideline on the trail side of the court.

• When the trail is on-ball, the lead's off-ball responsibilities include the area below the free-throw line extended, including the lane, out to the free-throw lane line on the trail side of the court.

• The lead's on-ball responsibilities include the area below the free-throw line extended and the free-throw lane line (away from the lead) to the sideline nearest the lead. If the lead is ball-side, the lead's area of responsibility grows. It includes the area below the free-throw line extended to the the three-point arc.

• When the lead is on-ball, the trail's off-ball responsibilities include the area above the free-throw line extended to the division line and the free-throw lane line (nearest the trail) to the sideline nearest the trail. The trail's off-ball area of responsibility decreases when the lead is on-ball, ball-side. It is the area above the free-throw line extended and outside the three-point arc.

• Moving ball side improves the lead's view of low-post action.

• The trail has a much better look on drives to the lane that start on the trail's half of the court when the lead is on the far side of the court.

• By aggressively penetrating toward the endline when players drive the lane, the trail can take some of the pressure off the lead by being in great position to judge the play.

Generally, in a fullcourt setting:

• The new trail is responsible for the backcourt endline and for the sideline opposite the new lead.

• The new lead is responsible for the frontcourt endline.

• *Referee* recommends that the sideline opposite the trail in the backcourt is a shared responsibility.

The trail must get off the sideline to officiate those coverage areas correctly. It takes a lot of movement and an understanding of good angles. Proper coverage requires good eye contact and a "feel" for where your partner is looking. Specific officiating movements designed to better cover particular plays force coverage adjustments, as illustrated throughout this book.

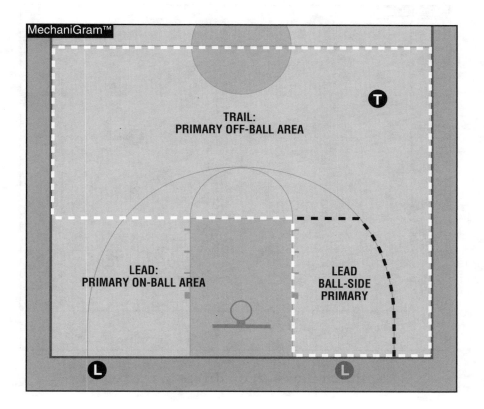

Court coverage: basic frontcourt responsibilities

In the frontcourt, basic coverage shifts depending on which official is on-ball.

In the MechaniGram, the lead's on-ball responsibilities include the area below the free-throw line extended to the far edge of the free-throw lane line (away from the lead) when the lead is oppostie the trail and the floor is balanced. If the lead is ball-side, the lead's area of responsibility grows. It includes the area below the free-throw line extended to the the three-point arc.

When the lead is on-ball, the trail's off-ball responsibilities include the area above the free-throw line extended to the division line and the lane area from the free-throw lane line (nearest the trail) to the sideline nearest the trail. The trail's off-ball area of responsibility decreases when the lead is on-ball, ball-side. It is the area above the free-throw line extended and outside the three-point arc.

The MechaniGram illustrates basic guidelines for coverage. Specific officiating movements designed to better cover particular plays force the officials to adjust coverage, as illustrated throughout this book.

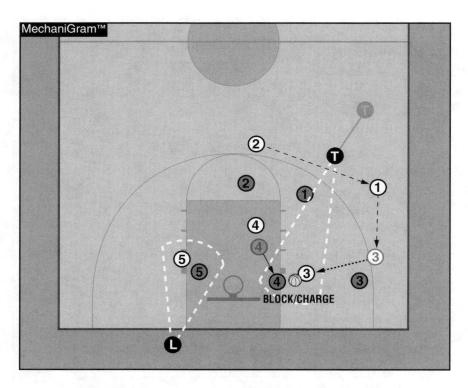

Splitting the court on drives to the basket

Sometimes, the lead doesn't have enough time to get ball side, avoid quicksand and get a good look on drives toward the basket. When players make quick passes away from the lead that cover a great distance, it's difficult to react in time to get a good angle.

When that happens, there's a simple solution: "You take the stuff on your side of the hoop and I'll take the stuff on my side of the hoop."

There's a great myth among referees that the lead is the only official who can call block/charge near the lane. That's wrong. That attitude places too much pressure on the lead because there's too much to watch. It also leaves the lead straightlined and guessing on many plays that aren't on the lead's side of the floor.

When the lead is on the far side of the court, the trail has a much better look on drives to the lane that start on the trail's half of the court. But it takes an aggressive, hard-working trail to make the call correctly and with conviction.

As the trail, penetrate toward the endline to get the proper angle on the drive to basket. Referee the defense. Make the call. It's really that simple.

In the MechaniGram, the officials start the play with the floor balanced. ② quickly passes to ①, who quickly passes to ③. ③ immediately drives around ❸ toward the basket. The action is too fast for the lead to move ball side. As ③ drives toward the basket, ❹ steps in to take a charge. The trail penetrates toward the endline, gets a good angle and makes the judgment on the contact.

Developing an aggressive mindset as a trail official will help overall court coverage. Don't leave the lead alone. Do your part by taking the "stuff" on your side of the basket when the lead can't see clearly.

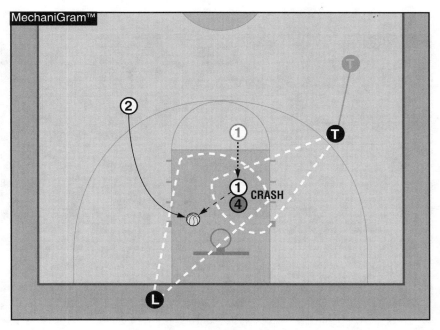

Pass/crash in the lane

A player driving a crowded lane, passing off to a teammate, then crashing into a defender can be one of the most difficult plays to officiate. Why? There's a lot going on in a small area in a short period of time.

For the lead, the play is especially tough to handle alone. Did the passer get fouled? Did the passer foul? Block? Charge? Did the passer foul after releasing the ball or was it a player-control foul? Did the dribbler travel? Did the player filling the lane catch the pass cleanly and travel or did the player merely fumble and recover? Did the violation occur before the foul? Oh, and by the way … just who is shooting the one-and-one at the other end? That's way too much for one official to handle in most cases.

The trail must help. By aggressively penetrating toward the endline when players drive the lane, the trail can take some of the pressure off the lead by being in great position to judge the play.

The common phrase that sums up responsibilities is, "Lead takes the pass, trail takes the crash." That's generally accurate when the pass is toward the lead. However, when the pass is toward the trail (especially out toward the perimeter), the trail should take the pass and the lead take the crash.

The trail should watch the dribbler penetrate. Watch for the dribbler being fouled on the drive or while passing. Also, the trail watches for the dribbler crashing into a defender after releasing a pass that goes toward the lead. Referee the defense to see if the defender obtained legal guarding position. Be especially wary of dribblers who leave their feet to make a pass. Don't bail out an out-of-control player by making a no-call.

With the trail watching that action, the lead can concentrate primarily on the pass toward the lead and the player receiving it. Don't fall into the trap, however, of leaving all crashes to the trail. For the lead, the pass is primary, but the crash is secondary. You'd rather have a call on the crash from the lead than a no-call that lets a foul get away. Sometimes, the proper pass/crash angle is difficult for the trail to obtain, especially if there's heavy lane traffic. Be prepared to make a call as the lead if you have to.

If the dribbler passes the ball toward the trail, the trail takes the pass and the lead takes the crash. Be especially wary of dribblers who leave their feet and then make long passes out to the perimeter toward the trail.

In the MechaniGram, ① drives the lane. When ④ steps up to stop the drive, ① passes to ②, who was filling the lane. The trail penetrates toward the endline to get a good angle on the play. The trail has primary coverage on the crash. The lead watches ② catch the pass and lay it in. The lead also has secondary coverage of the crash.

Whatever call is made and whoever makes it, sell it! It's a real "bang-bang" play that can have major implications. For example, if the dribbler goes airborne to make the pass, the player filling the lane catches the pass and is about to lay it in when the airborne player crashes into a defender, that foul wipes away the basket. The trail must have the intestinal fortitude to come in strong and make that call.

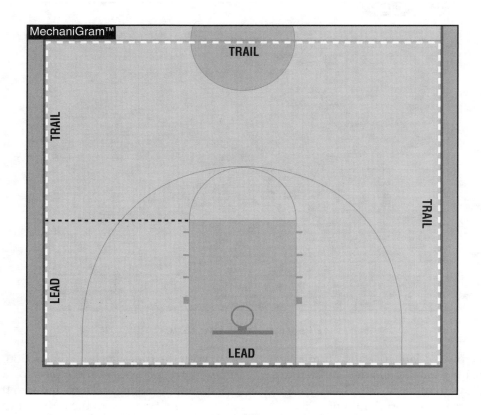

Boundary coverage: basic frontcourt responsibilities

Covering boundary lines is among the most difficult tasks using a crew of two officials. By correctly placing so much emphasis on off-ball coverage for the lead, (see "Court coverage," p. 73), some boundary line coverage sometimes gets sacrificed.

The NFHS manual states that in the frontcourt the lead is responsible for the sideline nearest the lead and the endline. The trail is responsible for the division line and the sideline nearest the trail. While in theory that sounds easy, the actual practice is very difficult and sacrifices off-ball coverage in the lane area.

Here's an example. A trouble spot for two-person crews is a player who has the ball near the sideline above the free-throw line extended and opposite the trail. The trail correctly moves toward the center of the court to officiate the action on the player with the ball, such as fouls, traveling violations, etc. (See, "Trail movement off sideline," p. 92).

The problem: The manual states that sideline is the lead's responsibility. Well, if the lead has to look beyond the free-throw line extended to watch for a potential sideline violation and the trail has to watch for fouls, etc., who is watching the other players? No one. There are too many off-ball problems that can occur if no one is supervising those players.

Referee recommends that the trail also have opposite sideline responsibility above the free-throw line extended. Sometimes, the trail must move well beyond the center of the court to see an out-of-bounds violation. Stay deep (toward the division line) on the play to get a good angle.

Even with great hustle toward the far sideline, it is a tough look for the trail. The problem compounds if there's a swing pass back toward the other sideline. The trail must hustle back toward that sideline to get a good look there. Staying deep gives the trail a chance.

Reality is, however, that most out-of-bounds calls are fairly obvious ones. The defender knocking the ball into the crowd or the dribbler kicking the ball into the bench can be called even from a bad angle. The close ones (for example when a player holding the ball pivots away from defensive pressure and narrowly steps on the sideline) are difficult but are few in comparison.

Though not the best sideline coverage, you're making a conscious sacrifice. You might occasionally miss an out-of-bounds call. Obviously, we don't want to miss calls. However, that's better than missing an off-ball elbow to a player's head because no one was watching. It's a trade-off we must make: Off-ball coverage to control rough physical play is more important than an occasional missed sideline violation.

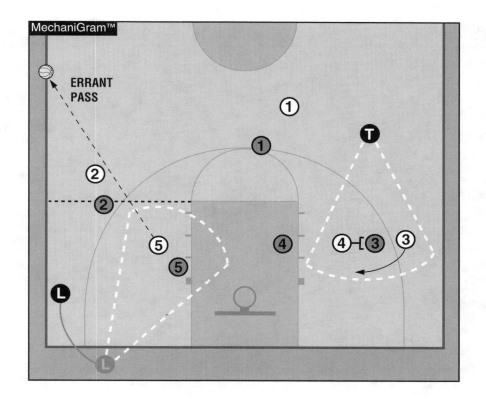

Boundary coverage: frontcourt lead exception

Though *Referee* recommends that the trail is responsible for the opposite sideline above the free-throw line extended (see "Boundary coverage: frontcourt," p. 76), there is an exception.

When the floor is balanced, the lead is on-ball and a pass is thrown from the lane to a player above the free-throw line extended, the lead has initial responsibility of the entire sideline. Why? When the lead is on-ball, the trail is off-ball (see "Court coverage," p. 73). The trail may not see an errant pass out-of-bounds above the free-throw line extended because the trail and lead haven't switched coverages yet. The trail can't effectively watch off-ball and see a quick pass made to the opposite sideline. The lead must help.

In the MechaniGram, ⑤ has the ball in the low post. The lead is on-ball. The trail is correctly watching off-ball, including ④ screening ❸. While the trail is off-ball, ⑤ throws an errant pass in the direction of ②. The ball goes out-of-bounds above the free-throw line extended.

Since the lead was watching the play already and the trail was watching off-ball, the lead makes that call by moving toward the sideline and getting a good angle on the play. Though *Referee* suggests that would normally be the trail's call above the free-throw line extended, this coverage exception ensures quality off-ball coverage.

Note: If the errant pass is deflected by the defense and out-of-bounds above the free-throw line extended (the ball remains in the frontcourt), the lead makes the call, but *Referee* recommends that the trail swings over and administers the throw-in. The NFHS manual states the lead is responsible for all throw-ins on the lead's sideline in the frontcourt. Check with your governing bodies to see if you can use the *Referee* recommendation.

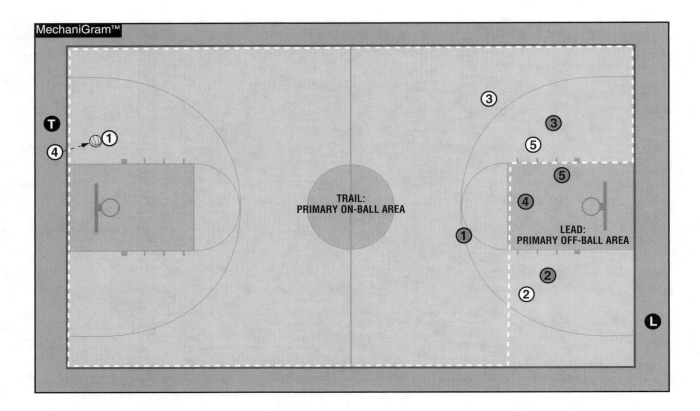

Court coverage: backcourt, no defensive pressure

When play moves from one endline toward the other, the trail has primary responsibility in the backcourt. For example, after a made basket the trail is responsible for the throw-in and watches the players move to the other end of the court.

In any transition effective coverage means significant movement by the trail. Similar to halfcourt coverage, the trail must move off the sideline (see "Trail movement off sideline," p. 92).

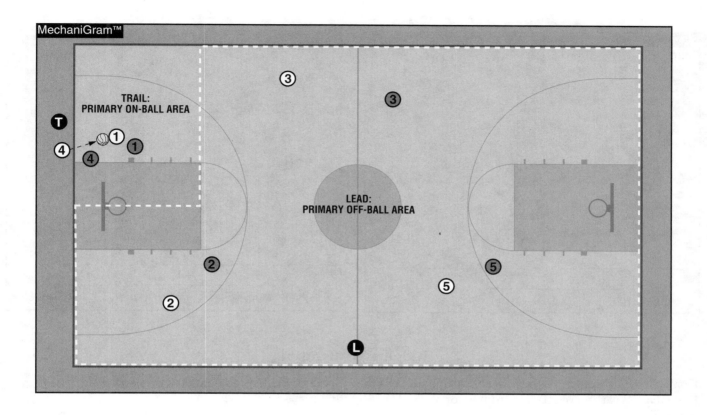

Court coverage: backcourt, defensive pressure

When play moves from one endline toward the other, the trail has primary responsibility in the backcourt. However, when there's defensive pressure in the backcourt, sometimes the lead must help.

There is a general rule when the lead helps the trail in the backcourt. If there are four or fewer players in the backcourt, the trail works alone there. More than four players, the lead helps.

When there's more than four players in the backcourt, the lead is positioned near the division line. If all the players are in the backcourt, the lead may move closer to the backcourt endline for better angles. If some players are in the frontcourt, however, the division-line area is the best position.

When near the division line, the lead must stay wide and constantly glance from backcourt to frontcourt. That "swivel" glance allows the lead to help the trail with backcourt traffic plus watch players in the frontcourt.

No call

Goaltending

Judging goaltending

Goaltending is arguably one of the most difficult calls in basketball. It can get officials in trouble for a couple of reasons:

1. It doesn't happen very often (especially during high school and lower-level games).

2. Officials are usually not watching the ball after it has been released on a try.

In almost all situations, the trail is responsible for goaltending. However, the lead can call goaltending if the trail doesn't see it. That's *very* rare because the lead shouldn't be watching the flight of the ball from the endline; the lead should be watching strong-side rebounding, etc. Another exception: When the trail moving to new lead on a transition play is behind the fastbreak play, the new lead has primary goaltending responsibility.

Because goaltending is somewhat rare, it becomes a reactionary call that can take you by surprise. Too often the trail is correctly watching other things: fouls in the act of shooting, three-point lines, fouls after the try has been released, weak-side rebounding, etc. When a defensive player leaps to block the shot, an official's reaction is sometimes just a bit slow, reducing judgment to guesswork.

The NFHS rule on goaltending reads, "Goaltending occurs when a player touches the ball during a field goal try or tap while:

a. The ball is in downward flight.

b. The entire ball is above the level of the basket ring.

c. The ball has a possibility of entering the basket in flight.

d. The ball is not touching an imaginary cylinder which has the basket ring as its lower base."

To correctly rule on goaltending, you must judge the arc of the ball. That's easier said than done because of all the other things you have to observe. In theory it's simple: ball is upward, no-call; ball is downward, goaltending. The reality is much different, especially when the ball is near its apex, or the top of the arc. The short- to medium-range jump shots are most difficult, generally because they happen so quickly.

One simple tool officials can use to help themselves judge goaltending correctly is knowing where the defender is in relation to the shooter and the basket. Simply stated, if the defender is closer to the shooter than to the basket when the ball is touched, you've likely got a no-call because the ball is likely still on its way up (PlayPic A). If the defender is closer to the basket than to the shooter when the ball is touched, it's probably goaltending because the ball is likely on its way down (PlayPic B).

Understand that advice is merely a *guideline* to help officials, it is not a cure-all. Judging goaltending still requires a knowledge of where the ball was touched in its arc, but knowing where the defender was when the ball was touched can help when making that tough call or no-call.

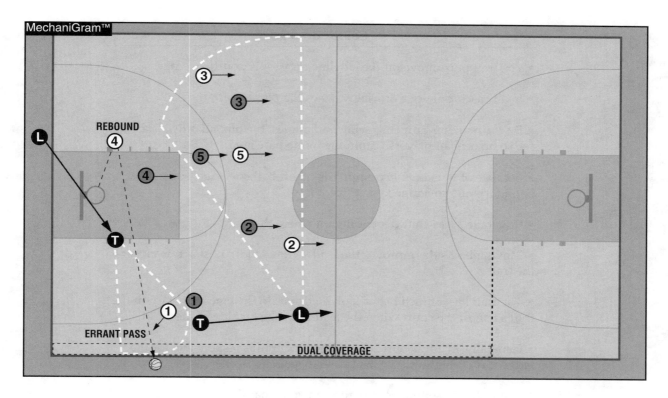

Boundary coverage: backcourt

In the backcourt, the new trail is responsible for the backcourt endline and the sideline opposite the new lead. The new lead is responsible for the frontcourt endline. That's the easy part. Who's got the sideline opposite the new trail and who's got the division line?

The sideline opposite the trail in the backcourt is a shared responsibility. Simply stated, when the new lead is looking in the area where the sideline violation occurs, the new lead makes the call. Actual practice can be a bit of a challenge though.

Proper coverage is necessitated by good eye contact and a "feel" for where the new lead is looking. One general rule of thumb: If you were on-ball immediately before a play near the sideline, you've likely got sideline responsibility. (One notable exception is when the new lead is helping with backcourt pressure, is positioned on the sideline and the ball goes out-of-bounds near the new lead. It would be odd to have the new trail make an out-of-bounds call from an appreciable distance when the ball went out-of-bounds in close proximity to the new lead.)

If the new lead is already looking in the area (on-ball or off-ball) where the out-of-bounds violation occurs, the new lead can make that call. If the new lead is running into the frontcourt watching players in transition (off-ball) and the play happens behind the new lead, the new trail has sideline responsibility.

In the MechaniGram, ④ grabs a rebound. ②, ⑤ and ③ sprint toward the frontcourt to attempt a fastbreak. The trail, becoming the new lead, sprints upcourt with the players, watching off-ball. ① breaks toward the corner opposite the new trail. ④ throws an errant pass to ① that goes out-of-bounds. Since the new trail was already on-ball and the new lead was sprinting away from the play watching off-ball, *Referee* recommends that the out-of-bounds call belongs to the new trail.

Help each other out. If the new lead whistles an out-of-bounds violation on the new lead's sideline but doesn't know who caused the violation, blow the whistle, stop the clock and look for help from the new trail.

With a transition play near the division line, the new lead has initial responsibility until the new trail is in position to get a good look at the division line. Eye contact and a feel for where your partner is watching play an important role in who has division line responsibility.

Court Coverage

- The trail must move off the sideline for proper court coverage.

- In all cases, only one official watches the player with the ball.

- By maintaining proper spacing and angles, the on-ball official can also see some off-ball players within the immediate area.

- Because of the necessary emphasis on off-ball coverage, some boundary line coverage is sacrificed.

- Coverage areas shift depending on where the ball is.

- Moving ball-side improves the lead's view of low-post action closer to the trail.

- The trail has a much better look on drives to the lane that start on the trail's half of the court when the lead is on the far side of the court.

- Generally, in a fullcourt setting, the new trail is responsible for the backcourt endline and for the sideline opposite the new lead.

- In a fullcourt setting, *Referee* recommends that the sideline opposite the trail in the backcourt is a shared responsibility.

Quiz

Without referring back, you should be able to answer the following true-false questions.

1. The lead should be positioned directly under the basket when a shot is taken.

2. *Referee* recommends that the trail is responsible for the sideline opposite the trail above the free-throw line extended.

3. On a pass/crash play with the pass going toward the lead, ideally the lead takes the pass and the trail takes the crash.

4. The lead should never call goaltending.

5. When there are less than four players in the backcourt, the general advice is that the trail is solely responsible.

1 - False, 2 - True, 3 - True, 4 - False, 5 - True

Chapter 10

Lead Position

The lead position

The lead is normally positioned on the endline. That unique look means plays generally come toward the lead. The lead has a great opportunity to see drives to the basket, post-up play and rebounding action. Movement along and away from the endlines to improve angles is critical to the lead's success.

In most situations, the lead's primary responsibility is off-ball coverage. That means rough post play mainly falls on the shoulders of the lead. A strong lead usually means a game under control; a weak lead tends to let games get too rough.

The most basic yet necessary skill for working the lead is training yourself to watch off-ball. All our lives as sports fans, watching games in person or on TV, we've been watching action around the ball. For example, most fans watch the player dribbling rather than the action in the lane. As a lead, you've got to stop watching like a fan and start watching off-ball. It's tempting to see what's going on with the ball, especially when you hear the crowd react to something, but you must fight that temptation and remain focused on off-ball coverage.

Moving off the endline and avoiding straightlining are important elements to successful lead officiating. If you're too close to the endline you lose perspective because your sightlines are too narrow. With six or more off-ball players moving through the lane area attempting to gain position, straightlining is a major concern. A one- or two-step adjustment left or right improves your sightline angles tremendously.

Generally, in a halfcourt setting:

• The lead must use ball side mechanics by anticipating a weak side play and moving across the endline to get an angle on the weak side low-post action.

• The lead will only move ball side when the perimeter player with the ball is near or below the free-throw line extended.

• Keep your head and shoulders turned toward the players in the lane when moving.

• Never position yourself directly under the basket.

• When the ball drops below the free-throw line extended on the lead side of the court, the lead has two responsibilities: Watch the post players on the near low block and watch the perimeter player with the ball.

• To improve on-ball coverage, back off the endline and move toward the sideline when necessary.

With movement along and away from the endline and off-ball concentration, the lead has a much better chance of officiating plays correctly.

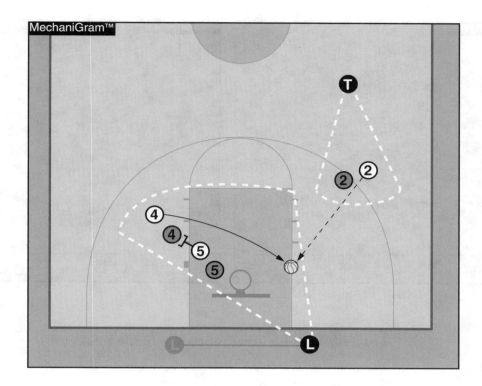

Lead must use ball side mechanics

Many teams today use off-ball screens to free post players near the basket. In the MechaniGram, ⑤ screens ④ so ④ can flash ball side and receive a drop pass from ②. If the play works effectively, the post player is open, catches the ball and scores an easy lay-up. Defensive players will either try to cut off the post player's movement to the open spot or race to challenge the post player's shot.

The lead must anticipate the play (that does not mean anticipate a foul!) and move across the endline to get an angle on the action moving toward the open spot. In the MechaniGram above, the lead official has moved across the endline to clearly see the post player catch the ball and attempt a shot. The lead's in a great position to see the oncoming defensive players and any potential violations or fouls. Generally, the lead will only move ball side when the perimeter player with the ball is near or below the free-throw line extended.

Keep your head and shoulders turned toward the players in the lane when moving. Remember, you still have responsibilities for watching the screen and other action in your primary area. If you put your head down and sprint across the lane to the new spot, you will miss off-ball contact. Move with dispatch, but move under control and with your eyes on your primary off-ball area. If the ball moves out of the post area, simply move back to your original position to balance the floor with the trail.

The lead moves for two reasons: The lead is in a better position to see the play clearly (if the lead stayed on the off-ball side he would be looking through bodies and guessing) and the lead is closer to the play, which helps sell the call or no-call. Perception is important. If you look like you're close to the play and in good position, your ruling has a better chance of being accepted.

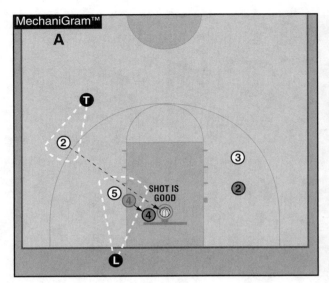

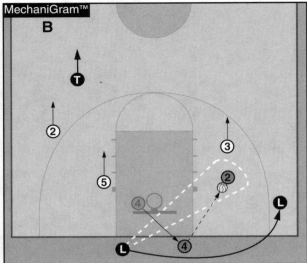

Lead ball side: movement after made basket

When the lead is ball side watching action in the post and a goal is scored, there's no need to rush back to the lane line opposite the trail and balance the floor. If immediately after the made basket you can balance the floor without interfering with the ensuing play and without missing action around the throw-in area, do so.

However, in most situations there is not enough time to balance the floor without interfering and missing action. If you don't have time to get over, don't panic. You've still got a pretty good angle to watch all the action.

Watch for players interfering with the ball after the made basket. Watch the player collect the ball and move out-of-bounds for the throw-in. Then, watch the thrower, the throw-in and action in the lane area. You can do all that from the lane line on the trail side of the floor.

After the throw-in is made, quickly swing behind the thrower toward the far sideline to balance the floor.

In MechaniGram A, the lead is ball side watching the post players when ② makes a jump shot. ④ grabs the ball and moves out-of-bounds for a throw-in. The lead does not have enough time to balance the floor before the throw-in. In MechaniGram B, ④ is out-of-bounds and throws an inbounds pass to ②. The lead, still on the opposite side, watches the thrower and throw-in, then quickly swings behind the thrower to balance the floor.

Too close

Good angle

Lead movement toward sideline

When the ball drops below the free-throw line extended on the lead side of the court, the lead has two responsibilities: Watch the post players on the near low block and watch the perimeter player with the ball. It is difficult to see both areas.

To give yourself a chance, back off the endline and move toward the sideline. Your shoulders should not be parallel to the endline. Angle them slightly; that movement increases your field of vision and gives you a chance to see both areas.

In PlayPic A, the lead is too close to the play and is not close enough to the sideline.

In PlayPic B, the lead is in better position after moving off the endline, moving closer to the sideline and angling the shoulders. Primary coverage is on-ball; secondary coverage is off-ball (see "Court coverage," p. 73). With that improved position, the lead has a chance to see both in his field of view.

Lead Position

• The lead is normally positioned on the endline.

• Movement along and away from the endlines to improve angles is critical to the lead's success.

• In most situations, the lead's primary responsibility is off-ball coverage.

• The lead must avoid straightlining.

• The lead must maintain proper spacing.

• The lead must use ball side mechanics by anticipating a weak side play and moving across the endline to get an angle on the weak side low-post action.

• The lead only moves ball side when the perimeter player with the ball is near or below the free-throw line extended.

• When moving across the lane, keep your head and shoulders turned toward the players in the lane so you can watch them effectively.

• The lead should never be positioned directly under the basket.

• To improve angles, move toward the sideline when necessary.

Quiz

Without referring back, you should be able to answer the following true-false questions.

1. The lead must avoid the quicksand area.

2. When on-ball, the lead's shoulders should be parallel to the endline.

3. When moving ball side across the lane, the lead should run with head down to get to the new position quickly.

4. If you're closer to the play and in good position, your ruling has a much better chance of being accepted.

5. The lead should always be positioned directly on the endline.

Chapter 11

Trail Position

The trail position

Effective court coverage requires significant movement by the trail. The trail must get off the sideline to view plays opposite the trail near the far sideline and above the free-throw line extended. Angles are just as important as distance. Stay deep on plays to keep good angles and avoid being in passing lanes.

Most of the time in a halfcourt setting, the trail has on-ball responsibility. Keep proper spacing and avoid being straightlined when watching on-ball.

The trail must help the lead on drives to the basket, rebounding action and plays that occur opposite the lead. There's a common myth that anything that happens in the lane area is the lead's responsibility. As the following PlayPics and MechaniGrams show, effective court coverage is dependent on an aggressive trail working for angles in areas that the lead can't see. Think about where the lead is positioned and what the lead is likely to see clearly from that position, then adjust your coverage to see where the lead is not likely to see things — like weak side rebounding, action near the free-throw line, etc.

Generally, in a halfcourt setting:

• When an offensive player has the ball opposite the trail, the trail must move away from the closest sideline and get proper angles.

• When moving toward the center of the court, the trail must stay deep (toward the division line) to avoid passing lanes.

• When a swing pass occurs with the trail in the middle of the court, the trail must use an inside-out look; a one- or two-step adjustment toward the center of the court gives you the proper angle.

• When a player takes a shot within the trail's coverage area, the trail's first responsibility is to watch the airborne shooter all the way back to the floor to ensure there are no offensive or defensive fouls.

• After a shot is taken, the trail must penetrate toward the endline to improve rebounding angles.

• The trail must watch the area in the lane when a post player spins away from the lead.

Work hard as the trail to cover the court and help the lead. When a shot goes up or you're off-ball, you've got just as much responsibility in the lane area as the lead. Resist the urge to move downcourt toward the division line when there's a shot attempt. Help out with rebounding action and drives to the basket to ensure quality court coverage.

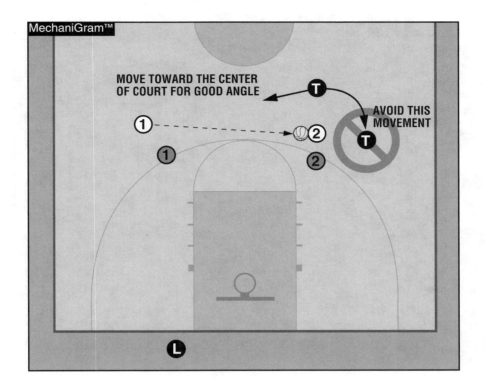

MechaniGram™

MOVE TOWARD THE CENTER
OF COURT FOR GOOD ANGLE

AVOID THIS
MOVEMENT

The 'inside-out' look

With a crew of two officials, the trail official often has to get off the sideline and move toward the center of the court to officiate action on the far side of the floor. When that happens, the trail can get caught in the middle on a swing pass from one side of the court to the other. Adjustments must be made.

When a swing pass moves from the sideline opposite the trail across the top of the key to the near-side wing, the trail can get straightlined because of the position off the sideline. When a quick swing pass straightlines you and gives you a poor angle, you must make an adjustment to improve the angle.

A simple one- or two-step adjustment *toward the center of the court* gives you the proper angle. You must fight the urge to run around the entire play toward the sideline, using six steps or more and wasting precious time. By the time you run around the play, the offensive player could take a shot (was the shooter's foot on or behind the three-point arc?), violate or be fouled — and you may not have seen it (see "Inside-out look," p. 19).

After adjusting one or two steps toward the center to improve your angle, watch the entire play from there, including a jump shot follow-through and landing. After you've taken care of that responsibility, you can move toward the sideline and endline, working for your next good angle on rebounding action.

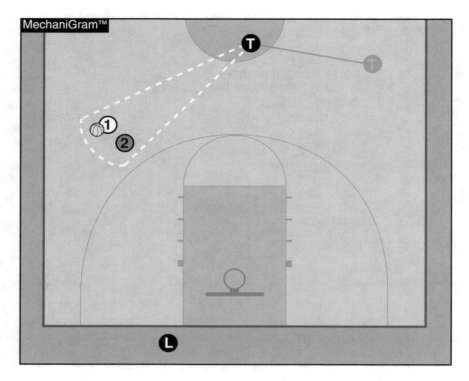

Trail movement off sideline

Effective court coverage requires significant movement by the trail.

When an offensive player has the ball on the side of the floor opposite the trail, the trail must move away from the near sideline and get proper angles. By staying too close to the near sideline, the trail cannot effectively see action near the ball and must make judgments from a distance — way too far away to convince anyone the trail saw the play correctly.

In the MechaniGram, ① with the ball is far away from the trail official — though the player is still the trail's responsibility — and there's defensive pressure. To see the play well, the trail must move off the near sideline and work to get a good angle.

Avoid moving straight toward the play: You could interfere with the play by stepping into a passing lane. Take an angle toward the division line to decrease your chances of interfering with the play. In extreme cases, you may even position yourself in the backcourt.

By moving off the sideline and angling toward the backcourt, you're in a much better position to see the play.

Trail movement off sideline

Effective court coverage requires significant movement by the trail.

When an offensive player has the ball on the side of the floor opposite the trail, the trail must move away from the near sideline and get proper angles. By staying too close to the near sideline, the trail cannot effectively see action near the ball and must make judgments from a far distance — way too far to convince anyone the trail saw the play correctly.

In PlayPic A, the player with the ball is near the sideline opposite the trail and above the free-throw line extended — still the trail's responsibility (see "Court coverage," p. 73). The trail is too far away and must adjust toward the center of the court.

In PlayPic B, the trail adjusts toward the center of the court for the proper distance and angle. Notice the trail also stays deep to avoid passing lanes.

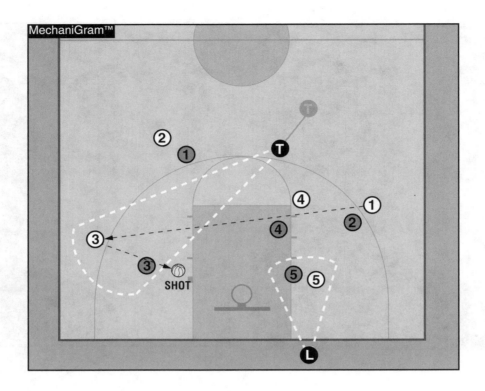

Trail must pick up shooter on skip pass

In two-person mechanics, the lead official should move to the ball side of the lane when the player with the ball is below the free-throw line extended and a potential post pass is evident (see "Lead must use ball side mechanics," p. 85).

Though ball side mechanics are effective for controlling post play, one weakness is coverage of a skip pass to the opposite wing player for a quick shot. A skip pass is a quick pass from one side of the floor to the other, designed to take advantage of a sagging defense. Taboo years ago, it's now seen at virtually every level.

Though the opposite wing player is primarily observed by the lead official (even though the lead moved ball side), when a skip pass occurs the trail should adjust a step or two toward the wing player (to the center of the floor) and get a good angle to rule on three-point attempts, fouls and possibly obvious out-of-bounds infractions. Though a long-distance look, that's better than having the lead guess because the lead's looking through lane traffic or sprinting head-down to the other side of the court and missing the banging going on in the post.

If there is no quick shot and the lead can adjust back to the other side of the court without haste, the lead then picks up the ball (assuming it is below the free-throw line extended) and the trail moves back toward the sideline, getting good angles to watch off-ball. The lead must continue to watch off-ball in the lane area while moving until completely across the lane and in a good position to pick up the player with the ball.

In the MechaniGram, the lead has moved ball side. ① throws a skip pass to ③, who quickly shoots. Since the lead is ball side and doesn't have enough time to balance the floor, the trail picks up ③, even though ③ is below the free-throw line extended. The trail should penetrate slightly toward the play to improve the angle.

A good pregame conference and good eye contact during the game give you a better chance to officiate the skip pass correctly.

Trail must pick up shooter on skip pass

Though lead ball side mechanics are extremely effective for controlling post play (see "Lead must use ball side mechanics," p. 85), one weakness is coverage of a skip pass to the opposite wing player for a quick shot. A skip pass is a quick pass from one side of the floor to the other, designed to take advantage of a sagging defense.

Though the opposite wing player is primarily observed by the lead official (even though the lead moved to ball side), when a skip pass occurs the trail should adjust a step or two toward the wing player (toward the center of the floor) and get a good angle to rule on three-point attempts, fouls and obvious out-of-bounds infractions. Though a long-distance look, that's better than having the lead guess because the lead's looking through lane traffic or sprinting head-down to the other side of the court and missing the banging going on in the post.

In PlayPic A, the trail is primary on-ball, watching the perimeter player with the ball. The lead has moved ball side to watch post play. The perimeter player then throws a skip pass to a teammate near the opposite sideline. In PlayPic B, the trail adjusts toward the center of the court and picks up the shooter. The trail must help on that skip pass — even though the shooter is below the free-throw line extended — because the lead is ball side and does not have enough time to balance the floor.

After the shot is released, the trail watches the shooter return to the floor, looking for fouls, etc. Next, the trail penetrates toward the endline for improved rebounding angles (see "Trail movement on jump shot," p. 99).

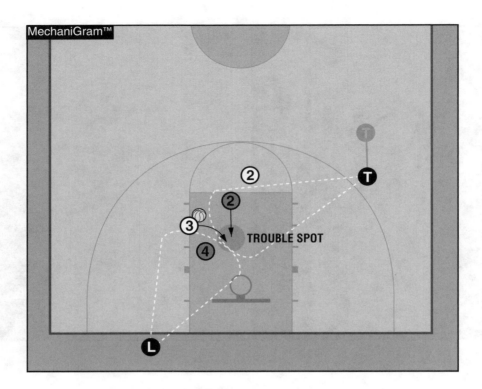

Trail must work 'backside' in lane area

A trouble spot for the lead develops when a player with the ball on the low block spins toward the middle of the lane away from the lead. The quick spin move often leaves the lead straightlined and without a good look on the play.

Many times, a defender near the free-throw line will drop down into the lane and challenge the move toward the basket. That's when you'll likely see that defender slap at the offensive player, trying to poke the ball away. That steal attempt is sometimes a foul — one that goes unseen by the now-straightlined lead.

The trail must help out and watch the area in the lane when a post player spins away from the lead. Commonly referred to as the lead's "backside," the trail has a much better look at the play after penetrating toward the endline for an improved angle.

In the MechaniGram, ③ has the ball on the low block in front of the lead. ③ then spins toward the middle of the lane and drives toward the basket. ❷ drops down and attempts the steal. The lead watches the post up action and the initial spin move. The trail penetrates toward the endline, gets a good angle and watches ❷ defend the play. The lead's backside is protected.

Come in strong and sell the call if you're the trail and you see a foul. Move toward the call to cut down the distance on the play. Perception is important. If you look like you're close to the play and in good position your ruling has a better chance of being accepted.

Trail must work 'backside' in lane area

A trouble spot for the lead occurs when a player with the ball on the low block spins toward the middle of the lane away from the lead. The quick spin move often leaves the lead straightlined and without a good look at the play.

A defender near the free-throw line will often drop down into the lane and help defend against the move toward the basket. That's when you'll likely see that defender slap at the offensive player, trying to poke the ball away. That steal attempt is sometimes a foul — one that goes unseen by the now-straightlined lead.

The trail must help out and watch the area in the lane when a post player spins away from the lead. Commonly referred to as the lead's "backside," the trail has a much better look at the play after penetrating toward the endline for an improved angle.

In PlayPic A, the lead is watching low post action. In PlayPic B, the offensive player spins away from the lead and a second defender moves toward the offensive player to attempt a steal — it's a congested, straightlined view for the lead.

PlayPic C illustrates the trail's excellent backside view as the second defender slaps the offensive player. That's the trail's call since the spin move went away from the lead.

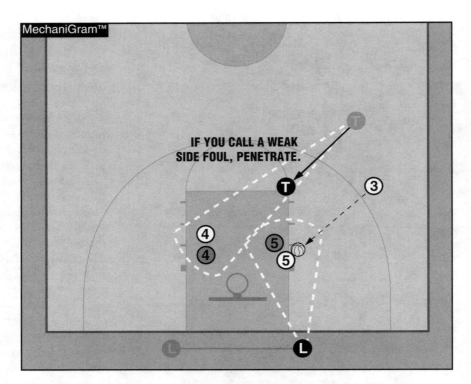

IF YOU CALL A WEAK SIDE FOUL, PENETRATE.

Trail looks weak side when lead moves ball side

There are many benefits of the lead moving ball side for post action (see "Lead must use ball side mechanics," p. 85). One potential problem, however, is weak side rebounding action. With the lead on the same side of the floor as the trail, the lane area opposite both officials can present problems.

With the lead ball-side and already watching post play near the closest lane line, it is difficult for the lead to watch players away from that area in the lane. First, primary concentration is — and should be — on the post play. Second, it is difficult for the lead to see the opposite side of the lane because the lead is looking through lane congestion and is easily straightlined.

When the lead moves ball side, it is the trail's responsibility to observe weak side rebounding action. Though somewhat of a long-distance look, with the proper penetration toward the endline to get a good angle the trail can effectively watch weak side rebounding action.

In the MechaniGram, the trail watches ③ deliver a drop pass to ⑤, who has effectively posted up on the low block. The lead already moved ball side anticipating the play. ⑤ seals off the defender and pivots strongly to the basket. The lead watches the post-up action.

Anticipating the play, the trail adjusts for a good angle and looks opposite. From that spot, the trail can look through the lane and watch ④ battle ④ on the weak side for rebounding positioning.

If you're the trail and you see a foul on the weak side, penetrate toward the lane and sell the call. By moving into the lane area aggressively (roughly around the intersection of the lane line and the free-throw line), the trail will cut the distance. Perception is important. If you look like you're close to the play and in good position, your ruling has a better chance of being accepted.

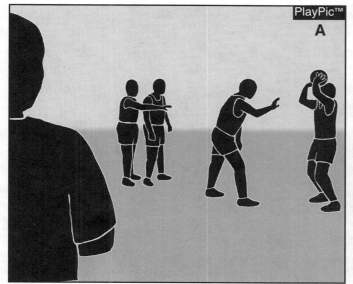

Trail movement on jump shot

The trail has more responsibilities than simply watching the shooter. Too often a shot goes up and the trail's first thought is to start moving to the other end of the floor to avoid getting beat down court. When the trail leaves, the lead is left with offensive players crashing the boards and defensive players doing all they can to grab the rebound. That's too much for one person to handle.

The trail must help with rebounding action. When a player takes a jump shot within the trail's coverage area, the first responsibility is to watch the airborne shooter all the way back to the floor to ensure there are no offensive or defensive fouls (PlayPic A). While watching that action, the trail should be moving a couple of steps toward the endline (PlayPic B).

Once everything is OK with the shooter and surrounding action, the steps toward the endline allow the trail to help the lead by watching rebounding action. A step or two to improve your angle is all that's necessary to successfully watch rebounding action (PlayPic C). Avoid going below the free-throw line extended. The trail is likely to see an offensive player pushing (or crashing into) a defensive player from behind — something that is difficult for the lead to see from the endline (PlayPic D).

Do the game, your partner and yourself a favor and resist the urge to sprint to the other end of the floor when the shot goes up. Move toward the endline to get rebounding angles.

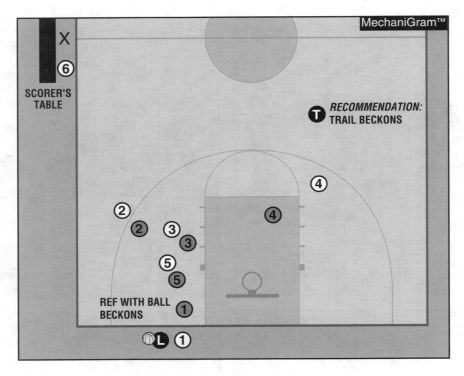

Substitutes beckoned

NFHS mechanics state the official with the ball beckons substitutes into the game. Before putting the ball in play, the official with the ball glances at the scorer's table (at the "X" on the floor) to see if any substitutes have reported and are ready to enter. If the substitute is ready, the official with the ball beckons the player into the game.

Both officials count all players before putting the ball back in play.

Referee recommendation: The trail beckons all substitutes into the game. There's one exception: When there's backcourt pressure, the new trail administers from the endline and the new lead is positioned near the division line to help with the press (see "Lead helps in backcourt," p. 180), the new lead beckons substitutes into the game.

The reason for the recommendation: When the lead has the ball for a throw-in, the lead is farther away from the scorer's table than the trail. There are many players in the vicinity of the throw-in that must be watched by the lead to ensure good dead-ball officiating. If the lead is looking for substitutes at the scorer's table, who is watching the players near the throw-in spot? One could say the trail, but the trail is too far away to effectively use preventive officiating.

The trail has an open view of the benches and the scorer's table and often has fewer players to watch than the lead just before the lead administers a throw-in. The

lead should focus on the players close by while the trail beckons substitutes.

Following that procedure, the trail puts up a "stop sign" signal to the lead and beckons in the substitute. The lead knows not to put the ball in play after making eye contact with the trail and seeing the stop sign. When the replaced player is in the bench area, the trail drops the stop sign and makes eye contact with the lead. The officials are then ready for the throw-in.

If you like the recommendation and want to try it, check with the appropriate authorities to see if you can use it. Otherwise, follow the prescribed mechanic.

Whistle. A note on blowing the whistle when beckoning substitutes: Some officials blow the whistle while beckoning on every substitution. The practice is not discussed in the NFHS manual.

Proponents say the whistle along with the beckoning motion gets the substitute's attention faster, making for a quicker substitution. The whistle along with the stop sign lets your partner know you've got a substitute.

Opposers say the whistle draws unnecessary attention to the official.

Referee recommendation: If there's confusion at the table, you think your partner doesn't see your stop sign or the gym is so loud few can hear you, blow your whistle. Otherwise, the stop sign and the eye contact should suffice.

Trail beckons substitutes: signals

If you and your partner determine to use the *Referee* recommendation in your pregame discussion, the trail must let the lead know so the lead doesn't put the ball in play too quickly.

Use the stop sign signal to the lead and simultaneously beckon in the substitute (PlayPics A and B). The lead knows not to put the ball in play after making eye contact with the trail and seeing the stop sign. When the replaced player is in the bench area, the trail drops the stop sign and makes eye contact with the lead. The officials are then ready for the throw-in.

Trail Position

• Effective court coverage requires significant movement by the trail.

• The trail must get off the sideline to view plays opposite the trail near the far sideline and above the free-throw line extended.

• Most of the time in a halfcourt setting, the trail has on-ball responsibility.

• The trail must keep proper spacing and avoid being straightlined when on-ball.

• Angles are just as important as distance.

• The trail must help the lead on drives to the basket.

• When moving toward the center of the court, the trail must stay deep to avoid passing lanes.

• An inside-out look is effective when a swing pass occurs.

• When a player takes a shot within the trail's coverage area, the trail's first responsibility is to watch the airborne shooter all the way back to the floor to ensure there are no offensive or defensive fouls.

Quiz

Without referring back, you should be able to answer the following true-false questions.

1. The trail should always stay as close to the sideline as possible to avoid being in the way of play.

2. When the lead is ball side, the trail must pick up the shooter on a skip pass.

3. When a post player spins away from the lead and into the lane toward the trail, the trail must help.

4. The trail should always watch the ball, no matter where it is on the court.

5. As soon as a shot is released, the trail should begin moving to the other end of the court to not get beat by a fastbreak.

1 - False, 2 - True, 3 - True, 4 - False, 5 - False

Chapter 12

Court Positioning

Court positioning

Court positioning and duties during dead-ball times, such as the pregame warmup, halftime, timeouts and injuries are important.

Pregame: stay away from the coaches

During the pregame warmup, go directly to the side of the court opposite the scorer's table. Each official should stand approximately 28 feet from the nearest endline. For NFHS games, enter the court no later than the 15-minute mark.

Do not go directly to the scorer's table when you enter. Why? You want to avoid the coaches, who are usually near their team benches. If you stand near the scorer's table, many coaches view that as an invitation to chit-chat or ask questions. Don't give the coaches the chance to "shmooze" you by telling you how great it is to see you, etc. Don't give a coach the chance to ask questions that the coach can later use against you. For example, if a coach before the game asks you about handchecking, then doesn't like your handchecking call in the game, the coach could bring up the pregame conversation by saying something like, "That's not how you said you were going to call it." Don't give them the opportunity or satisfaction.

Many pregame conversations with coaches are unneeded and usually are designed to test you. They may try to use your words against another official. How often have you heard the coach's rules question start with, "Last week, we had a ref call … that's not right, is it?" The coach either knows the rule and is testing you or is likely not relaying the play to you accurately. Don't give them the chance; stay away from the table.

It is an unwritten taboo to let coaches come across the floor to the sideline opposite the table to talk to officials before the game. Some newer or younger coaches may not know that unwritten rule. If it happens, gently educate them that coming over to talk to you is inappropriate because of the duties you must perform.

Even if the coach's questions and concerns are legitimate and not as sinister as previously described, think about the perception. If you've got an extended, friendly conversation going on with one coach, what's the other coach to think? Even if that official wouldn't think of calling a game one-sided, that perception is now in the front of the offended coach's mind. Avoid perception problems by staying away from coaches during the pregame warmup.

Stretching

Do all your stretching exercises before entering the court. There's too many other things to be doing and watching while on the court to conduct a workout session. Plus, it just looks bad … sort of paints an overhustling, overzealous picture of the official. If one team leaves the court to enter the locker room, then one official can leave the court to stretch. If both teams leave the court at the same time, both officials should also leave the court. There's no sense in standing out there watching nothing. When a team returns, at least one official must return to the observatory position.

Watch the teams

The referee observes the visiting team warmup, the umpire watches the home team. Why? Maybe it's for psychological reasons. The referee is the official in charge and if the referee is watching the visitors, the visiting coach may think less about not getting a fair shake on the road, a common fantasy among coaches.

Though there's usually not a lot of pressure on the officials during the pregame warmup, it's not the time to mentally relax. Watch for player and team tendencies while they warmup. For example, if a center is practicing a move to the basket, take note of which way the player likes to spin toward the basket. If the team is setting many off-ball screens while running their halfcourt offense, remember that during the game. Look for the best shooter; determine if the best ballhandler likes going right or left. Those clues and others will help you anticipate plays and get proper angles during the game.

Count the active players at that time. The umpire relays that number to the referee, who uses that information when checking the scorebook.

Pregame procedure

There are additional pregame duties to perform for both officials. They include checking the scorebook and conducting a captains' and coaches' meeting.

Checking the scorebook

The NFHS manual states that the referee checks the scorebook and reviews scorer and timer responsibilities 12 minutes before the game.

When the referee goes over the scorer's table to check the scorebook, the umpire moves to the intersection of the division line and sideline opposite the table and watches both teams.

As the referee, go directly to the table and avoid the coaches. Again, some coaches view your presence as an opportunity to strike up a conversation; don't.

Introduce yourself to the table crew. You might want to start up a conversation to find out how much experience they have. If they don't have much, prep them on their duties. Even if they do have years of experience, it's still a good idea to go over some things.

The reason you go over with about 12 minutes on the clock is so you can use preventive officiating if there's a scorebook problem. If you arrive at the table and one (or both) of the teams doesn't have a roster turned in or doesn't have starters designated, let the coach know immediately. Then the team can correct the problem before the 10-minute mark when penalties are assessed. If you can prevent a team from earning an administrative technical foul at that point, do it.

Use common sense applying penalties related to the scorebook. Some coaches have their roster typed up before the game with starters indicated. If that sheet is submitted to the scorer but the information has not been transferred to the scorebook by the scorer before the 10-minute mark, do *not* assess a penalty. The roster with designated starters is good enough; the information does not have to be in the scorebook, the scorer simply has to have the information. Another example of good common sense: If a coach is attempting to turn in his lineup, the scorer is not at the table, and the 10-minute mark elapses, do *not* penalize the team. Sometimes the scorer is out in the hallway eating popcorn, etc. The team shouldn't be penalized because they were trying to comply. Avoid administrative technical fouls whenever possible.

Count players. When looking at the book, count the number of players listed for each team and make sure it corresponds with the number of players physically present. If there's a discrepancy, count again. If a team lists more players than you counted, no problem. If a team lists fewer players than you counted, inform that coach immediately so a correction can be made before the 10-minute mark. Check to make sure there are no duplicate names or numbers listed and that the teams are wearing the right even or odd numbers. Some teams have even-numbered jerseys at home and odd-numbered jerseys on the road. Sometimes, the coach supplies the wrong information to the scorer, who lists all the wrong numbers because of it. If you notice it, fix it. Again, in almost all cases you're trying to avoid the administrative technical foul.

After all is well with the scorebook, sign it. An advanced tip used occasionally at higher levels: Have an assistant coach initial the book, indicating that team's information is accurate. The theory: If there's ever a scorebook problem related to names or numbers later, you can explain to the head coach that the listing was confirmed by the assistant before the game. It might get you out of trouble. Before applying the trick, check with the appropriate governing body to see if you can use it.

A/P arrow. After you check the scorebook, check the lights on the table alternating-possession arrow (if applicable). Simply flip the switch back and forth to see that both lights work. If they don't work properly, there's enough time to find a solution without delaying the start of the game.

Ball. Next, while at the table, secure a game ball and approve it. Sometimes the ball is already at the table. Other times you might have to use one that the home team is warming up with or pull one from a ball rack.

Use the bounce test. While on the court, hold the ball about six feet above the floor, then let the ball bounce. The ball should bounce just slightly more than four feet high. The referee should carry an inflation needle. If there's too much air in the ball, let a little out, then test again. If there's not enough air, either have it blown up or pick another ball.

An advanced tip occasionally used at higher levels: If the ball is not at the table, have the home team captain or point guard select a ball from the ones the home team is using to warm up. If it meets your approval, give the ball to the visiting team's captain or point guard for approval. Though their input is not "official," that's a great way to build a rapport with both team leaders before the game. Plus, they're the ones that have to play with it so they might as well be happy. The vast majority of the time, the captain or point guard will approve the ball and appreciate your asking their opinion. Before applying that little trick, check with the appropriate governing body to see if you can use it.

On occasion, the game ball mysteriously disappears before tip-off — after the ball was checked and approved by the referee. Usually, the approved ball is left unguarded near the scorer's table. Sometimes, the approved ball is inadvertently tossed in a large bin full of many balls, or is carried by an unsuspecting team manager into the locker room. For the most part, that's not a major issue because it's an innocent mistake.

Believe this: Once in a while, the missing game ball is *not* a mistake. Coaches or other team personnel may switch the approved game ball illegally — even though they may think it's not that big a deal. Teams may switch to a ball that has less air (to slow the ball down, allowing a turnover plagued team to control the less-bouncy ball better), more air (to allow more and higher rebounds for a team with a rebounding advantage), or an older ball — one that has a better "feel" to it, even if it doesn't comply with regulations. That's especially true now that all balls must bear the NFHS Authenticating Mark.

Even though the ball switch —intentional or not — may happen only a few times in your career, there's a relatively easy way to find the *real* game ball after it's gone. When at the scorer's table checking the ball, write a small "x" in an easily detectable place on the ball. When the ball gets "lost," simply look for the one with the "x."

"X" marks the spot

Speaking of "Xs," now is a perfect time to check for the required "X" on the floor. If it's not there, it is acceptable to ask host management to use athletic tape to mark the required spot.

Meeting the captains and coaches

Another pregame responsibility is meeting with both teams' captains and coaches. The referee escorts the visiting captain(s) to the center circle, while the umpire escorts the home captain(s). The captains stand on their side of the court parallel to the division line; the referee stands between the two rows of players on one side (parallel to a sideline) while the umpire stands opposite the referee. The NFHS manual says to hold the meeting "at an appropriate time."

During that huddle with captains and coaches, the referee gives instructions and answers questions. Keep the meeting very brief; the meeting should never last more than one minute. There's no need to explain common rules or obvious things — like telling them the boundary line is the blue line all the way around the court when there's only that blue line on the court! The players are more interested in warming up than listening to you talk. Use the time with the captains to clear up any confusion, but don't hold a rules clinic.

Explain to the captains that they are leaders and that you may come to them for some help in dealing with players. Giving them that responsibility shows them that you're willing to work with them to avoid potential problems. Ask the captains if they've got any questions (most of the time they don't) and ask your partner if your partner has anything to add. Ask both coaches to verify their player's equipment is legal and uniforms will be worn properly and that all participants will exhibit good sportsmanship throughout the contest. Let the captains shake hands and it's over.

After the meeting, return to normal observatory positions across from the scorer's table. Officially, the referee again watches the visiting team and the umpire watches the home team. Something to think about: After the meeting, have the referee and umpire switch watching responsibilities; the referee now watches the home team and the umpire the visitors. That allows both officials to watch both teams, looking for team and player tendencies as described earlier. If you stay with the same team, you're only getting clues and watching strategies for one team. The more information you have about both teams, the better off you'll be during the game. If switching at that time makes sense, check with your governing body to see if you can do it.

Introductions and anthem

It is common practice for the officials to position themselves directly in front of the scorer's table facing the center circle watching introductions. *Referee* recommendation: If governing bodies allow, follow that procedure.

Some officials correctly feel that the period immediately prior to the contest belongs to the players — the players are the ones being introduced in front of parents, classmates and fans. Many officials step behind the scorer's table or well off to one side rather than interfere with the introductions or with players who run across that area to shake the opposing coach's hand.

If you're wearing jackets, keep them on during the introductions and anthem and remove them just prior to tip off. Keep them at the table.

Halftime procedures

Halftime positioning is specifically addressed in the manual. In a 2003-05 mechanics change for NFHS games, the officials are positioned halfway between the farthest point of the center circle and the sideline opposite the scorer's table. Previously, officials gathered at the center restraining circle. After both teams have left their benches and gone to their respective locker rooms, both officials walk over to the scorer's table and take care of duties.

Some of the time, coaches will wait for you to come to the scorer's table to voice their displeasure with the officiating. Wait for them to leave before go over to the table, even if it takes an inordinate amount of time. Eventually, they'll give up and go to the locker room and resume coaching.

While at the table, the referee should ask the scorers if everything adds up and settle any differences that may exist. Make sure the alternating-possession arrow is correctly switched. Leave the game ball at the table. Ensure that both teams will be notified by management when halftime is about to end. In NFHS games, teams are notified three minutes before the end of the halftime break. Remind management to notify the officials too, but be aware of the time so you can report to the court if you are not notified.

After performing duties at the scorer's table, grab your jackets and leave together for your locker room. During halftime, relax. Then, review the first half and discuss necessary adjustments. Return to the court with about three minutes remaining in the intermission. Assume the same observatory position as you did to start the game. Just prior to the end of the intermission, the umpire goes to the table, gets the game ball and bounces it to the referee, who is positioned at the intersection of the division line and the far sideline for the ensuing throw-in.

NFHS 60-second timeouts
The officials assume 60-second timeout positions facing the scorer's table. Starting in the 2003-04 season, the administering official will stand on the block nearest the throw-in spot opposite the team benches. The non-administering official is at the same location on the other end of the court.

NFHS 30-second timeouts
Also starting in the 2003-04 season, positions for 30-second timeouts have changed from years past. Both officials will stand at the top of the near three-point arc, on both halves of the court.

Timeouts: Who reports?
In NFHS mechanics, the granting official reports the timeout. Do not grant a timeout after a foul until the necessary information has been given to the scorer, or until substitutes have been beckoned, disqualified players have been replaced or until injured players have been replaced.

The reporting official should verbally indicate the team color and verbally and visually indicate the requesting player's number (or head coach) and instruct the timer to begin the timeout period.

On-court injuries
When an injury occurs and the coach or medical personnel are beckoned onto the court, move away from the area immediately. For liability reasons, you don't want to get involved in injury situations. You must avoid the urge to help.

Plus, if you're nearby, it's easier for someone to fire an emotional cheap shot at you. For example, if you're nearby, the angry coach on the way out to attend to the injured player may say, "This is your fault! The game's too rough!" There's even more of a chance for an emotional response if a parent is summoned from the stands onto the court. Avoid it all by moving well away from the injured player.

Postgame exit
There's an easy way to sum up postgame exits: When the final horn sounds, get out of there! Assuming the scorebook is correct, there are no more duties for you to perform. Do not worry about where the basketball goes; it's not your responsibility. Jog to your locker room and avoid confrontations. A game management representative should meet you near the exit from the court to ensure you get to your locker room safely.

Stay away from the scorer's table; it's too easy to be a target of emotional coaches, players or fans. If you've done everything correctly and there's not a controversial ending, there's no need to be over there. If the score is close, there are usually timeouts toward the end of the game. That's the time for the referee to go over and make sure all the information in the scorebook is correct. If not, settle it then, not after the final horn. Handling that during a timeout means you don't have to go over after the final horn. (For more on end of game situations and controversial endings, see "Last-second shot," p. 264).

The majority of games don't end with controversy and close scores. When things are normal, as soon as the horn sounds, jog toward the locker room. There's no need to go back to the table to get your jacket because you carried it in at halftime. There's no need to sign the book because you signed it before the game and, by rule, the game is over when you leave the visual confines of the playing area. There's no need to watch the postgame handshake; it's not your responsibility. The quicker you're off the floor, the safer you will be. The officials' jurisdiction ends when *both* officials "leave the visual confines of the playing area."

All of the sections described involve dead-ball officiating. There are many things to be done during dead-ball time. It's not the time to mentally relax. Handling dead-ball situations professionally and with common sense separates the great officials from the average ones.

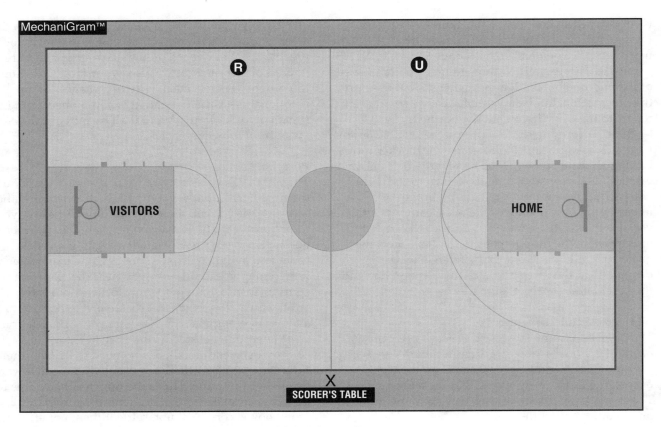

Court positioning: pregame

Position yourselves on the side of the court opposite the scorer's table. Each official should be approximately 28 feet from the nearest endline. The referee observes the visiting team warm up, the umpire watches the home team (see "Court positioning," p. 104).

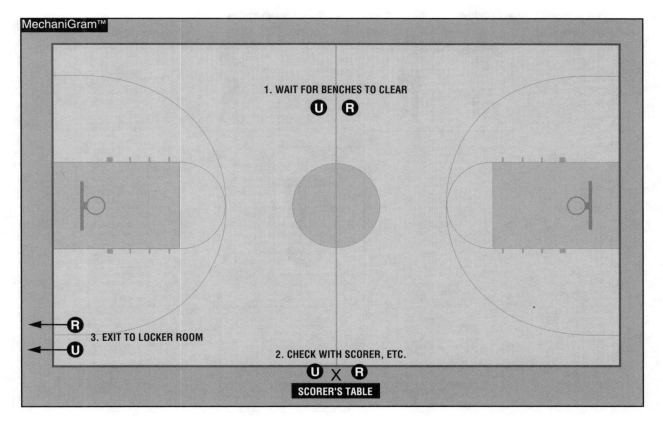

MechaniGram™

1. WAIT FOR BENCHES TO CLEAR

U   R

3. EXIT TO LOCKER ROOM

R

U

2. CHECK WITH SCORER, ETC.

U X **R**

SCORER'S TABLE

Court positioning: halftime

In a 2003-05 mechanics change, the officials are now positioned halfway between the farthest point of the center circle and the sideline opposite the scorer's table (1). After both teams have left their benches and gone to their respective locker rooms, both officials walk over to the scorer's table and the referee takes care of specified duties (2). After performing duties at the scorer's table, the officials leave together for their locker room. (3)

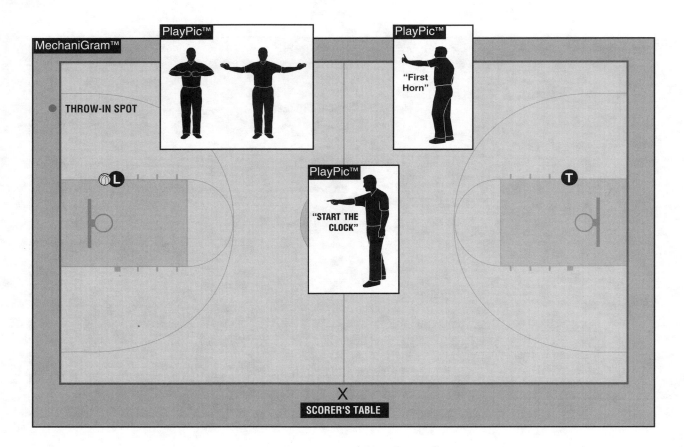

Court positioning: NFHS 60-second timeout

The officials assume timeout positions facing the scorer's table. Starting in the 2003-04 season, the administering official will stand on the block nearest the throw-in spot opposite the team benches. The non-administering official is at the same location on the other end of the court.

At the 45-second point, you should hear the timer sound the first buzzer or horn. Take a step or two toward the team bench and give the "first horn" signal. It's a good idea to identify a person in the team bench area during pregame who is responsible for seeing that signal — assistant coach, trainer, playing captain, etc.

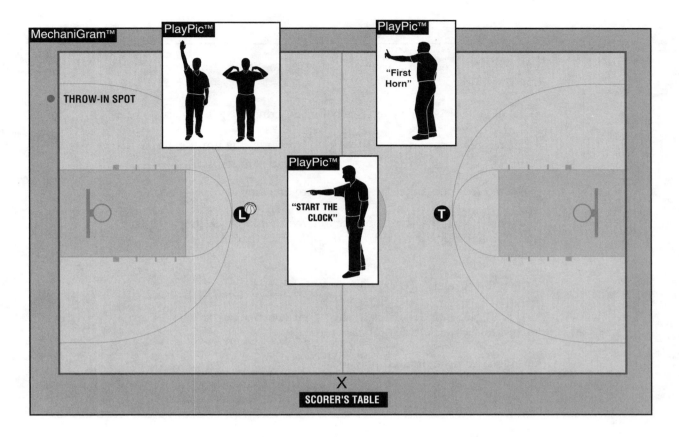

Court positioning: NFHS 30-second timeout

A new mechanic for positions during 30-second timeouts will be used. Now, both officials will stand at the top of the near three-point arc, on both halves of the court.

Players may not sit on the team benches, nor may cheerleaders take the floor during a 30-second timeout.

At the 20-second mark, you should hear the timer sound the first buzzer or horn. Take a step or two toward the team bench and give the "first horn" signal. It's a good idea to identify a person in the team bench area during pregame who is responsible for seeing that signal — assistant coach, trainer, playing captain, etc.

Court Positioning

• During the pregame warmup, go directly to the side of the court opposite the scorer's table.

• Do all your stretching exercises before entering the court.

• The referee observes the visiting team warmup, the umpire, the home team.

• The referee checks the scorebook before the game.

• After checking the scorebook, the referee should check the lights on the alternating-possession arrow (if applicable) then secure and approve a game ball.

• Keep the coaches' and captains' meeting brief.

• At halftime, wait for teams to clear their bench areas before moving toward the scorer's table or locker room.

• Move away from injured players.

• You must stay alive when the ball is dead.

Quiz

Without referring back, you should be able to answer the following true-false questions.

1. Before the game, each official should be positioned about 28 feet from the nearest sideline.

2. The NFHS manual says officials should be positioned on the low blocks during a 60-second timeout.

3. The NFHS 30-second timeout position places each official near the top of the key.

Chapter 13

Case Studies

Introduction to case studies

One of the things that makes a great official is a complete understanding of the game. That goes beyond rules and mechanics. Great referees anticipate plays. They always seem to be in the right place at the right time. It's not an accident or just luck. It's preparation and an understanding of the game. That puts them in the right spot at the right moment.

Studying the game

Part of that preparation is studying the game itself. Just what are the teams trying to do on the court? The novice or unprepared referee doesn't think beyond, "This team is trying to score more points than the other team."

The great referees think about offensive styles, defensive schemes, tempo and tendencies. For example, they'll know or recognize that team A likes to push the ball up the right side of the floor and establish a fast-paced tempo. They run multiple off-ball low-post screens to free up post players on the low block. They like to dump the ball into the post then pass it back out to the perimeter for three-point shots. They will crash the boards, then apply pressure defensive traps all over the court. They play an aggressive, trapping man-to-man defense and front the post. They will switch to a 2-3 zone defense only for a throw-in on the frontcourt endline.

The different approaches are obvious: The more you know about the game and a team's tendencies, the better prepared you are.

Recognizing and knowing what coaches and players are trying to do elevates your game. When you have that knowledge, you can adjust your court coverage accordingly. In "Court coverage philosophy" (p. 28), you read how anticipation and "playing the odds" are critical to successful two-person officiating. The obvious question is, how do you get better at anticipating plays? You study the game and the specific plays.

As the game of basketball becomes more complex, officials must be more aware of specific basketball plays. When officials recognize offensive plays and defensive strategies, they make better court coverage adjustments.

Gaining the knowledge

How do you gain the knowledge about specific plays and teams? One way is to talk to other officials. If you know referees that have had a team you're about to officiate, ask them questions about style and tempo. Another way is to carefully watch the players during the pregame warmup (see "Watch the teams," p. 104).

The most common: Learning and adjusting while the game is in progress. You must develop the ability to see what's happening on the court and adjust accordingly. Whether the lead or the trail, you're not just watching a bunch of players move. Learn to watch specific, orchestrated offensive and defensive plays while on the court. Then, make the necessary adjustments.

Always read the defense first. Why? Defensive schemes are easier to recognize. Plus, offensive plays are based on defensive strategies, not vice versa. Once you've read the defense, think about the offensive plays that are likely to be used against that specific defense. Adjust accordingly.

For most referees that don't have an extensive playing or coaching background, it takes time to develop those skills. Practice while watching other games (on TV or in person). See what's happening on the floor and recognize the plays and defensive schemes. Think about what is likely to happen once you've recognized the play.

Here's an example of how a well-schooled official thinks on the court. Team A is down 10 points with 1:40 remaining in the game. They haven't applied backcourt defensive pressure all game; they've stayed in a halfcourt 2-3 zone. A team A player nails a three-point shot and team A immediately calls and is granted a timeout. What's likely to happen when play resumes? Since team A is now down seven points with little time left, they obviously need the ball back quickly to get an opportunity to score again. Is that likely to happen if team A sits back in their halfcourt zone? Obviously not! Instead, team A is likely to apply a fullcourt press after the timeout. It may be a trapping defense. Team A is likely to try for a quick steal and if unsuccessful will immediately foul to force team B to make free throws to win the game.

Anticipating that action, the referees adjust their court coverage accordingly. A referee who doesn't understand the game or recognize specific plays will be caught by surprise; a well-schooled referee is prepared.

Reading the case studies

Remember the old "chalk talk" when you were a player? The coach frantically drew circles and lines and pounded the chalk until it became a fine white dust, all while yelling something like, "Remember on defense, it's *ball-you-man!*" *Basketball Guidebook* case studies take the chalk talk a giant step forward.

Case studies are separated into categories: Halfcourt vs. man-to-man; halfcourt vs. zone; three-point offenses; defensive traps and presses; delay offenses; and, last-second shots. Each includes actual game plays presented in four action frames showing the movements of players and officials. Text accompanies each frame, describing the player action so officials can learn to recognize those plays in their games, and referee movement, so officials know where to go and what they're trying to see.

Before each section of case studies, text describes what teams are trying to accomplish when using certain strategies. You'll also read about officiating trouble spots and court adjustments when those plays occur.

Use these case studies to learn what plays look like and what you're supposed to do once you recognize them. As you become a student of the game, you're officiating will dramatically improve.

Notes

Chapter 14

Jump Ball

The jump ball

The jump ball sets the tone for the rest of the game. It's the first action directly related to the game and that first impression can be a lasting one. A good toss and you've started the game off properly.

Some may think that the opening toss isn't that big a deal because it only occurs once. Consider the ramifications of a poor toss:

- The referee already appears incompetent to players and coaches.
- If the toss is too far to one side, you've planted the seed to the offended team that the officiating isn't fair.

A bad toss creates bad perceptions for officials, which are often difficult to overcome.

The procedure

After the introductions and anthem, the referee takes the ball and moves to a spot near the far sideline, facing the scorer's table. Allow ample time for the players to get settled into their spots. While that occurs, the umpire checks with the table personnel to ensure they are ready. The umpire then takes a position at the intersection of the sideline and the division line directly in front of the table making certain not to block the view of the scorer and timer. Before entering the center restraining circle, the referee makes eye contact with the umpire, who signals to the referee that table personnel and the umpire are ready to go. Both officials make sure the teams are facing the correct direction.

While still outside the circle, the referee notifies both team captains that play is about to begin. Tell the players to hold their spots to avoid violations. Blow the whistle with a sharp blast before entering the circle.

Before tossing the ball, you may want to use a bit of preventive officiating with the jumpers. Tell them to jump straight up and not into each other and tell them not to tap the ball on the way up. Just before the toss, the umpire uses the "do not start clock" signal (open hand raised above head). The referee tosses the ball high enough so the players tap the ball on its downward flight.

The umpire must maintain a wide field of vision while the referee administers the toss. The umpire watches both jumpers and all other players around the circle to spot fouls and violations.

The umpire has initial responsibility of judging the toss. If it's a good one, start the clock as soon as the ball is touched by a jumper. If the toss is a bad one, the umpire blows the whistle and calls for a re-jump, using the jump ball signal. Why does the umpire call back a bad toss? For safety reasons, the referee should not have the whistle in the mouth during the toss. By the time the referee judges a bad toss, finds the whistle and blows it, players are likely moving downcourt with the ball. That's an awkward delay.

Some referees tell umpires that the referee is the only one that should call for a re-toss. Because of the delay and the poor vantage point for judging the direction of the toss, that's not realistic. Trust the umpire to use good judgment.

What constitutes a bad toss? For starters, very few tosses should be called back. Again, you don't want to start out the game out of sync. However, if a toss is clearly favors one side or the toss is so far back over the referee's head that neither jumper can touch it, blow it back. Don't nit-pick; only call for a re-jump when the toss is obviously poor. When in doubt, let it go.

Different styles

There are three accepted tossing styles, the one-handed toss, the "quick" toss and the two-handed toss. The following pages illustrate those styles. No matter which style is best for you, practice it regularly so your games start correctly.

Balls out-of-bounds

One trouble spot during jump-ball coverage is a ball that is knocked out-of-bounds behind the referee on the sideline opposite the umpire. Most of the time, the referee doesn't have enough time to get out of the center restraining circle and see what's going on behind the referee. Four principles apply:

1. If the referee knows the ball is out-of-bounds and knows who touched it last, make the call.

2. If the umpire knows the ball is out-of-bounds and knows who touched it last, make the call.

3. If the referee knows the ball is out-of-bounds but is unsure who touched it last, stop the clock. Then, check with the umpire. If the umpire knows who touched it last, the umpire signals the direction.

4. If neither official is sure who touched it last, immediately signal for a re-jump.

Don't guess a direction; you're better off re-jumping than guessing wrong.

After the jump

As the jump ball occurs, the referee must think safety. Cover up if necessary by placing your tossing arm in front of your face and your off hand in front of your groin area.

After the toss, the referee should stay near the center restraining circle until the players clear the area. If you try to move to the sideline too quickly, you'll likely run into players and risk injury.

The umpire must read the direction of the toss. If the ball is tapped toward the frontcourt and a fastbreak ensues, the umpire must sprint toward the endline and become the lead. The referee reads the umpire's movement, lets the players clear the center restraining circle area, then backs out toward the sideline and becomes the trail.

If the ball is tapped safely into the backcourt and is not near the backcourt endline, the umpire watches action around the catch from near the starting position. Then, if there's no immediate defensive pressure (usually there isn't because the defensive team is moving downcourt), the umpire moves to the frontcourt endline and becomes the lead. If the catch of the tapped ball is challenged or there is immediate defensive pressure, the umpire must watch that action until the referee can. Once the referee has picked up on-ball coverage, the umpire moves to the frontcourt endline and becomes the lead. The referee becomes the trail.

If the ball is tapped backward toward the backcourt endline, the umpire must move with the ball toward the backcourt endline to judge potential out-of-bounds violations. The referee must read the umpire's movements, move out toward the sideline and move to the frontcourt endline and become the lead. The umpire, already positioned in the backcourt, is the trail.

The direction of the tap dictates officiating movements. No matter where you end up, be sure the floor is balanced so two officials don't end up on the same side of the court.

After the ball is possessed, the trail should glance at the alternating-possession arrow to make sure it is pointing in the right direction. If it isn't, wait for the first dead-ball and correct it.

General tips

Remember these points during jump-ball administration:

• Before administering the jump ball, notify both team captains that play is about to begin.

• Check with the umpire to make sure the umpire is ready.

• Both officials should count the players of both teams.

• Blow the whistle outside the center restraining circle before entering.

• For a one-handed toss, make sure your elbow is directly below the ball and perpendicular to the floor to ensure a straight toss.

• Place your foot between the jumpers' pivot feet to create space.

• Keep the ball at your side.

• Bend your knees slightly; using your leg strength will help toss the ball high.

• For a one-handed toss, keep your palm open to the sky to ensure a wrist spin doesn't create a bad toss.

• The toss should be straight and slightly higher than the players can jump so the players tap the ball on the way down.

If you practice the jump-ball toss often, read your partner's movements to ensure proper court coverage and communicate effectively with table personnel and your partner, your games will get off to a good start.

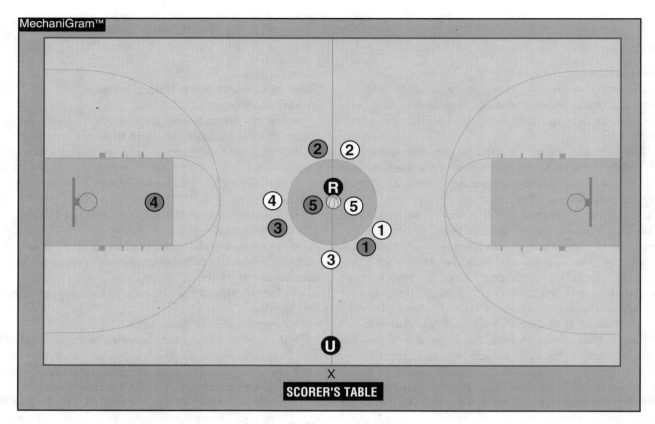

Jump ball positioning

The umpire is positioned near the intersection of the sideline and the division line directly in front of the table. Before entering the center restraining circle, the referee makes eye contact with the umpire, who signals to the referee that table personnel and the umpire are ready to go. Both officials make sure the teams are facing the correct direction.

While still outside the circle, the referee notifies both team captains that play is about to begin. Tell the players to hold their spots to avoid violations. Blow the whistle with a sharp blast before entering the circle.

Before tossing the ball, you may want to use a bit of preventive officiating with the jumpers. Tell them to jump straight up and not into each other, and tell them not to tap the ball on the way up. Just before the toss, the umpire uses the "do not start clock" signal — raised open hand. The referee tosses the ball high enough so the players tap the ball on its downward flight. The umpire starts the clock when the ball is tapped.

The umpire must maintain a wide field of vision while the referee administers the toss. The umpire watches both jumpers and all players around the circle to spot fouls and violations.

Jump ball: one-handed toss

Before administering the jump ball, the referee notifies both team captains that play is about to begin. Check with the umpire to make sure the umpire is ready. Blow the whistle outside the center restraining circle before entering (PlayPic A).

Place your foot between the jumpers' pivot feet. Keep the ball at your side (PlayPic B). This is the time to give final instructions to the jumpers. Tell them to not tap the ball on its way up and to not jump into each other and commit a foul.

Put the ball in one hand above your head. Make sure your elbow is directly below the ball and perpendicular to the floor to ensure a straight toss (PlayPic C). Bend your knees slightly; using your leg strength will help you toss the ball high.

After the ball is balanced, push with your legs slightly and extend your arm with the ball directly upward

(PlayPic D). Do not drop the ball downward before you toss; any movement will cause the players to react and jump. Your only movement is upward. Keep your palm open to the sky to ensure a wrist spin doesn't create a bad toss.

Think of your own safety. Do not put the whistle in your mouth during the toss. You don't want the lanyard to get caught on a player's arm and damage your teeth. Also, immediately after the toss, cover up if necessary by placing your tossing arm in front of your face and your off hand in front of your groin area.

The toss should be straight and slightly higher than the players can jump so the players tap the ball on the way down. In your spare time, practice the toss by throwing it up through the bottom of the basket without touching the ring.

Jump ball: two-handed toss

Before administering the jump ball, the referee notifies both team captains that play is about to begin. Check with the umpire to make sure the umpire is ready. Blow the whistle outside the center restaining circle before entering (PlayPic A).

Place your foot between the jumpers' pivot feet. Extend each elbow toward a jumper while holding the ball at your chest (PlayPic B). That move creates enough space between the jumpers to ensure a good toss. This is the time to give final instructions to the jumpers. Tell them to not tap the ball on its way up and to not jump into each other and commit a foul.

Extend both arms upward and release the ball (PlayPic C). The toss should be straight and slightly higher than the players can jump so the players tap the ball on the way down.

Think of your own safety. Do not put the whistle in your mouth during the toss. You don't want the lanyard to get caught on a player's arm and damage your teeth. Also, immediately after the toss, cover up if necessary by placing your tossing arm in front of your face. One disadvantage to the two-handed toss is you don't get a chance to cover your groin area.

Jump ball: quick toss

If you use the one-handed toss and are having trouble with players "quick jumping" the toss and tapping the ball on the way up, consider using the quick toss.

Before administering the jump ball, the referee notifies both team captains that play is about to begin. Check with the umpire to make sure the umpire is ready. Blow the whistle outside the center restraining circle before entering.

Place your foot between the jumpers' pivot feet. Put your tossing hand directly between the jumpers facing upward. Bend your knees slightly; using your leg strength will help you toss the ball high. Keep the ball behind you and slightly hidden so the players can't time the jump (PlayPic A). This is the time to give final instructions to the jumpers. Tell them to not tap the ball on its way up and to not jump into each other and commit a foul.

Take the jumpers by surprise using a quick-motion toss. Quickly transfer the ball into the tossing hand (PlayPic B). Quickly extend the ball upward using a leg-and-elbow push (PlayPic C). A smooth, quality quick toss is done in one fluid movement. The toss should be straight and slightly higher than the players can jump so the players tap the ball on the way down.

The quick toss is a great way to keep the players from jumping early, but it's also the least accurate of the tossing techniques. Practice it many times before using it in a game.

Think of your own safety. Do not put the whistle in your mouth during the toss. You don't want the lanyard to get caught on a player's arm and damage your teeth. Also, immediately after the toss, cover up if necessary by placing your tossing arm in front of your face and your off hand in front of your groin area.

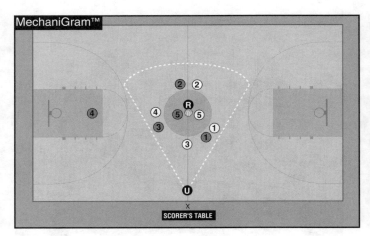 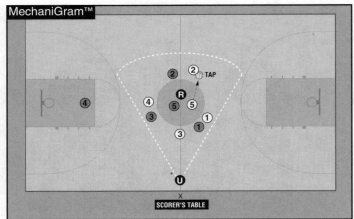

Action on the court:

⑤ and ⑤ prepare for jump ball.	⑤ tips ball to backcourt ②.

Umpire Responsibilities

Position near division line. **Primary: Off-ball.** Watch all players around center restraining circle.	**Primary: On-ball.** Watch ⑤ tap ball. **Secondary: Off-ball.** Watch players around center restraining circle.

Referee Responsibilities

Prepare for jump ball.	Toss ball.

KEY

L LEAD OFFICIAL
T TRAIL OFFICIAL

PRIMARY
COVERAGE
AREA

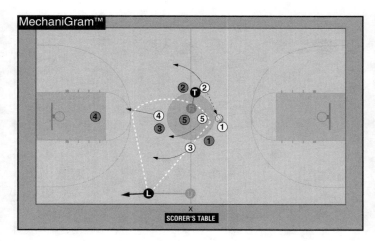

MechaniGram™

SCORER'S TABLE

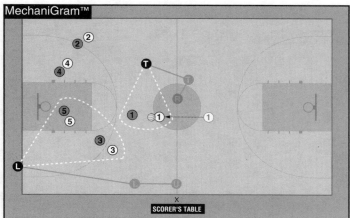

MechaniGram™

SCORER'S TABLE

---

② passes to backcourt ①, then ② moves toward frontcourt. ⑤, ④ and ③ move to frontcourt.

① dribbles to frontcourt to start a play.

Read direction of play.
Become lead and move toward frontcourt.
Primary: Off-ball. Watch players move to frontcourt.

Move downcourt to endline.
Primary: Off-ball. Watch players move to frontcourt.

After ② passes to ① and moves downcourt, move slowly toward near sideline and become trail.
Primary: On-ball. Watch ① with ball.

Move into frontcourt.
Primary: On-ball. Watch ① with ball.

 OFFENSE    PASS   ⊢── SCREEN

DEFENSE   DRIBBLE

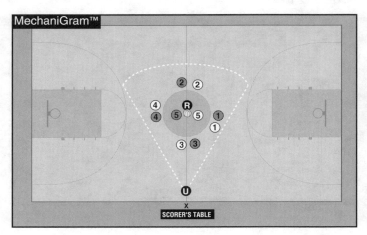

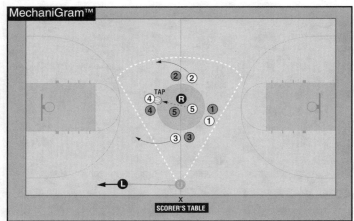

Action on the court:

⑤ and **⑤** prepare for jump ball.

⑤ tips ball to frontcourt ④. ② and ③ break downcourt.

Umpire Responsibilities

Position near division line.
Primary: Off-ball. Watch all players around center restraining circle.

Primary: On-ball. Watch ⑤ tap ball.
Secondary: Off-ball. Watch players around center restraining circle.
Read direction of play.
Read fastbreak.
Become lead and break to frontcourt quickly.

Referee Responsibilities

Prepare for jump ball.

Toss ball.

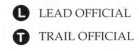

KEY

L LEAD OFFICIAL

T TRAIL OFFICIAL

PRIMARY COVERAGE AREA

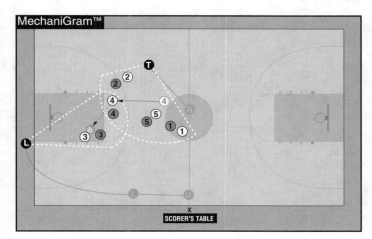

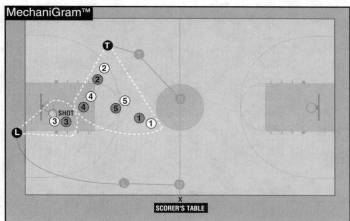

④ dribbles to frontcourt. ④ passes to ③ filling the lane on fastbreak.	③ catches pass and shoots.
Move to endline quickly and get good angle. **Primary: On-ball.** Watch ④ pass to ③.	**Primary: On-ball.** Watch ③ catch pass and shoot.
After players move downcourt, move toward near sideline and become trail in frontcourt. **Primary: On-ball.** Watch ④ with ball. **Secondary: Off-ball.** Watch players above free throw line.	**Primary: Off-ball.** Watch players above free throw line. Penetrate toward endline for angles. Observe weak-side rebounding.

① OFFENSE   ⊘◄----① PASS   ⊢— SCREEN

① DEFENSE   ⊘①◄········① DRIBBLE

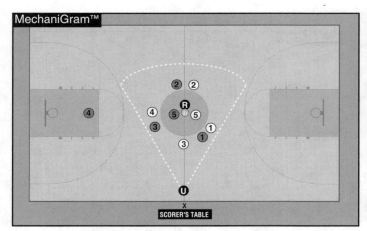

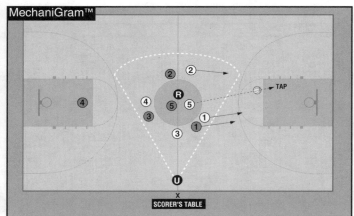

Action on the court:

⑤ and ⑤ prepare for jump ball.	⑤ tips ball far into backcourt toward endline. ②, ① and ❶ chase the loose ball.

Umpire Responsibilities

Position near division line. **Primary: Off-ball.** Watch all players around center restraining circle.	**Primary: On-ball.** Watch ⑤ tap ball. **Secondary: Off-ball.** Watch players around center restraining circle.

Referee Responsibilities

Prepare for jump ball.	Toss ball. Read that the ball is tapped hard toward the endline.

KEY

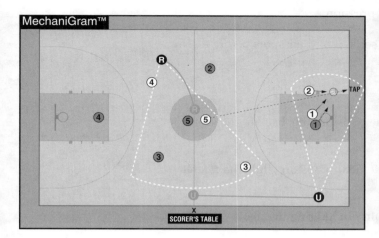

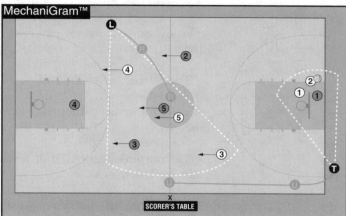

Loose ball continues toward endline as ②, ① and **①** converge.	② secures ball in the backcourt. Players near midcourt move toward frontcourt.
Read that the ball is tapped hard toward the endline. Move quickly toward endline. **Primary: On-ball.** Watch players move toward loose ball.	Move downcourt to endline. **Primary: On-ball.** Watch ② secure ball in backcourt. Umpire is now the trail. **Secondary: Off-ball.** Watch ① and **①** begin moving upcourt.
Read that the umpire has aggressively moved toward the endline. Swing out toward sideline opposite the umpire. **Primary: Off-ball.** Watch players in the midcourt area.	Continue movement toward sideline opposite the umpire. After ② secures ball and play moves upcourt, begin moving toward frontcourt endline. The referee is now the lead. **Primary: Off-ball.** Watch midcourt players move toward frontcourt.

 OFFENSE   PASS   ⊢— SCREEN

 DEFENSE    DRIBBLE

Review

Jump Ball

• A good toss gives a good first impression.

• Allow ample time for players to settle into their spots before tossing the ball.

• The referee tosses the ball.

• The umpire is positioned near the division line, back to the scorer's table.

• The umpire must maintain a wide field of vision while the referee administers the toss.

• The umpire has initial responsibility of judging the toss.

• Before administering the toss, the referee should notify both captains and the umpire that play is about to begin.

• The umpire must read the direction and speed of the tap and move toward the correct position accordingly.

• The referee must read the umpire's movement and adjust toward the correct position accordingly.

Quiz

Without referring back, you should be able to answer the following true-false questions.

1. The umpire should be positioned toward the endline that the umpire thinks the tap will go, not on the division line.

2. Before tossing the ball, you should use preventive officiating with the jumpers.

3. Before entering the center restraining circle the referee should give a whistle blast.

4. When performing a one-handed toss, the ball should be lowered just before the toss.

5. The quick toss is a great way to keep players from jumping early.

1 - False, 2 - True, 3 - True, 4 - False, 5 - True

Chapter 15

Free Throws

Free throws

Free-throw administration requires teamwork between the lead and the trail. Smooth running free-throw administration looks sharp. It also ensures the ball will quickly and correctly become live with the clock running following free-throw activity.

Coverage areas

For NFHS mechanics, the lead watches players on the opposite lane line (closer to the trail) for potential violations, etc. That coverage is commonly referred to as "looking opposite." The lead also watches the lane space nearest the endline on the lane line nearest the lead.

The trail watches players on the opposite lane line (closer to the lead) except the opposite low block area. The trail also watches the free thrower. The officials look opposite because it's easier to see players stepping toward you and violating than it is to see them step away from you, especially when other players are blocking your view.

The change means better coverage of the low block area opposite the trail. Before the change, the trail had to watch the shooter and the opposite low block — a difficult task at best, especially if a player occupied the lane space nearest the free-throw line on the trail side. The trail was straightlined when a player was positioned there. It's a much better look for the lead since the lead is standing near there anyway.

Adjust your angles as a lead and trail to properly cover the free-throw action.

In NFHS mechanics, the trail's secondary coverage is always players above the top of the key. Be especially wary of trouble players in that area; a cheap-shot artist or trash-talker might think that's an ideal time to start a problem because the trail isn't watching.

Lead positioning

The lead is always positioned off the court. That allows the lead to see players along the near lane line without having obstructed vision.

In the NFHS manual, the lead is positioned "approximately four feet from the nearer lane line well off the endline." That position is maintained regardless of the number of free throws.

Trail positioning

The trail has a specific spot to ensure proper coverage.

• The trail is always positioned facing the scorer's table.

• The trail is positioned at a spot just behind the free-throw line extended halfway between the trail-side lane line and the trail-side sideline. Many officials incorrectly back up all the way to the sideline; it's impossible to correctly watch the players on the opposite lane line from there.

• Do not take a spot even with the free-throw line extended; move about one or two strides toward the division line. That angle allows you to clearly see the free thrower and the opposite lane line.

The only exception to that position is technical foul administration (see "Technical foul administration," p. 135).

Lead movements

Before administering the free throws, the lead has the ball and is positioned in the lane under the basket.

• Look for late-arriving substitutes at the scorer's table and beckon them in if appropriate.

• Signal the number of remaining free throws to the players in the lane and the free thrower. Simultaneously verbalize the number of free throws.

• Before bouncing the ball to the free thrower, make sure there are no players moving into or leaving lane spaces.

• When the free thrower is ready to catch the ball, bounce the ball to the free thrower.

• Move to the appropriate spot for free-throw coverage (see "Lead movement," p. 136).

• After the shot is airborne, adjust your position along the endline a step or two to get a good angle on strong side rebounding.

If the last shot is good and an immediate throw-in follows, raise your arm using the "do not start clock" signal and begin your throw-in count when the ball is at the disposal of the thrower-in. Don't be too quick to start your count; unless there's an intentional delay, wait to begin your count until after the thrower-in has crossed the endline and is out of bounds.

Trail movements

The trail has specific movements during free throws.

• Do not step into the lane; the lead administers the free throw alone.

• Maintain normal trail free-throw position (see "Trail movement," p. 137).

• After the free thrower has caught the ball from the lead, pick up the visible 10-second count with the arm farthest from the basket.

• Immediately after the free thrower releases the shot, use the "do not start clock" signal with open hand raised directly above your head. Use the arm farthest from the basket so the timer sees the signal.

• During the flight of the try and with your arm still raised, penetrate slightly toward the endline using a two-step crossover move. That movement ensures good angles on rebounding action.

• If the shot is good, lower your arm. There is no need to signal a made free throw.

• If the shot is no good and the ball is to remain live, use the "start the clock" signal as soon as the ball touches or is touched by a player.

Since the trail is always facing the scorer's table, the trail must be aware of reporting substitutes. If a sub is entering between free throws, tell the lead to wait to administer the final free throw until the substitution is complete.

If a sub has legally reported during the last free throw and the free throw was made — which could be anywhere from the time the ball was placed at the disposal of the free thrower until the ball was at the disposal of the thrower-in following the made free throw — the trail should immediately blow the whistle and give the "do not start clock" signal. You must react quickly because many times the throw-in team grabs the ball after the made free throw and wants to make a quick throw-in. Once you've stopped the ensuing play, beckon in the substitute. Make sure the lead does not administer the throw-in until after the substitution is complete.

Technical foul administration

Technical foul administration is one area of coverage where things seem to vary greatly in different state and local associations and different leagues.

For NFHS mechanics, the two officials switch on the technical foul, just as they would with any foul. Technical foul free throws are administered in the same manner as other free throws.

The NFHS manual also states, "If the situation requires, the lead official may administer both free throws while the trail official moves to a position which provides maximum supervision." That's sound advice because during technical foul free throws, often players bunch up near the division line. Since technical fouls are usually emotional in nature, there could be lingering problems among players.

Referee recommendation: If the technical foul was called on a player who did something unsportsmanlike toward an opponent and those players remain on the floor during the free throws, let the lead administer the free throws alone while the trail moves toward the division line to watch those players. Having a presence near the division line may be enough to stop the problem.

When the trail remains near the free-throw line during administration, back up farther toward the sideline than you normally would to ensure you see all players near the division line. There's no need to be in tight like during a normal free throw because there are no players lined up along the lane line to watch. The trail's primary responsibility is the remaining nine players and the benches; secondary responsibility is the free thrower. You're simply playing the odds. You're more likely to have problems among the other players or the benches than you are to have a violation on the free thrower.

Despite what the manual says, in some cases, the official who called the technical foul becomes the *lead*. The theory: The lead is always facing away from the benches and is far away from players who are standing near the division line during free throws. If a technical foul was just whistled on a coach, the lead's back is to the coach and a confrontation is less likely to occur. The official involved in the call can't see the bench. If the coach can't look at the lead face-to-face, the coach is likely to stop arguing with that official. If the technical foul was on a player who is now near the division line, the lead who called the technical foul is far away and avoids a confrontation. The trail, who did not call the technical foul, watches the bench area and the division line players for potential problems.

Check with the appropriate governing body to see what procedure should be used. Discuss the procedures in your pregame with your partner so technical foul free-throw administration runs smoothly.

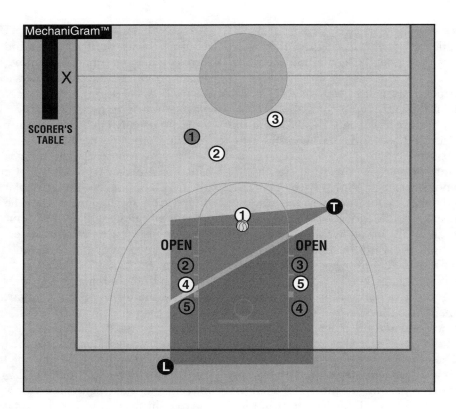

Free throw coverage

The lead watches players on the opposite lane line (closer to the trail) for potential violations, etc. The lead also watches the lane space nearest the endline on the lane line nearest the lead.

The trail watches players on the opposite lane line (closer to the lead) except the opposite low block area. The trail also watches the free thrower.

The positioning means better coverage of the low-block area opposite the trail.

In the MechaniGram, the lead looks opposite and watches ③, ⑤ and ④, plus ⑤ nearest the lead. The trail looks opposite and watches ② and ④, plus free thrower ①. The trail's secondary coverage includes all the players behind the free-throw line extended.

As a point of emphasis, you should look for defensive players using hands or arms to disconcert the free thrower. Warn the players to prevent such actions, if you can. If the defender's actions warrant a violation, award a substitute free throw if the charity toss is missed. If that doesn't stop the illegal actions, use the technical foul.

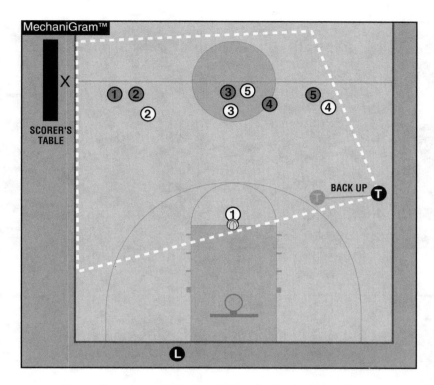

Free throws: technical foul administration

Technical foul administration is one area of coverage where things seem to vary greatly in different state and local associations and different leagues.

In NFHS mechanics, the two officials switch on the technical foul, just as they would with any foul. Technical foul free throws are administered in the same manner as other free throws.

The NFHS manual also states, "If the situation requires, the lead official may administer both free throws while the trail official moves to a position which provides maximum supervision." That's sound advice because during technical foul free throws, players often bunch up near the division line. Since technical fouls are usually emotional in nature, there could be lingering problems among players.

Referee recommendation: If the technical foul was called on a player who did something unsportsmanlike toward an opponent and those players remain on the floor during the free throws, let the lead administer the free throws alone while the trail moves toward the division line to watch those players. Having a presence near the division line may be enough to stop the problem.

When the trail remains near the free-throw line, back up further toward the sideline than you normally would to ensure you see all players near the division line.

There's no need to be in tight like during a normal free throw because there are no players along the lane line. The trail's primary responsibility is the remaining nine players and the benches; secondary responsibility is the free thrower. You're simply playing the odds. You're more likely to have problems among the other players or the benches than you are to have a violation on the free thrower.

Despite what the manual says, in some cases, the official who called the technical foul becomes the *lead*. The theory: The lead is always facing away from the benches and is far away from players who are standing near the division line during free throws. If the technical foul was just whistled on a coach, the lead's back is to the coach and a confrontation is less likely to occur. The official involved in the call can't see the bench. If the coach can't look at the lead face-to-face, the coach is likely to stop arguing with that official. If the technical foul was on a player who is now near the division line, the lead who called the technical foul is far away and avoids a confrontation. The trail, who did not call the technical foul, watches the bench area and the division line players for potential problems.

Discuss the procedures in your pregame with your partner so technical foul free throw administration runs smoothly.

Free throw: lead movement

Before administering the free throw, the lead has the ball and is positioned in the lane under the basket. Look for late-arriving substitutes at the scorer's table and beckon them in if appropriate. Signal the number of remaining free throws to the players in the lane and the free thrower (PlayPic A). Simultaneously verbalize the number of free throws. Before bouncing the ball to the free thrower, make sure there are no players moving into or leaving lane spaces.

When the free thrower is ready to catch the ball, bounce the ball to the free thrower (PlayPic B).

The NFHS manual states that the lead is positioned "approximately four feet from the nearer lane line well off the endline" (PlayPic C). That position is maintained regardless of the number of free throws.

After the shot is airborne, adjust your position along the endline a step or two to get a good angle on strong side rebounding (PlayPic D).

Free throws: trail movement

Do not come into the lane to administer the free throw; the lead administers all free throws.

Pick up the visible 10-second count with the arm furthest from the basket (PlayPic A). Using your outside arm ensures the arm movement doesn't distract the shooter and shows the count clearly to bench personnel, etc. When showing a visible count as a trail during a free-throw attempt, the count should be less demonstrative than your normal visible count so as to not distract the shooter and draw unnecessary attention to the official.

On the last free throw, use the "stop the clock" signal with open hand raised directly above the head immediately after the shooter releases the shot (PlayPic B). Use the same arm (furthest from the basket) to ensure the timer clearly sees the signal. During the flight of the try and with your arm still raised, penetrate slightly toward the endline using a two-step crossover move. That movement ensures good angles on rebounding action. If the shot is good, lower your arm. If the shot is no good and the ball is to remain live, use the "start the clock" signal as soon as the ball is touched by or touches a player.

There is no need to signal a made free throw.

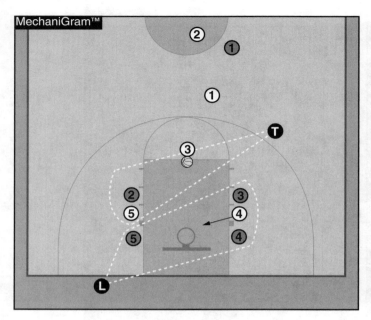

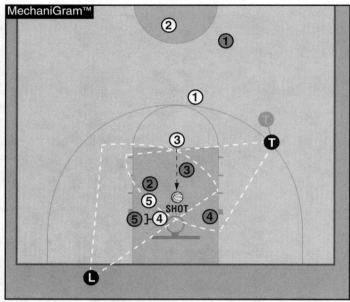

Action on the court:

③ releases free-throw attempt. ④ legally breaks into lane toward opposite lane line.

④ screens ⑤. ⑤ cuts off screen toward basket.

Lead Official Responsibilities

Primary: Off-ball. Watch ③, ④ and ④ on opposite lane line and ⑤ on near lane line. Look for defenders disconcerting the thrower.

Primary: Off-ball. Watch players near closest lane line.
Watch ④ screen ⑤.

Trail Official Responsibilities

Primary: On-ball. Watch ③ attempt free throw.
Secondary: Off-ball. Watch ② and ⑤ on opposite lane line. Look for defenders disconcerting the thrower.

As free throw is released, penetrate toward endline.
Primary: Off-ball. Watch players around free-throw line area.
Secondary: Off-ball. Watch players in lane area.

KEY

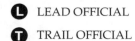

L LEAD OFFICIAL
T TRAIL OFFICIAL

PRIMARY COVERAGE AREA

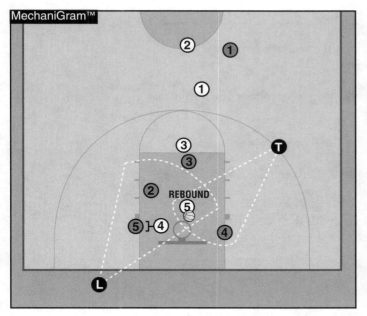

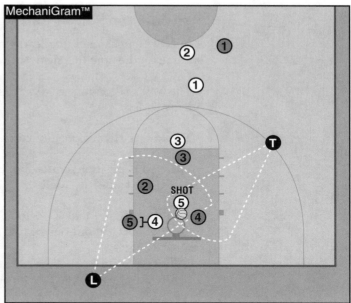

④ screens ⑤. ⑤ rebounds miss.

⑤ shoots.

Primary: Off-ball. Observe strong-side rebounding. Watch ④ screen ⑤.
Then: Primary: On-ball. Watch ⑤ rebound miss.

Primary: On-ball. Watch ⑤ shoot.
Secondary: Off-ball. Watch players in lane area. Observe strong-side rebounding.

Primary: On-ball. Watch ⑤ rebound ball.
Secondary: Off-ball. Watch players in lane area.

Primary: On-ball. Watch ⑤ shoot.
Secondary: Off-ball. Watch players in lane area. Observe weak-side rebounding.

---

① OFFENSE    PASS   ⊢— SCREEN

① DEFENSE    DRIBBLE

Review

Free Throws

• In NFHS mechanics, the lead watches the lane space nearest the endline on the lane line nearest the lead.

• The trail's secondary coverage is always players above the free-throw line extended.

• The trail is always positioned facing the scorer's table.

• The trail is positioned at a spot halfway between the trail-side lane line and the trail-side sideline.

• As a trail, do not take a position even with the free-throw line extended; move about one or two strides toward the division line to improve angles.

• Before administering a free throw, "sweep the floor."

• After a shot is airborne, adjust your position to improve rebounding angles.

• There is no need to signal a made free throw.

• Both officials should look for defenders disconcerting the thrower.

Quiz

Without referring back, you should be able to answer the following true-false questions.

1. Before bouncing the ball to the free thrower, the lead should make sure there are no players coming into or leaving marked lane spaces.

2. The trail must administer free throws during technical foul administration.

3. The trail should count silently when applying the free-throw count.

Chapter 16

Throw-ins

Throw-ins

Proper throw-in administration is critical to ensure your games run smoothly. There are probably more unwanted game interruptions during throw-ins than during any other segment of the game. Efficient movement and strong communication by the officials gets the ball back in play quickly and correctly.

Throw-in spots

Stoppages of play inside the key circle, plus the area from the free-throw line corners to the endline corners and below, result in throw-ins along the endline nearest the stoppage of play. All throw-ins from the endline shall be outside the free-throw lane lines extended. Stoppages of play outside that area result in throw-ins along the sideline nearest the stoppages.

Be precise with throw-in spots. The ball should be put in play exactly where it went out of play. Many officials incorrectly move the throw-in spot, either out of laziness or ease of administration. Don't fall into that trap; a moved throw-in spot impacts the ensuing throw-in. Most of the time, specific plays are called by coaches based on the location of the throw-in spot. Moving it creates an unfair advantage for one of the teams.

If a throw-in is immediately preceded by a timeout, make sure both officials are aware of the throw-in spot. Coaches will often ask the closest official where the throw-in spot is so the coach can discuss an appropriate play with his players during the timeout. It's awkward at best when the coach asks for the throw-in spot and you don't know. Be ready.

The boxing-in method

On all throw-ins, the officials use the boxing-in method. That means the thrower-in (and likely, most of the players) is always between the two officials; the thrower is "boxed in" for proper court coverage.

The lead administers all throw-ins on the frontcourt endline and along the lead's sideline if below the free-throw line extended. When the lead administers:

• The thrower is always between the lead and the thrower's goal.

• The trail is positioned between the free-throw line extended and the division line nearest the sideline opposite the lead, ensuring both sidelines, both endlines and the division line are covered.

The trail administers all throw-ins on the trail's sideline, the lead's sideline in the backcourt and the backcourt endline. When the trail administers the

throw-in in the frontcourt:

• The thrower shall be between the trail and the frontcourt basket.

• Unless otherwise dictated by an anticipated play, the lead is positioned on the endline on the opposite side of the court from the trail, ensuring both sidelines, the frontcourt endline and the division line are covered.

When the trail administers the throw-in in the backcourt:

• The thrower is always between the trail and the thrower's goal.

• Depending on backcourt pressure, the lead is positioned near the division line on the sideline opposite the trail, ensuring both sidelines and both endlines are covered.

If the throw-in is to be taken on the lead's sideline above the free-throw line extended, the lead becomes the new trail and the trail becomes the new lead.

Though general boxing-in principles apply in all throw-in situations, certain plays may dictate position adjustments. For example, if the lead anticipates a play that requires a ball side move by the lead, the lead may start the play ball side. When ball side, the lead must react quickly to cover the far sideline away from the trail if the anticipated play doesn't happen and the ball is thrown toward the lead's sideline. As the lead, move ball side at the start of the play only if you're confident that look is a good one for the anticipated throw-in play. Though moving ball side before a throw-in occurs is rare, you might consider it, for example, when a sideline throw-in is below the free-throw line extended and a post player is positioned on the low block nearest the thrower. Moving ball side on that throw-in play gives you a good look at the post action.

Administering a throw-in

Before administering a throw-in, make eye contact with your partner to make sure both officials are ready. That's especially necessary when a throw-in follows substitutions. Sometimes, the administering official is eager to put the ball in play and doesn't check first with the partner. Meanwhile, the partner is beckoning in subs and making sure replacements are off the court. When the ball is incorrectly given to the thrower *during* a substitution, chaos ensues. Avoid trouble by making eye contact before every throw-in.

After a substitution and before the throw-in, both officials should use preventive officiating and count the number of players on the court. Do not administer the throw-in until both teams have the correct number of players on the court. If the officials are doing their jobs properly, there should *never* be a technical foul for having too many players on the court.

The official may hand or bounce the ball to the thrower. The bounce may occur on throw-ins from the sideline or backcourt endline. It is not recommended for the lead to bounce the ball to the thrower for an endline throw-in remaining in the frontcourt.

To ensure proper court coverage, the administering official, if handing the ball to the thrower:

• Hands the ball to the thrower with the inside hand (closest to the thrower).

• Raises the other arm to give the "start clock" signal to the timer.

• Must move away from the thrower to avoid straightlining. Staying too close to the thrower blocks court vision. Take at least one step laterally away from the thrower so your field of vision increases.

• The administering official may also need to step back from the endline or sideline, increasing visual clearance and assuring proper perspective.

For the lead official, post play on throw-ins is often physical as players jockey for inside position and set screens to free teammates. The lead must see potential infractions by the thrower, potential infractions or fouls by the player defending the thrower and action nearest the throw-in.

Communication with players
Talk to the players involved in the throw-in. Use signals and words to help them understand what they can and can't do. That preventive officiating will help players and officials stay out of trouble.

Endline throw-ins can sometimes cause confusion for players. By rule, a player may move along the endline with the ball for a throw-in after a made basket. Teams may run the endline after a foul or violation after a made goal. All other throw-ins are designated spot throw-ins that restrict the thrower's movements. Sideline throw-ins don't cause as much confusion because sideline throw-ins are always designated spot throw-ins.

To end the endline confusion, when a player is awarded a designated-spot throw-in on the endline, tell the thrower that before handing over the ball. Say something like, "It's a spot throw-in," so the player knows not to run the endline. It's also a good idea to point down at the spot while talking to the player. That shows everyone you've told the player it is a designated-

spot throw-in (and your signal is likely to be on video to back you up!).

If the player may run the endline, tell the thrower that before handing over the ball. Say something like, "You can run it," so the player knows of the option. It's also a good idea to wave your arm in front of you parallel to the endline (similar to a three-second call signal but with your arm swinging parallel to the endline). That shows everyone you've told the player

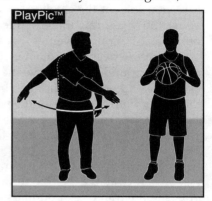

it is not a designated-spot throw-in (again, you'll be seen on video handling it correctly).

When a defensive player is guarding the throw-in closely and is positioned very close to the boundary line, use preventive officiating. Before handing the ball to the thrower, tell the defensive player to avoid a violation and not break the plane of the boundary line. It's a good idea to hold your hand up, using a stop sign signal, over the boundary line plane while talking to the player. That shows everyone you've warned the player not to violate (and it's on video).

Take the time during throw-ins to let players know exactly what is going on and prevent minor infractions.

Switching on throw-ins
The lead has primary on-ball coverage when the ball is below the free-throw line extended opposite the trail (see "Court coverage," p. 73). When a throw-in occurs on the sideline below the free-throw line extended opposite the trail, the lead administers the throw-in using the boxing-in method by bouncing the ball to the thrower.

If the throw-in is to be taken on the lead's sideline above the free-throw line extended, the lead becomes the new trail and the trail becomes the new lead.

The NFHS manual mandates officials switch on all fouls. The non-calling official freezes the action, likely near the division line. Then, after the calling official reports the foul, the non-calling official moves into the backcourt to administer the throw-in.

Switch for throw-ins above free-throw line extended
The NFHS manual states, "If the designated spot for the throw-in is above the free-throw line extended, the lead official administering the throw-in will now become the

new trail. The original trail now becomes the new lead The original trail now becomes the new lead. The same procedure is used on the opposite side."

Referee recommends that, in most situations, the trail is responsible for the sideline opposite the trail and above the free-throw line extended so the lead can watch off-ball (see "Court coverage," p. 73).

The same coverage problems discussed on p. 72 occur on out-of-bounds plays above the free-throw-line extended and opposite the trail. If the trail is watching the player with the ball and the lead is watching the sideline above the free-throw line extended to see if the player violates, who is watching the rest of the players? No one.

Referee recommends that the trail has sideline responsibility above the free-throw line extended and opposite the trail (see "Boundary coverage," p. 76). That coverage recommendation extends to the ensuing throw-in. Since the trail is already watching the action near the sideline above the free-throw line extended, the trail administers the throw-in if the play remains in the frontcourt. Assuming no play dictates otherwise, the lead moves near the far lane line to box in the throw-in and cover the far sideline. The benefits: The lead can focus on watching off-ball and the ball is put back in play quickly.

If you are following the NFHS sideline coverage strictly, the lead will make the out-of-bounds call above the free-throw line extended then move up the sideline and administer the throw-in, becoming the new trail. The trail would move down to the endline and become the new lead.

Be sure to discuss throw-in coverage and responsibilities thoroughly in your pregame conference with your partner.

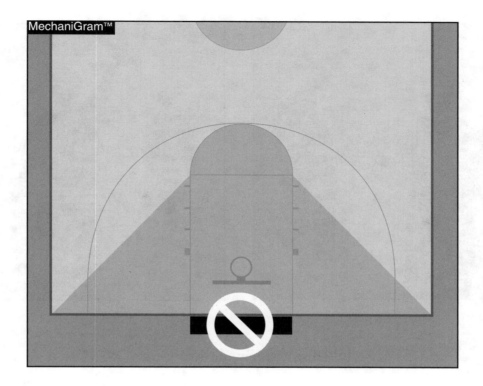

Throw-in spots

Stoppages of play inside the key circle, plus the area from the free-throw line corners to the endline corners and below, result in a throw-in along the endline nearest the stoppage of play. Stoppages of play outside that area result in throw-ins along the sideline nearest the stoppage of play.

Do not administer a throw-in within the lane line extended.

Administering a throw-in

On all throw-ins, the officials use the boxing-in method. On all frontcourt endline throw-ins, the lead is positioned outside the thrower between the thrower and the sideline (see, "Throw ins: boxing-in method when lead administers," p. 147).

Officials may bounce or hand the ball to the thrower. The bounce to the thrower-in should only occur from the sideline or the backcourt endline.

To ensure proper court coverage when handing the ball to the thrower, use the inside hand. Before handing or bouncing the ball to the thrower, tell the players to ball is about to become live with short commands, like "ready" or "play it." That gives all players a fair start. Then the administering official must move away from the thrower. Staying too close to the thrower obscures court vision. Move for proper angles to avoid straightlining. Take at least one step laterally away from the thrower so your field of vision increases. You should also step back from the endline or sideline, increasing visual clearance and assuring proper perspective.

For the lead official, post play on throw-ins is often physical as players jockey for inside position and set screens to free teammates. The lead must see potential infractions by the thrower, potential infractions or fouls by the player defending the thrower and action nearest the throw-in.

In PlayPic A, the official hands the ball to the thrower with the hand closest to the thrower. In PlayPic B, the official steps away from the thrower and begins the throw-in count. The count is silent.

The step away from the thrower allows the official to see the thrower and provides a better angle on the players jockeying for position.

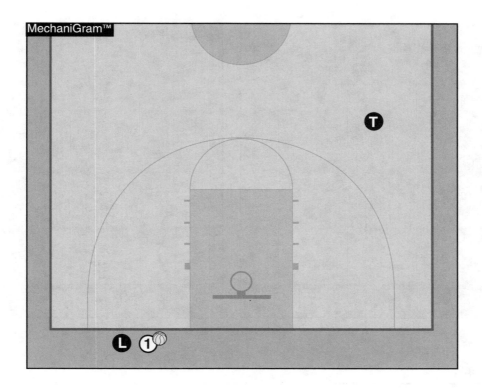

Throw-ins: boxing-in method when lead administers

The lead administers all throw-ins on the
frontcourt endline. The thrower is always between
the lead and the thrower's goal. The trail is
positioned between the free-throw line extended
and the division line, opposite the lead, to ensure
both sidelines, both endlines and the division line
are covered.

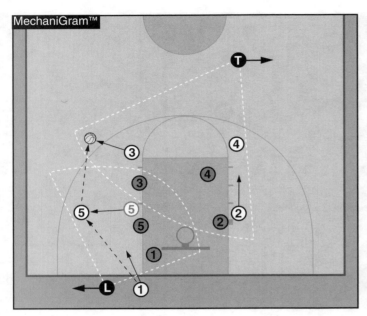

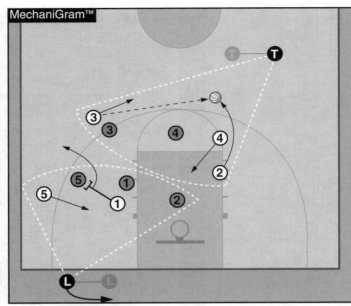

Action on the court:

⑤ breaks toward sideline. ① passes to ⑤ then moves toward low block. ③ breaks toward sideline. ⑤ passes to ③.

② cuts toward top of the key. ③ passes to ② then moves toward top of key. ④ cuts toward low block. ① screens ❺ then moves beyond three-point arc.

Lead Official Responsibilities

Hand ball to thrower using boxing in method.
Primary: On-ball. Step away from thrower; watch thrower.
Secondary: Off-ball. Watch ⑤ break toward sideline.
Then: Primary: On-ball. Watch ⑤ receive pass from ①.
Watch ⑤ pass to ③.
Then: Primary: Off-ball. Watch players in lane area.

Primary: Off-ball. Watch players in lane area.
Watch ① screen ❺.
Anticipate play.
Begin moving ball-side to opposite lane line.

Trail Official Responsibilities

Start deep.
Anticipate throw-in direction.
Primary: Off-ball. Watch ② move toward top of key.
Watch ③ break toward sideline.
Then: Primary: On-ball. Watch ③ receive pass from ⑤.

Primary: On-ball. Watch ③ pass to ②.

KEY

L LEAD OFFICIAL   PRIMARY COVERAGE AREA
T TRAIL OFFICIAL

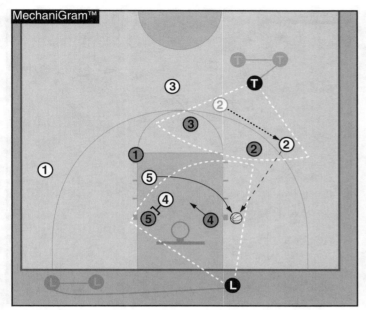

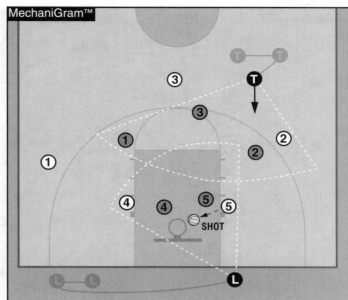

② dribbles toward sideline. ④ screens ⑤. ⑤ cuts off screen to low block. ② delivers drop pass to ⑤.	⑤ catches drop pass from ② and shoots.
Move ball-side to opposite lane line. **Primary: Off-ball.** Watch ④ screen ⑤. Watch ⑤ cut to low block. **Then: Primary: On-ball.** Watch ⑤ catch drop pass from ②.	**Primary: On-ball.** Watch ⑤ shoot.
Primary: On-ball. Watch ② dribble toward sideline. Penetrate toward center of court for inside-out angle. Watch ② drop pass to ⑤.	**Primary: Off-ball.** Watch players around free-throw line area. Penetrate toward endline for angles. Observe weak-side rebounding.

 ① OFFENSE    ① PASS   ⊢— SCREEN

① DEFENSE   ① DRIBBLE

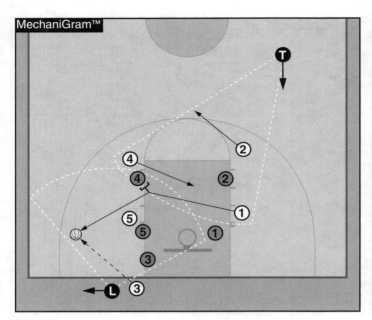

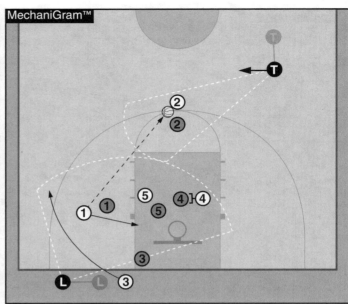

Action on the court:

① screens ④ then rolls toward sideline. ③ passes to ①. ② moves toward top of key. ④ cuts off screen toward opposite lane line.

① passes to ② then cuts toward opposite sideline. ③ moves toward three-point line. ④ screens ④.

Lead Official Responsibilities

Hand ball to thrower using boxing in method.
Primary: On-ball. Step away from thrower; watch thrower.
Secondary: Off-ball. Watch ① screen ④.
Then: Primary: On-ball. Watch ① catch pass from ③.

Primary: On-ball: Watch ① pass ball to ②.
Then: Primary: Off-ball. Watch ① cut toward opposite sideline.
Watch ④ screen ④.

Trail Official Responsibilities

Anticipate throw-in direction.
Penetrate toward endline.
Primary: Off-ball. Watch ① screen ④.
Watch players around free-throw line area.

Primary: On-ball. Watch ② catch pass from ①.

KEY

L LEAD OFFICIAL
T TRAIL OFFICIAL

PRIMARY COVERAGE AREA

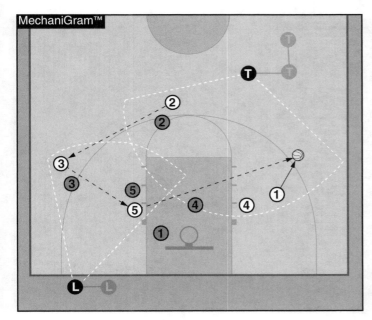

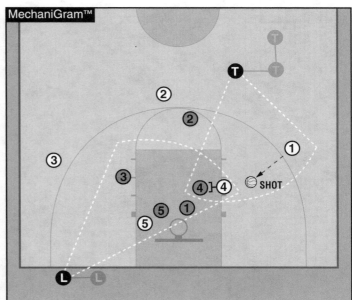

② passes to ③. ③ passes to ⑤. ⑤ passes to ①.	④ screens ❹. ① shoots three-point shot.
Primary: On-ball. Watch ③ catch pass from ②. Watch ③ pass to ⑤. Watch ⑤ pass to ①.	**Primary: Off-ball.** Watch players in lane area. Watch ④ screen ❹. Observe weak-side rebounding.
Primary: On-ball. Watch ② pass to ③. **Then: Primary: Off-ball.** Watch players around free-throw line area. Watch ① move toward three-point arc. **Then: Primary: On-ball.** Watch ① receive pass from ⑤.	**Primary: On-ball.** Watch ① shoot three-point shot. **Secondary: Off-ball.** Watch ④ screen ❹. Observe strong-side rebounding.

① OFFENSE	🏀◄----① PASS	⊢— SCREEN
❶ DEFENSE	🏀①◄········① DRIBBLE	

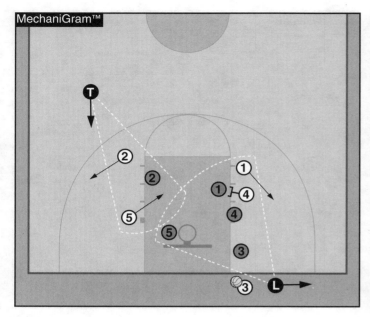 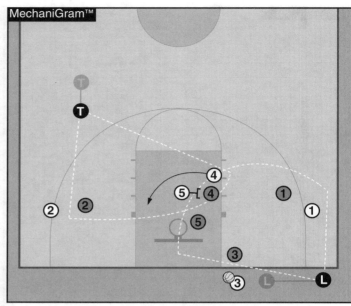

Action on the court:

④ screens ①. ① cuts off screen to three-point arc.
⑤ cuts toward lane. ② moves toward three-point arc.

⑤ screens ④. ④ rolls to basket.

Lead Official Responsibilities

Hand ball to thrower using boxing in method.
Primary: On-ball. Step away from thrower; watch thrower.
Secondary: Off-ball. Watch players in lane area. Watch ④ screen ①.

Primary: On-ball. Watch thrower.
Secondary: Off-ball. Watch players in lane area. Watch ⑤ screen ④.

Trail Official Responsibilities

Primary: Off-ball. Watch players around nearest lane line.
Anticipate play.
Penetrate toward endline for angles.

Primary: Off-ball. Watch ⑤ screen ④.

KEY   **L** LEAD OFFICIAL   **T** TRAIL OFFICIAL   PRIMARY COVERAGE AREA

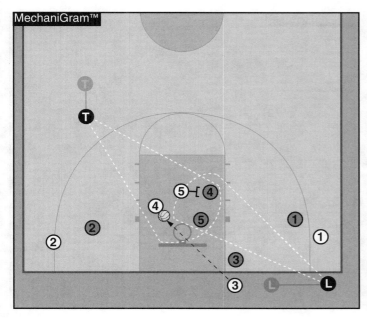

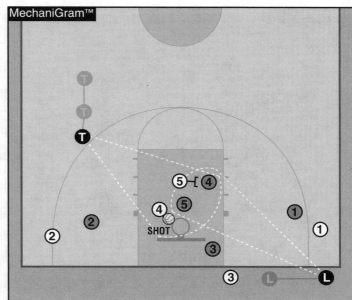

⑤ screens ④. ③ passes to ④.	④ shoots.

Primary: On-ball. Watch ③ pass to ④.
Secondary: Off-ball. Watch ⑤ screen ④.

Primary: On-ball. Watch ④ shoot.
Secondary: Off-ball. Watch ⑤ screen ④.

Primary: Off-ball. Watch ⑤ screen ④.

Primary: Off-ball. Watch ⑤ screen ④.
Secondary: On-ball. Watch ④ shoot.
Penetrate toward endline for angles.
Observe weak-side rebounding.

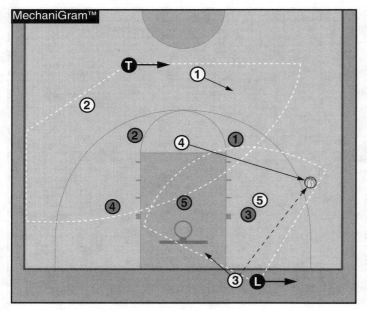
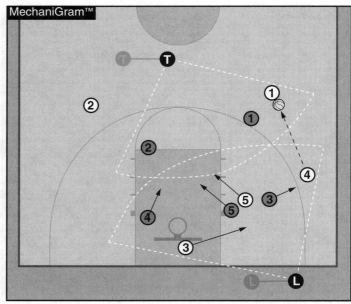

Action on the court:

③ inbounds to ④ and begins to break into the lane.

④ passes to ①. ③ cuts toward ④. ⑤ moves toward the free-throw line.

Lead Official Responsibilities

Hand ball to thrower using boxing in method.
Primary: On-ball. Step away from thrower; watch thrower.
Secondary: Off-ball. Watch players in lane area.
Then: Primary: On-ball. Watch ④ catch pass from ③.

Step toward sideline.
Primary: On-ball. Watch ④ pass to ①.
Secondary: Off-ball. Watch players in lane area.

Trail Official Responsibilities

Primary: Off-ball. Watch players around free-throw line area.
Adjust toward center court for angles.

Primary: On-ball. Watch ① catch pass from ④.
Secondary: Off-ball. Watch players around free-throw line area.

KEY

L LEAD OFFICIAL
T TRAIL OFFICIAL
PRIMARY COVERAGE AREA

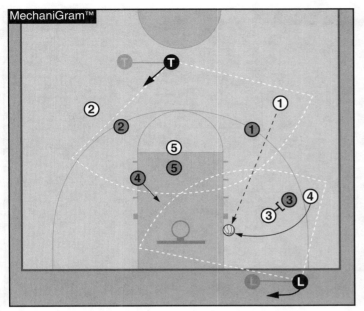

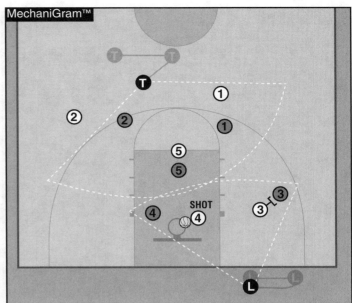

③ screens ❸. ④ cuts toward basket. ① delivers lob pass.

④ catches lob pass and shoots.

Anticipate play; move slightly toward basket.
Primary: Off-ball. Watch ③ screen ❸.
Watch ④ cut off screen toward basket.

Primary: On-ball. Watch ④ catch lob pass and shoot.
Secondary: Off-ball. Watch players in lane area.

Anticipate play.
Penetrate toward endline for angles.
Primary: On-ball. Watch ① pass to ④.
Secondary: Off-ball. Watch players around free-throw line area.

Primary: Off-ball. Watch players in lane area.

 OFFENSE   PASS   ⌐— SCREEN

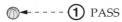 DEFENSE    DRIBBLE

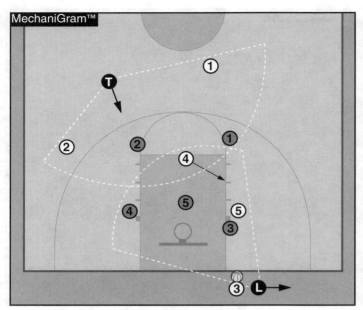

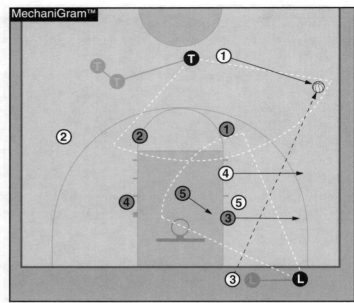

Action on the court:

④ breaks toward sideline.	① breaks toward sideline. ④ continues toward sideline. ③ passes to ①.

Lead Official Responsibilities

Hand ball to thrower using boxing in method. **Primary: On-ball.** Step away from thrower; watch thrower. **Secondary: Off-ball.** Watch players in lane area.	Step toward sideline as pass is delivered. **Primary: Off-ball.** Watch players in lane area.

Trail Official Responsibilities

Primary: Off-ball. Watch players around free-throw line area. Anticipate throw-in toward opposite sideline. Penetrate slightly toward endline for angles.	Adjust toward center court for angles. **Primary: On-ball.** Watch ① catch pass from ③. **Secondary: Off-ball.** Watch players around free-throw line area.

KEY   **L** LEAD OFFICIAL   **T** TRAIL OFFICIAL   PRIMARY COVERAGE AREA

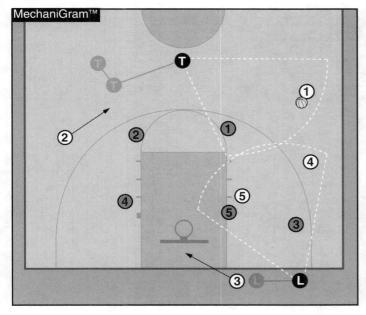

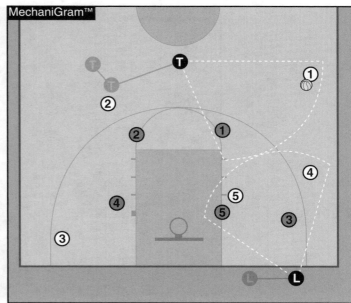

② moves toward top of the key. ③ moves toward sideline away from the ball.

① sets the offense and begins to run a play.

Primary: Off-ball. Watch players in lane area.

Primary: Off-ball. Watch players in lane area.

Primary: On-ball. Watch ① with ball.
Secondary: Off-ball. Watch players around free-throw line area.
Stay deep; avoid passing lane between ① and ② as ② moves toward top of the key.

Primary: On-ball. Watch ① with ball.
Secondary: Off-ball. Watch players around free-throw line area.

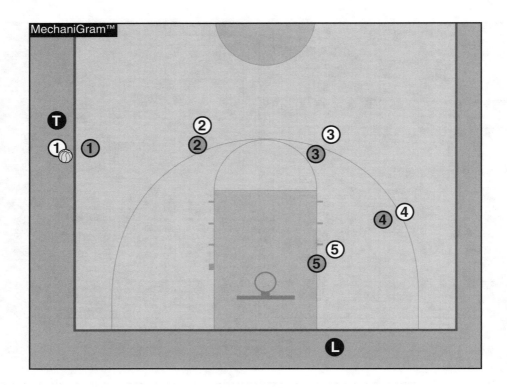

Throw-ins: boxing-in method when trail administers in frontcourt

When the trail administers the throw-in, the thrower is always between the trail and the frontcourt basket. Unless otherwise dictated by an anticipated play, the lead is positioned on the endline opposite the trail to ensure both sidelines, the frontcourt endline and the division line are covered.

There are two ways the officials might have wound up in the positions shown in the MechaniGram. Under NFHS mechanics, the old lead would have been responsible for out-of-bounds calls along the sideline where the ball went out. Since the ball is being taken out above the free-throw line extended, the lead would move to new trail, while the trail would move to new lead.

Referee recommended mechanics dictate that the officials would have switched sides of the court, trail continuing in the trail position, lead continuing in the lead position. Make sure you discuss those options in the pregame discussion with your partner.

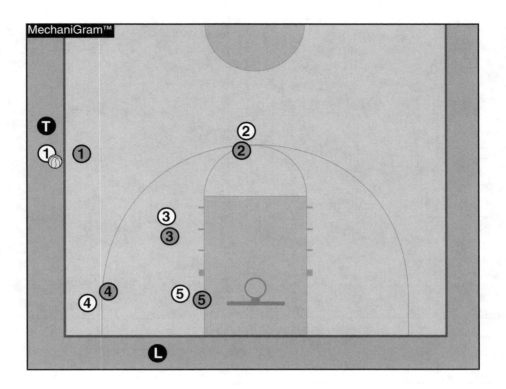

Throw-ins: lead ball-side when trail administers in frontcourt

When the trail administers the throw-in, the thrower is always between the trail and the frontcourt basket. Normally, the lead is opposite the trail (see "Box-in method" p. 158), however the players' location on the court now dictates the lead to be ball-side for the throw-in, while taking a position on the endline.

Even though the lead is ball-side, the lead is still responsible for two boundary lines: the endline and sideline opposite the trail. The lead is making a conscience decision to be ball-side, sacrificing the lead's sideline coverage for superior off-ball coverage.

If the lead were to balance the court by staying opposite the trail, the lead would be too far away from the players to officiate properly. Not to mention putting unjust pressure on the trail to officiate the throw-in and all 10 players.

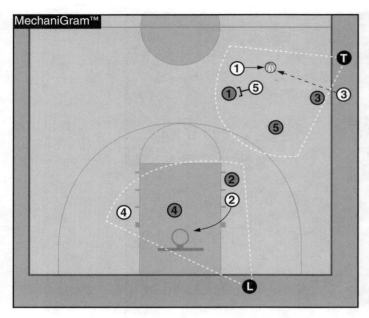

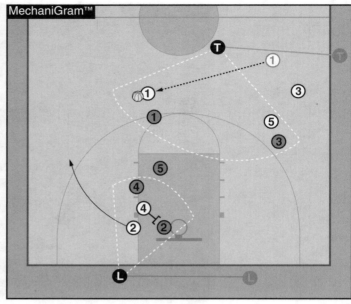

Action on the court:

⑤ screens ❶. ① cuts toward sideline. ③ passes to ①. ② cuts into free-throw lane.

① dribbles to top of the key. ④ screens ❷. ② moves toward three-point arc.

Lead Official Responsibilities

Start play ball side anticipating ball may come directly to dominant player ②.
Primary: Off-ball. Watch players in lane area.

As ① dribbles toward the top of the key, move to lane line opposite trail to balance the floor.
Primary: Off-ball. Watch players in lane area. Watch ④ screen ❷.

Trail Official Responsibilities

Administer throw-in using boxing-in method.
Primary: On-ball. Step away from thrower unless you bounce pass the ball; watch thrower.
Secondary: Off-ball. Watch ⑤ screen ❶.
Primary: On-ball. Watch ① catch pass from ③.

Move onto the court.
Primary: On-ball. Watch ① dribble toward top of the key.

KEY

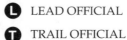 

L LEAD OFFICIAL

T TRAIL OFFICIAL

PRIMARY COVERAGE AREA

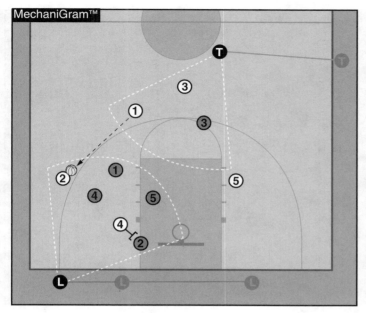

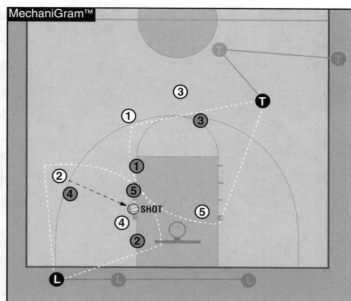

④ screens ❷. ① passes to ②.	② shoots three-point shot.

As ball is passed to ②, adjust to sideline for proper angle. **Primary: On-ball.** Watch ② catch pass from ①. **Secondary: Off-ball.** Watch ④ screen ❷.	**Primary: On-ball.** Watch ② shoot. **Secondary: Off-ball.** Watch players in lane area. Observe strong-side rebounding.

Primary: On-ball. Watch ① pass to ②. **Then: Primary: Off-ball.** Watch players around free-throw line area.	Penetrate toward endline for angles. **Primary: Off-ball.** Watch players in lane area. Observe weak-side rebounding.

① OFFENSE   PASS   ⊢— SCREEN

❶ DEFENSE    DRIBBLE

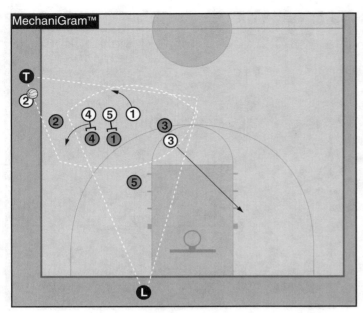

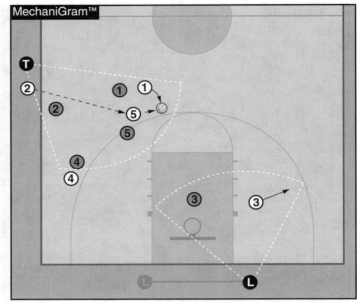

Action on the court:

② has ball for throw-in. ⑤ screen ❶. ④ screens ❹, then ④ rolls toward three-point arc. ① rolls off double screen toward division line. ③ cuts toward opposite three-point arc.

② passes to ⑤. ① cuts toward top of the key and catches short pass from ⑤.

Lead Official Responsibilities

Start play ball side since all 10 players are on that side of the court.
Extend field of vision beyond free-throw line.
Primary: Off-ball. Watch ④ screen ❹ and ⑤ screen ❶.
Watch ③ cut toward three-point arc.

Anticipate play.
As ① catches pass from ⑤ and begins dribble, move back to lane line opposite trail to balance the floor.
Primary: Off-ball. Watch players in lane area.

Trail Official Responsibilities

Administer throw-in using boxing-in method.
Primary: On-ball. Step away from thrower unless you bounce pass the ball; watch thrower.
Secondary: Off-ball. Watch ④ screen ❹.
Watch ⑤ screen ❶.

Primary: On-ball. Watch ② pass to ⑤.
Watch ⑤ catch pass from ②.
Watch ⑤ pass to ①.

KEY

L LEAD OFFICIAL

T TRAIL OFFICIAL

PRIMARY COVERAGE AREA

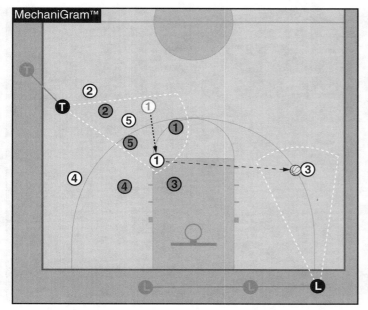

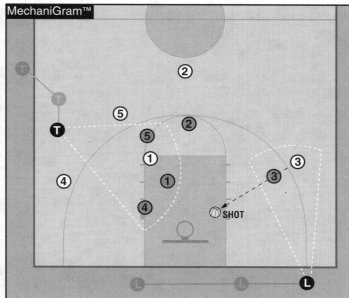

① dribbles to free-throw line. ① passes to ③.	③ shoots three-point shot.
Primary: On-ball. Watch ③ catch pass from ①. Adjust toward near sideline to improve angle.	**Primary: On-ball.** Watch ③ shoot. Observe strong-side rebounding.
Move onto the court. Penetrate toward endline for angles. **Primary: On-ball.** Watch ① dribble toward free-throw line. Watch ① pass to ③.	Penetrate toward endline for angles. **Primary: Off-ball.** Watch players in lane area. Observe weak-side rebounding.

  OFFENSE 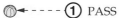 PASS ⊢—— SCREEN

 DEFENSE  DRIBBLE

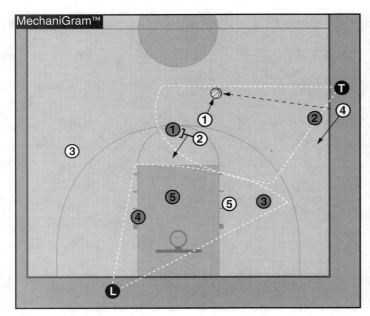

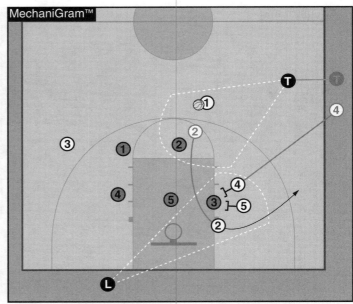

Action on the court:

④ has ball for throw-in. ② screens ①, then ② moves toward free-throw line. ① rolls off screen toward division line and catches pass from ④. ④ moves toward low-block.

④ screens ③. ⑤ screens ③. ② circles through lane and cuts off screens toward three-point arc.

Lead Official Responsibilities

Primary: Off-ball. Watch players in lane area.

Primary: Off-ball. Watch players in lane area.
Watch ④ screen ③.
Watch ⑤ screen ③.
Watch ② roll off screens toward three-point arc.

Trail Official Responsibilities

Administer throw-in using boxing-in method.
Primary: On-ball. Step away from thrower unless you bounce pass the ball; watch thrower.
Secondary: Off-ball. Watch ② screen ①.
Primary: On-ball. Watch ① catch pass from ④.

Move onto the court.
Primary: On-ball. Watch ① with the ball.
Secondary: Off-ball. Watch ② cut through lane.

KEY — **L** LEAD OFFICIAL   **T** TRAIL OFFICIAL   PRIMARY COVERAGE AREA

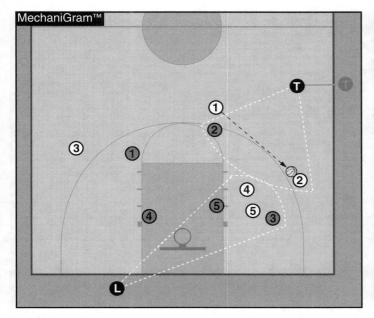

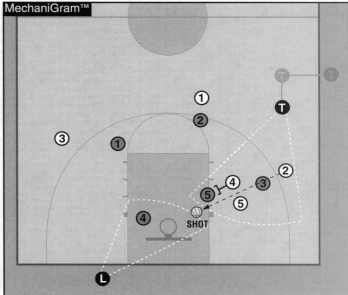

① passes to ②.	④ screens ⑤. ② shoots three-point shot.
Primary: Off-ball. Watch players in lane area.	**Primary: Off-ball.** Watch players in lane area. Observe strong-side rebounding.
Primary: On-ball. Watch ① pass to ②.	**Primary: On-ball.** Watch ② shoot three-point shot. **Secondary: Off-ball.** Watch ④ screen ⑤. Penetrate toward endline for angles. Observe weak-side rebounding.

① OFFENSE	🏀◀- - - - ①	PASS	⊣— SCREEN
① DEFENSE	🏀①◀········①	DRIBBLE	

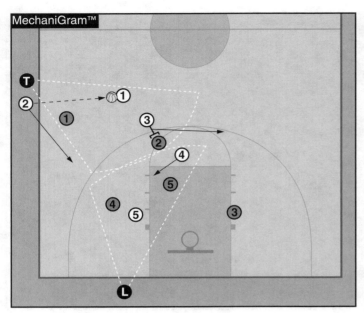

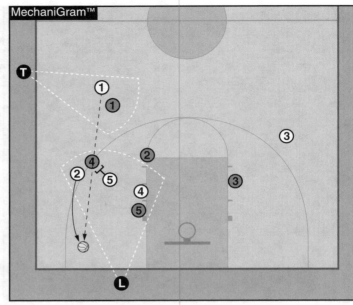

Action on the court:

② has ball for throw-in. ③ screens ② then ③ moves toward opposite side three-point arc. ② passes to ① then ② cuts toward corner. ④ cuts toward low block.

⑤ screens ④. ① passes over the defense to ②.

Lead Official Responsibilities

Start play ball side because the light-colored team has used this same play three times previously.
Primary: Off-ball. Watch players in lane area.

Primary: Off-ball. Watch players in lane area. Watch ⑤ screen ④.
Watch ② cut toward corner.
Then: Primary: On-ball. Watch ② catch pass from ①.

Trail Official Responsibilities

Administer throw-in using boxing-in method.
Primary: On-ball. Step away from thrower unless you bounce pass the ball; watch thrower.
Secondary: Off-ball. Watch ③ screen ②.
Then: Primary: On-ball. Watch ① catch pass from ②.

Primary: On-ball. Watch ① pass to ②.

KEY

L LEAD OFFICIAL
T TRAIL OFFICIAL

PRIMARY COVERAGE AREA

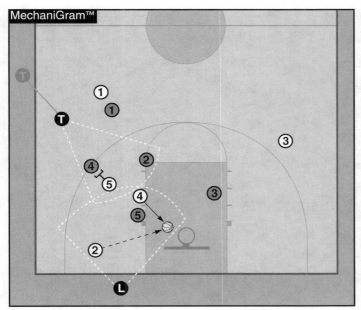

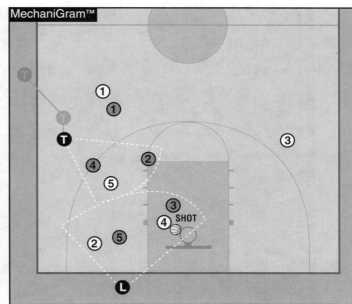

⑤ screens ④. ④ cuts toward basket. ② delivers drop pass to ④.	④ catches pass and shoots layup.
Primary: On-ball. Watch ② pass to ④. **Secondary: Off-ball.** Watch ④ cut toward basket.	**Primary: On-ball.** Watch ④ catch pass and shoot.
Move onto the court. Penetrate toward endline for angles. **Primary: Off-ball.** Watch ⑤ screen ④.	**Primary: Off-ball.** Watch players around free-throw line area. Penetrate toward endline for angles. Observe weak-side rebounding.

① OFFENSE	◉←----①	PASS	⊢—	SCREEN
① DEFENSE	◉①←·······①	DRIBBLE		

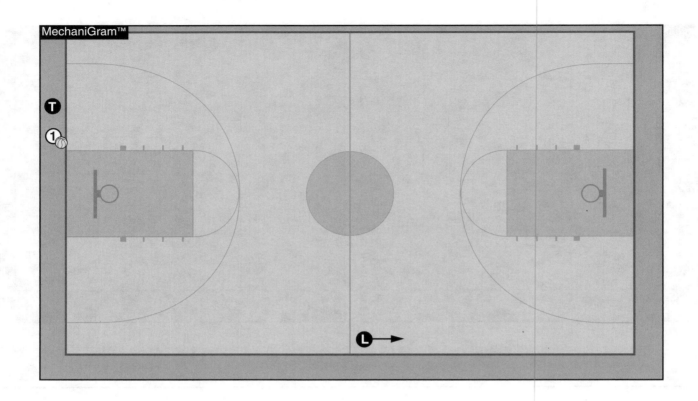

Throw-ins: boxing-in method when trail administers in backcourt

The trail administers all throw-ins in the backcourt. The thrower is always between the trail and the thrower's goal. Depending on backcourt pressure, the lead is positioned near the division line on the sideline opposite the trail, to ensure both sidelines and both endlines are covered.

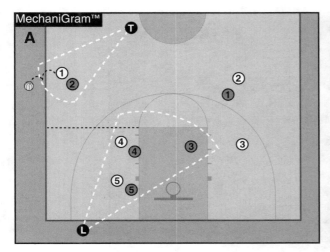

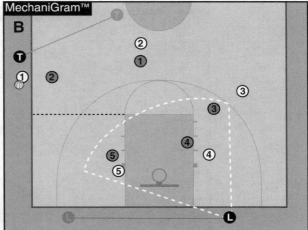

Throw-in: trail administers above free-throw line extended

The NFHS manual states, "In the frontcourt, the throw-in is administered by the official responsible for the boundary where the throw in occurs." The manual also states the lead has the entire sideline on the lead side of the court. *Referee* recommends that, in most situations, the trail administers all throw-ins that occur above the free-throw line extended on either side of the floor so the lead can watch off-ball (see "Court coverage," p. 72).

The same coverage problems discussed on p. 72 occur on plays that go out-of-bounds above the free-throw line extended and opposite the trail. If the trail is watching the player with the ball and the lead is watching the sideline above the free-throw line extended to see if the player violates, who is watching the rest of the players? No one.

Referee recommends that the trail has sideline responsibility above the free-throw line extended and opposite the trail (see "Boundary coverage," p. 76). Although counter to standard NFHS mechanics, that coverage recommendation extends to the ensuing throw-in. Since the trail is already watching the action near the sideline above the free-throw line extended, the trail administers the throw-in if the play remains in the frontcourt. Assuming no play dictates otherwise, the lead moves near the far lane line to box-in the throw-in and cover the far sideline. The benefits: The lead can focus on watching off-ball and the ball is put back in play quickly.

In MechaniGram A, the trail has moved beyond the center of the court to watch ① with the ball above the free-throw line extended. ② knocks the

ball out-of-bounds. The lead is watching off-ball. In MechaniGram B, the trail administers the throw-in. The lead moves toward the opposite sideline to employ boxing in principles.

The NFHS manual clearly states that the official responsible for the sideline administers the throw-in. That means the lead would make the out-of-bounds call, then move up the sideline and administer the throw-in, becoming the new trail. The trail would move down to the endline and become the new lead.

If your state or local association follow the NFHS manual exclusively, do it. Check with the appropriate authorities to see if you can use the *Referee* recommendation. Be sure to discuss it thoroughly in your pregame conference with your partner.

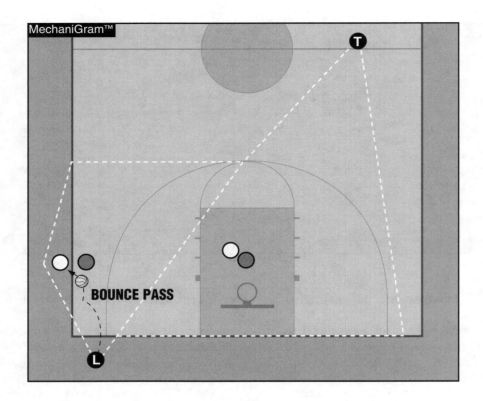

Throw-in below free-throw line extended

The lead has primary on-ball coverage when the ball is below the free-throw line extended opposite the trail (see "Court coverage," p. 72). When a throw-in occurs on the sideline opposite the trail below the free-throw line extended, the lead administers the throw-in using the boxing-in method by bouncing the ball to the thrower.

The adjustments means the lead and trail will not have to switch or move across the court to administer a throw-in below the free-throw line extended, a necessary practice in previous seasons.

In order for the lead to administer the sideline throw-in, significant coverage adjustments must be made. The lead must move closer toward the sideline before bouncing the ball to the thrower to ensure a proper visual field that includes the thrower and throw-in plane. The lead should also get deep (move back away from the endline) to increase the field of vision and see secondary coverage of post play on the low block (MechaniGram).

With the lead focused nearer the throw-in, the trail must move off the opposite sideline and onto the court to officiate all off-ball action, including action in the lane area. The trail must be aggressive if an off-ball foul in the lane is detected, moving toward the foul to close the distance.

As with all throw-ins, the lead and trail should make eye contact before the lead bounces the ball to the thrower.

Keep in mind the lead administers throw-ins below the free-throw line extended *when the ball goes out of bounds on the lead's side of the court*. If the ball goes out of bounds below the free-throw line extended on the trail's side of the court (opposite the lead), the trail administers that throw-in. There's no need for the lead to come across the court to administer that throw-in because the trail would also have to cross the court to apply boxing-in principles.

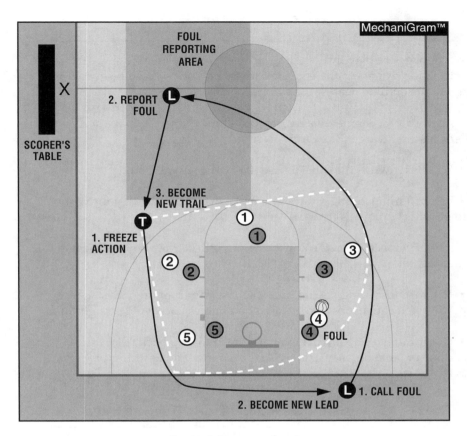

Switching on fouls

Officials switch on all fouls. Why switch? If not, the same official would be the lead on one end of the court and the trail on the other end of the court all the time. Switching allows the two officials to observe both teams and their respective offensive and defensive plays from the different perspectives.

When your partner moves to report a foul to the scorer (see "Foul reporting area," p. 67), keep all players within your field of vision. Penetrate toward the crowd of players slightly — maybe just a step or two depending on where the players are — and stop. You are the eyes and ears of two officials as your partner reports to the table. It is that dead-ball time when you can prevent many extracurricular illegal activities from brewing into bigger problems. Use your voice to let players know you're in the area. Your mere presence may stop a problem.

Do not worry about the basketball. Many times the ball will bounce away from the area. *It is not your responsibility to chase it!* Going after the ball leaves players unattended. The ball will eventually come back because you can't play without it.

If the players appear calm, begin moving toward the throw-in spot or begin preparing players for free throws. Move slowly and with your head up, watching the players as you move toward the spot. Use your voice to tell the players what's next. If you have the players ready for the next play, the ball will get back in play quickly and smoothly.

After the foul is reported to the scorer, the calling official assumes the new position. The effective switch means good dead-ball officiating and a smooth resumption of play.

Throw-ins

• Stoppages of play inside the key circle, plus the area from the free-throw line corners to the endline corners and below, result is throw-ins along the endline nearest the stoppage of play.

• If a throw-in is immediately proceeded by a timeout, make sure both officials are aware of the throw-in spot.

• On all throw-ins the officials use the boxing-in method.

• Before administering a throw-in, make eye contact with your partner to ensure everyone is ready.

• In NFHS mechanics, the administering official may bounce the ball to the thrower.

• The administrating official must move away from the thrower after placing it at the disposal to ensure good angles and avoid straightlining.

• The administering official may also need to step back from the endline or sideline, increasing visual clearance and assuring proper perspective.

Quiz

Without referring back, you should be able to answer the following true-false questions.

1. There's no need to count the number of players after a substitution and before a throw-in.

2. If a ball goes out-of-bounds in the lead's on-ball area along the sideline below the free-throw line extended, the lead and trail should switch positions for the ensuing throw-in.

3. In NFHS games, the throw-in count is always silent.

4. In NFHS games, the officials switch on all fouls.

1 - False, 2 - False, 3 - True, 4 - True

Chapter 17

Transitions

Transitions

Transition plays occur any time the ball moves from one end of the court to the other. On transition plays, the officials switch designations — from trail to lead and vice versa.

Unique challenges for both officials occur during transitions. Understanding specific movements and responsibilities gives you an opportunity to officiate the transition game properly.

Moving from backcourt to frontcourt

When play moves from one endline toward the other, the trail has primary responsibility in the backcourt. For example, after a made basket, the trail is responsible for the throw-in and watches the players move to the other end of the court.

In any transition, effective coverage means significant movement by the trail. Similar to halfcourt coverage, the trail must move off the sideline (see "Trail movement off sideline, p. 92).

When running upcourt, do not backpedal. Run with your torso turned slightly so you can see the action. Never run with your head down; you could miss a foul or severe contact. Backpedaling is too slow and holds a greater risk for injury.

When an offensive player has the ball on the opposite side of the floor from the trail official, the trail must move away from the closest sideline and get proper angles. By staying too close to the near sideline, the trail cannot effectively see action near the ball and must make judgments from a far distance — way too far to convince anyone the trail saw the play correctly.

The trail has primary sideline responsibility in the backcourt (see "Boundary coverage: backcourt" p. 81). Three factors make that possible: hustle, spacing and angles. The trail has to work hard at getting good angles and proper spacing.

When the ball is moving upcourt with defensive pressure toward the division line near the sideline opposite the trail, the trail should move up the court behind the play (about five feet) and *at least* in the center of the court. If the ball swings to the center of the court or the near sideline, simply move back toward the near sideline. That movement — from sideline toward the center of the court and back — ensures both sidelines are covered while your partner watches most of the players off ball.

When there's aggressive defensive pressure (trapping defenses, etc.) near the sideline opposite the trail, it may be necessary to move beyond the center of the court

and get even closer to the play. Save that extreme movement, however, when you anticipate a double-team near the opposite sideline. When beyond the center of the court, maintain proper spacing; you must still be able to move back toward the near sideline if necessary.

Avoid moving straight toward the play: You could negatively impact the play by being in a passing lane. Take an angle toward the backcourt endline to decrease your chances of interfering with the play.

By coming up the court off the sideline and angling toward the backcourt endline, you're in a much better position to see the transition from backcourt to frontcourt.

The bump-and-run

The bump-and-run is a mechanic used to move swiftly from the frontcourt after a violation. Though not covered in the NFHS manual, the bump-and-run is used in many high school games. In fact, most officials' camps teach it.

As the trail, when an offensive violation occurs in your coverage area (frontcourt or backcourt), stop the clock, signal the violation and the direction, then point to the spot for the throw-in. Next — after checking that there are no problems — sprint down court and become the new lead.

If you're the lead, eye the trail's signals, move toward the spot for the throw-in and administer it. You have now become the new trail. The lead "bumps" the trail down court and the trail moving to lead "runs" the floor.

The bump-and-run serves two main purposes: The trail has a better chance of avoiding problems near the violation and the officials move into place quicker and get the ball live faster.

For example, if a player or coach near the trail is unhappy, if the trail stood there to administer the throw-in and waited for the lead to get all the way down court, a heated conversation could occur simply because the official who made the call or no-call is still on the spot. The bump-and-run lets the official clear the area quickly and avoid unnecessary and potentially damaging conversations.

Also, the bump-and-run gets the ball live faster. Again, if the trail stayed put and administered the throw-in, the lead would have to run the length of the floor before the trail could hand the ball to the thrower. That's a long time even if the lead is fast! The bump-

and-run cuts the distance each official travels and gets the game going smoothly, allowing the crew to establish and maintain a quality tempo.

Movement adjustments
Sometimes, the ball moves quickly from one end of the court to the other in a transition. Every fastbreak play is the product of the transition game.

Because of the speed and open nature of the transition game, coverage adjustments are often necessary.

The buttonhook
There are times when officials get beat downcourt on fastbreaks. That's OK. In fact, if you're so worried about not getting beat, you're probably leaving the lead hanging alone with all the rebounding action — a definite no-no.

When you do get beat downcourt, there's no need to panic. There's a simple movement — the buttonhook — that can eliminate straightlining and allow you to officiate the play properly from behind. (It's called the buttonhook because the movement is similar to a football wide receiver's movement on a buttonhook pass pattern.)

Too often, officials who are trailing a fastbreak sprint as fast as they can (sometimes with their heads down) to stay even with the players. *Staying even with the players is about the worst thing you can do for your angles.* You either want to get ahead of the play and let it comfortably come to you (unlikely, unless you're a world-class sprinter) or let it go and momentarily officiate the play from behind. Staying even means you're looking through bodies and guessing.

When officiating a play from behind, move toward the middle of the court, roughly at the intersection of the lane line and the free-throw line. Momentarily pause there to watch the action (referee the defense). That movement allows you a good angle to observe potential contact. When that part of the play is over, move back out toward the sideline and endline to get into proper position.

Be aware of players coming from behind you. You should be well ahead of the second wave of players coming down court. They'll see you in the middle of the court and avoid contact. Make sure your position in the center of the court is momentary; you want to move out of there before the second wave comes down. If you feel pressure from players behind you, think safety first. Stay there a bit longer if you have to to let players go by before you move to the endline.

The buttonhook is a quick, simple movement that will eliminate the guesswork when trailing a play. It will help you get good angles (see "The buttonhook," p. 185).

Cutting the corner on a fastbreak
The benefits of getting good angles on transition plays are no different than getting good angles on any other play. Sometimes, because of the speed of the players, long outlet passes, etc., it is difficult to get a good angle on a transition play.

On some fastbreak plays, the trail moving to lead can improve an angle on a play nearer the opposite sideline by cutting the corner while moving into the frontcourt. That can only happen effectively if (1) the new lead is well-ahead of — and can *stay* ahead of — the drive to the basket and (2) there are no other players in the area filling the passing lanes. If (1) and (2) are not in effect, remain closer to the near sideline and consider buttonhooking on the play.

If (1) and (2) are in effect, begin cutting the corner at around or below the free-throw line extended. Take a sharp angle under the basket to the far lane line. Keep your head up and watch the oncoming players.

The improved angle is similar to the ball-side look during a halfcourt play (see "Lead must use ball side mechanics," p. 85).

It takes anticipation and speed to cut a corner on a fastbreak play, but the reward is an improved angle that defeats straightlining.

Helping out
Transition plays require significant teamwork from both officials. There's a lot to watch and action usually moves swiftly from backcourt to frontcourt. Whether the new trail or the new lead, be prepared to help your partner so the entire court is covered properly.

Lead helps in backcourt
There is a general rule when the lead helps the trail in the backcourt. If there are four or fewer players in the backcourt, the trail works alone there. More than four players, the lead helps.

When there are more than four players in the backcourt, the lead is positioned near the division line. If all the players are in the frontcourt, the lead may move closer to the backcourt endline for better angles. If some players are in the frontcourt, however, the division-line area is the best position.

When near the division line, the lead must stay wide and constantly glance from backcourt to frontcourt.

That "swivel" glance allows the lead to help the trail with backcourt traffic plus watch players in the frontcourt.

Pass/crash during transition
A pass/crash play that occurs opposite the new lead during a transition is one of the most difficult coverages for a crew of two officials. Why? Many times you'll see players leave their feet to make a pass then crash into defenders. The new lead is moving swiftly toward the frontcourt endline and can't get off the near sideline too far because players are moving downcourt too. After a steal or quick outlet pass, the new trail sometimes can't get upcourt and toward the near sideline quick enough to correctly see the pass/crash play. When a pass/crash play (or any other contact) occurs in that trouble spot, the new lead must be prepared to help. The same pass/crash principles that apply in the lane area (see "Pass/crash in lane," p. 75) apply all over the court.

The lead must quickly read the fastbreak and move toward the division line to become the new trail. There the new trail has a good look at an offensive player leaping, passing and crashing.

The trail who became the new lead must also quickly read the fastbreak and move into the frontcourt. The new lead's primary responsibility is players catching a pass. However, if the new trail did not get out on the break fast enough to see the crash, the new lead's secondary coverage area is the crash. When making that call, you must sell it and advance on the foul.

New lead helps on three-point attempt
The transition game is especially tough when quick outlet passes lead to quick shots at the other end of the court.

When quick, long passes advance the ball upcourt, the new lead must be prepared to help the trail determine whether or not a shot is a three-point try. The help occurs even though the shot attempt is in an area not normally covered by the lead, such as the top of the key. Why help? When there's a quick outlet pass that leads to another quick, long pass, the new trail usually doesn't have enough time to get into the frontcourt and get a good angle on a shot. Because of the distance and poor angle between the trail and the shot, the trail is left guessing.

The new lead must recognize the quick transition play and help the new trail by judging the shot.

When that type of transition play can occur near the end of a period, the new lead judges whether or not the shot was a three-pointer, but the trail still judges whether the shot was released in time, unless alternate coverage was previously discussed (see "Last-second shot," p. 264).

Be ready to help and hustle and your transition coverage will be a success.

Notes

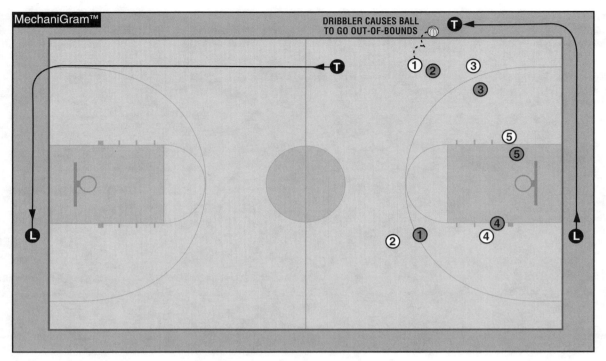

The 'bump-and-run'

The bump-and-run is a mechanic used by two-person crews to move swiftly from the frontcourt after a violation.

As the trail official, when an offensive violation occurs in your coverage area, stop the clock, signal the violation and the direction, then point to the spot for the throw-in. Next — after checking that there are no problems — sprint down court while viewing the action behind you and become the new lead official.

If you're the lead, eye the trail's signals, move toward the spot for the throw-in and administer it. You have now become the new trail. The lead "bumps" the trail down court and the trail moving to lead "runs" the floor.

In the MechaniGram, ① causes the ball to go out-of-bounds. The trail correctly stops the clock, signals a violation and the direction, then communicates the throw-in spot to the lead. The trail then moves down court and becomes the new lead.

On occasion, the trail may cut across the court when moving to lead. It saves time and allows your partner to put the ball in play quickly. Be careful, however; the trail-to-lead movement should not cut across the court if players are quickly moving down court because a collision may occur. Whether you remain near the sideline or cut across the court, the new lead's field of vision must keep players in sight — looking for potential problems — while moving down court. The

new lead must balance the court on the throw-in and assume responsibility for the sideline opposite the throw-in.

The bump-and-run serves two main purposes: The trail official has a better chance of avoiding problems near the violation and the officials move into place quicker and get the ball live faster.

For example, in the MechaniGram, the dribbler is unhappy because the dribbler thought there was a foul before turning the ball over. If the trail stood there to administer the throw-in and waited for the lead to get all the way down court, a heated conversation could occur simply because the official who made the call is still on the spot. The bump-and-run lets you clear the area and avoid unneeded and potentially damaging conversations.

Also, the bump-and-run gets the ball live faster. Again, if the trail stayed put and administered the throw-in, the lead would have to run the length of the floor before the trail could hand the ball to the thrower. That's a long time even if the lead is fast! The bump-and-run cuts the distance each official travels and gets the game going smoothly, allowing the crew to establish and maintain a quality tempo.

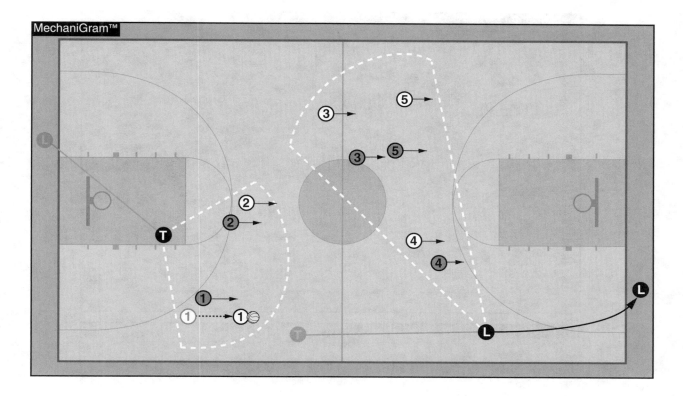

Transition: trail movement off sideline

Effective two-person court coverage requires significant movement by the trail off the sideline (see "Trail movement off sideline," p. 92). The same philosophies are true in the transition game when play is moving from the backcourt to the frontcourt.

When an offensive player has the ball on the side of the floor opposite the trail, the trail must move away from the near sideline and get proper angles. By staying too close to the near sideline, the trail cannot effectively see action near the ball and must make judgments from a distance — way too far to convince anyone the trail saw the play correctly.

In the MechaniGram, ① dribbles the ball upcourt opposite the new trail as ❶ applies defensive pressure. The rest of the players are advancing to the frontcourt as the new lead watches off-ball. To see the play well, the new trail must move far off the near sideline and work to get a good angle.

Stay deep. Avoid moving straight toward the play because you could interfere with the play by stepping into a passing lane. Take an angle toward the backcourt endline to decrease your chances of interfering with the play.

By moving off the sideline and angling toward the play, you're in a much better position to see the play.

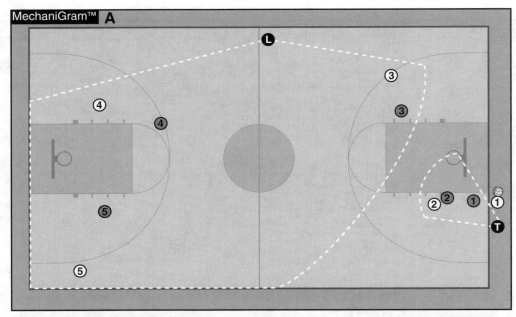

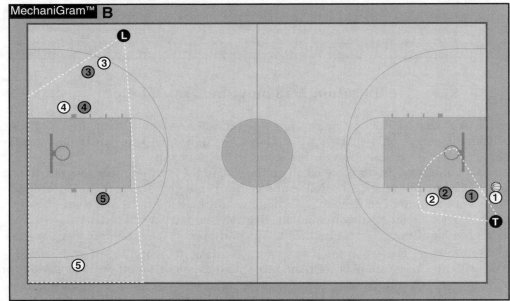

Lead helps in backcourt

There is a general rule that dictates when the lead helps the trail in the backcourt. If there are four or fewer players in the backcourt, the trail works alone there. More than four players, the lead helps.

When there's more than four players in the backcourt, the lead is positioned near the division line. If all the players are in the backcourt, the lead may move closer to the backcourt endline for better angles. If some players are in the frontcourt, however, the division-line area is the best position.

When near the division line, the lead must stay wide and constantly glance from backcourt to frontcourt. That

"swivel" glance allows the lead to help the trail with backcourt traffic plus watch players in the frontcourt.

In MechaniGram A, there are six players in the backcourt. The lead is positioned near the division line to help with backcourt players away from the trail. The lead must also watch players in the frontcourt.

In MechaniGram B, there are four players in the backcourt. The trail is responsible for all of those players. The lead moves into the frontcourt and watches all players there, eventually moving to the frontcourt endline.

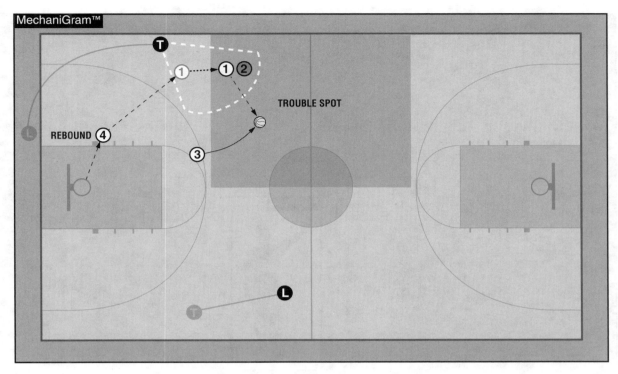

Pass/crash during transition

The same pass/crash principles that apply in the lane area (see "Pass/crash in lane," p. 75) apply all over the court. One trouble spot for officials is the pass/crash when a team in transition starts a break up the court. Many times you'll see players leave their feet to make a pass then crash into defenders. Block? Charge? No-call?

In the MechaniGram, ④ rebounds and throws an outlet pass to a streaking ①. ① catches the pass and dribbles up court trying to start a fastbreak. ③ is filling the passing lane down the center of the court. ② steps in to stop ① from advancing into the frontcourt. ① leaps into the air and passes to ③. ① then crashes into ②.

The lead must quickly read the fastbreak and move toward the sideline to become the new trail. There the new trail has a good look at ① leaping, passing and crashing.

The trail who became the new lead must also quickly read the fastbreak and move into the frontcourt. The new lead's primary responsibility is ③ catching the pass. In rare circumstances, if the new trail did not get out on the break fast enough to see the crash, the new lead's secondary coverage area is the crash. That is more likely, however, when the pass/crash occurs in the center of the court.

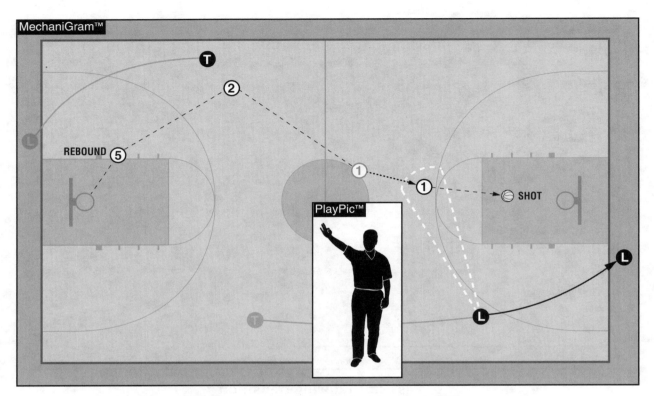

Transition: lead helps on three-point attempt

The transition game is difficult to cover with a crew of two officials. It's especially tough when quick outlet passes lead to quick shots at the other end of the court.

When quick, long passes advance the ball upcourt, the new lead must be prepared to help the trail determine whether or not a shot is a three-point try. The help occurs even though the shot attempt is in an area not normally covered by the lead. Why help? When there's a quick outlet pass that leads to another quick, long pass, the new trail usually doesn't have enough time to get into the frontcourt and get a good angle on a shot. Because of the distance and poor angle between the trail and the shot, the trail is left guessing.

The new lead must recognize the quick transition play and help the new trail by judging the shot.

In the MechaniGram, ⑤ grabs the rebound and throws a quick, long outlet pass to ②, who throws another quick, long pass to ①. ① catches the pass near the center restraining circle, dribbles to the top of the key and shoots. The lead moving to new trail doesn't have enough time to get a good look at the shot. The trail moving to new lead recognizes that and makes the judgment on the shot, even though a top-of-the-key shot is normally covered by the trail.

When that type of transition play occurs near the end of a period, the new lead judges whether or not the shot was a three-pointer, but the trail still judges whether the shot was released in time — unless alternate coverage was previously discussed (see "Last-second shot," p. 264).

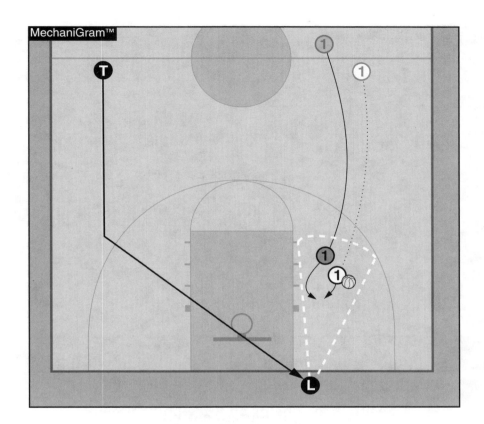

Transition: lead cuts corner

The benefits of good angles on transition plays are no different than getting good angles on any other play. Sometimes, because of the speed of the players, long outlet passes, etc., it is difficult to get a good angle on a transition play.

On some fastbreak plays, the trail moving to new lead can improve an angle on a play nearer the opposite sideline by cutting the corner while moving into the frontcourt. That can only happen effectively if (1) the new lead is well-ahead of — and can *stay* ahead of — the drive to the basket and (2) there are no other players in the area filling the passing lanes. If (1) and (2) are not in effect, remain closer to the near sideline and consider buttonhooking on the play (see "The buttonhook," p. 184).

If (1) and (2) are in effect, begin cutting the corner as you cross the free-throw line extended. Take a sharp angle under the basket to the far lane line. Keep your head up and watch the oncoming players at all times.

In the MechaniGram, ① with defensive pressure dribbles from the backcourt to the frontcourt and is driving in for a layup. The trail moving to new lead stays well ahead of the play and there are no other players in the area filling passing lanes. The new lead cuts the corner at the free-throw line extended and moves to the far lane line to judge the play. The improved angle is similar to the ball-side look during a halfcourt play (see "Lead must use ball side mechanics," p. 85).

It takes anticipation and speed to cut the corner on a fastbreak play, but the reward is an improved angle that defeats straightlining.

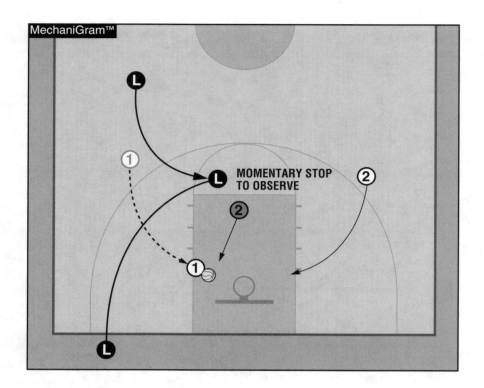

The buttonhook

There are times when officials get beat downcourt on fastbreaks. That's OK. In fact, if you're so worried about not getting beat you're probably leaving the lead official hanging alone with all the rebounding action — a definite no-no.

When you do get beat downcourt, there's no need to panic. There's a simple movement — the buttonhook — that can eliminate straightlining and allow you to officiate the play properly from behind. (It's called the buttonhook because the movement is similar to a football wide receiver's movement on a buttonhook pass pattern.)

Too often, an official who is trailing a fastbreak sprints as fast as possible (sometimes with their heads down) to stay even with the players. *Staying even with the players is about the worst thing you can do for your angles.* Either get ahead of the play and let it come comfortably to you (unlikely, unless you're a world-class sprinter) or let it go and momentarily officiate the play from behind. Staying even means you're looking through bodies and guessing.

When officiating a play from behind, swing toward the middle of the court, roughly at the intersection of the lane line and the free-throw line. Momentarily pause there to watch the action (referee the defense). That movement allows you a good angle to observe potential contact. When that part of the play is over, swing back out toward the sideline and endline to get into proper position.

Be aware of players coming from behind you. You should be well ahead of the second wave of players coming down court. They'll see you in the middle of the court and avoid contact. Make sure your position in the center of the court is momentary; you want to move out of there before the second wave comes down. If you feel pressure from players behind you, think safety first. Stay there a bit longer if you have to to let players go by before you move to the endline.

The buttonhook is a quick, simple movement that will eliminate the guesswork when trailing a play. It will help you get good angles.

The buttonhook

The buttonhook can eliminate straightlining and allow you to officiate the play properly from behind. (It's called the buttonhook because the movement is similar to a football wide receiver's movement on a buttonhook pass pattern.)

Too often, an official who is trailing a fastbreak sprints as fast as possible (sometimes with head down) to stay even with the players. *Staying even with the players is about the worst thing you can do for your angles.* Either get ahead of the play and let it come comfortably to you (unlikely, unless you're a world-class sprinter) or let it go and momentarily officiate the play from behind. Staying even means you're looking through bodies and guessing.

When officiating a play from behind, move toward the middle of the court, roughly at the intersection of the lane line and the free-throw line. Momentarily pause there to watch the action (referee the defense). That movement allows you a good angle to observe potential contact. When that part of the play is over, move back out toward your sideline and the endline to get into proper position.

In PlayPic A, the trail moving to new lead is behind the play and unable to get ahead of it. In PlayPic B, the new lead moves toward the middle of the court, roughly at the intersection of the lane line and the free-throw line, to officiate the play. After momentarily stopping to view the play, the lead moves back out toward the sideline and endline to get into proper position.

Be aware of players coming from behind you. Most likely, you're well ahead of the second wave of players coming down court. They'll see you in the middle of the court and avoid contact. Make sure your position in the center of the court is momentary; you're likely to move out of there before the second wave comes down. If you feel pressure from players behind you, think safety first. Stay there a bit longer if you have to to let players go by before you move to the endline.

The buttonhook is a quick, simple movement that will eliminate the guesswork when trailing a play. It will help you get good angles.

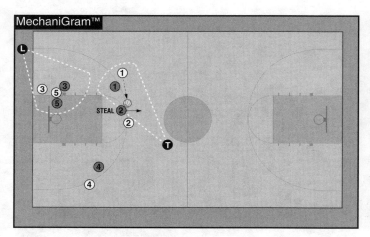

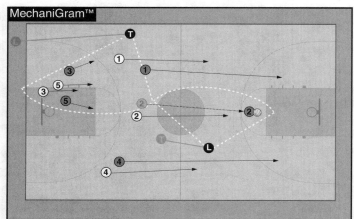

Action on the court:

① passes toward ②. ② steps into passing lane and intercepts pass.

② dribbles into frontcourt to free-throw line for fastbreak. ① and ④ fill passing lanes.

Lead Official Responsibilities

Primary: Off-ball. Watch players in lane area.

After steal occurs, move quickly toward division line and become new trail.
Primary: Off-ball. Watch backcourt players.

Trail Official Responsibilities

Primary: On-ball. Watch ① pass to ②.
Watch ② steal pass.

Become the new lead.
Trail the play.
Carefully angle toward sideline, avoiding players filling passing lane.
Primary: On-ball. Watch ② dribble to free-throw line.

KEY

L LEAD OFFICIAL

T TRAIL OFFICIAL

PRIMARY COVERAGE AREA

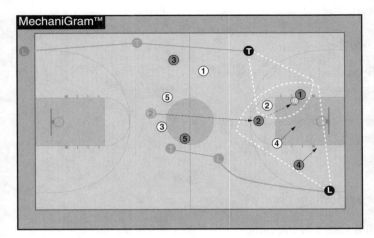

MechaniGram™

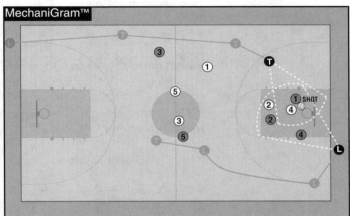

MechaniGram™

② passes to ①.	① drives in for layup.

Penetrate toward endline for angles. **Primary: On-ball.** Watch ① catch pass from ②. **Secondary: Off-ball.** Glance occasionally at players near division line.	Penetrate toward endline for angles. **Primary: On-ball.** Watch ① dribble toward the basket and shoot. **Secondary: Off-ball.** Glance occasionally at players near division line.

After players have filled passing lanes, circle out toward endline. **Primary: On-ball.** Watch ② pass to ①. **Secondary: Off-ball.** Watch ④ fill the passing lane.	Obtain endline position. **Primary: On-ball.** Watch ① dribble in for layup and shoot . **Secondary: Off-ball.** Watch players in lane area. Observe weak-side rebounding.

① OFFENSE   ◄----① PASS   ├── SCREEN

① DEFENSE   ◄·······① DRIBBLE

Transitions

• When play moves from one endline toward the other, the trail has primary responsibility in the backcourt.

• When running upcourt, do not backpedal.

• As the trail, avoid moving straight toward the lane: You could negatively impact a play by being in a passing lane.

• The bump-and-run is a mechanic used to move swiftly from the frontcourt after a violation.

• It's OK to get beat downcourt.

• Use the buttonhook when trailing a transition play.

• Cut the corner on a fastbreak if well ahead of the play.

Quiz

Without referring back, you should be able to answer the following true-false questions.

1. When there are more than four players in the backcourt, the new lead helps in the backcourt.

2. Either official can call a foul after a pass/crash play in transition.

3. The new trail is always responsible for three-point attempts in transition.

4. The trail must move off the sideline to ensure good angles.

5. When using the buttonhook, stay in the middle of the court briefly.

1 - True, 2 - True, 3 - False, 4 - True, 5 - True

Chapter 18

Halfcourt vs. Man-to-Man

Halfcourt vs. man-to-man

OFFENSIVE STRATEGY

Offensive plays versus man-to-man defenses include many screens (on-ball or off-ball), backdoor cuts toward the basket, drop passes into the post and drives to the basket.

Screens

On-ball screens free the dribbler to penetrate toward the basket or give the dribbler enough room make passes. The screener will occasionally roll toward the basket looking for a pass from the dribbler — particularly if the screener's defensive player moved to cut off the dribbler (commonly referred to as the "pick and roll").

Off-ball screens free players to catch passes. There are two types of off-ball screens: down screens and cross screens. Down screens occur when players move from the perimeter to the low block area to screen defenders. The offensive player near the low block cuts off the screen toward the perimeter, sometimes beyond the three-point arc.

Down screens usually start with perimeter players (guards and small forwards) near the low block and post players (centers and power forwards) near the perimeter. The post players screen for the perimeter players. Then, the post players usually post up on the low block, looking for a drop pass from the perimeter player.

If the post player doesn't receive a drop pass, often that post player will cross screen for another post player. A cross screen occurs when a post player cuts across the lane to screen for a teammate on the other side of the lane. The cross screen frees the teammate (often another post player), who moves into the open area (usually ball side) and looks for a drop pass, usually from the same perimeter player.

Backdoor cuts

Another common strategy: backdoor cuts, which are designed to take advantage of an over-aggressive defensive player. Backdoor cuts always move toward the basket and usually start well away from the basket. The most common backdoor cut sequence: an offensive player moves from near the lane toward the perimeter to catch a pass from near the top of the key. An overzealous defender tries to anticipate the play and beats the offensive player to the perimeter spot. One problem: the pass wasn't delivered. The offensive player reads the over-playing defender's move and, instead of

moving further away from the basket to catch the pass, cuts toward the basket. The offensive player near the top of the key reads the cut and delivers a pass to the streaking teammate, who catches the ball and beats the defender to the basket. Though backdoor cuts only occur a few times a game, it's a great way to "keep the defense honest."

Drop passes

Drop passes into the post usually occur from perimeter players (guards and small forwards) to post players (centers and power forwards). The passer reads how the defense is playing the post player and delivers the pass away from the defender. If the defender is playing on the high side of the post player (toward the free-throw line), the perimeter player looks to pass to the post player's hand toward the endline — away from the defense. If the defender is playing on the low side (toward the endline), the perimeter player looks to pass to the post player's hand toward the free-throw line — away from the defense. If the defender fronts the post (is positioned directly between the post player and the perimeter player), the perimeter player looks to throw the drop pass over the defender toward the basket. If the defender plays directly behind the post player, the drop pass is not being challenged.

Two related plays off of the drop pass are the high-low pass and the low block pass. The high-low pass moves from the free-throw line area to the low block, sometimes from one post player to another. The low block pass comes from a post player on the low block to a perimeter player. That often occurs after a drop pass when the perimeter player's defensive player double-teams the post player with the ball, leaving the perimeter player open for a possible shot.

Dribble penetration

Man-to-man defenses invite more individual penetration plays because there are usually fewer defenders to avoid on the way to the basket than against a zone defense. Good penetrators are usually adept at handling the ball with both hands and have a quick first step toward the basket. Since most players are right-handed and — especially at the lower levels — aren't that good at dribbling with their left hand, offenses tend run to the offensive player's right. After a dribbler beats a defender, the dribbler usually looks to score or pass to an open teammate as another defender moves to stop the dribbler.

DEFENSIVE STRATEGY

Man-to-man defense is characterized by defensive players who guard individual offensive players. The defenders tend to follow their assigned offensive player in the frontcourt, sometimes even well away from the basket. In most situations, defenders match up with offensive players of similar size and skill (guards usually defend guards, forwards guard forwards and centers defend centers). Defensive strategies against a man-to-man include forcing opponents to their weak side, double-teaming, pressuring the passer and defending the post.

Forcing weak side
Defensive players want to stop offensive players from going where the attackers want to go. That's especially true with dribblers. For example, if a dribbler is right-handed and is attempting to go right, a good defensive player will force the dribbler left to thwart the offensive move. The defender attempts to beat the dribbler to a spot and establish legal guarding position. If the strategy works, the dribbler either is called for a player-control foul or the offensive team's play is disrupted because the dribbler can't go where the dribbler wants to go.

Double-teaming
Double-teaming occurs when two defensive players defend against a single offensive player. That can occur on-ball or off-ball. One common on-ball double-team occurs when an offensive player is dribbling with back to the basket and looking over the shoulder. One defensive player "bodies up" the dribbler, effectively cutting off the dribbler's path. Another defender, usually from behind the dribbler, moves toward the dribbler to either attempt a steal from behind or force a bad pass.

Another common on-ball double team occurs when an offensive player has the ball in the low post. Usually the post defender "bodies up" the post player and stays between the post player and the basket. Then, another defender, usually a perimeter player, double-teams the post player, forcing a turnover or a pass out of the post area.

Off-ball double teams normally occur in the low post area. They are generally designed to stop a good post player from receiving a pass. One defensive player fronts the post while another plays directly behind.

Pressuring the passer
Since good passes are essential in most offensive plays, defenders want to make passing difficult. When an offensive player ends a dribble, you'll often see a defender apply more defensive pressure, making passing difficult.

Pressuring the passer is also a good defensive strategy against an effective drop-pass offense. Simply, if the passer has a clean look to make the drop pass to the post player, it's an easier pass to make. If the passer is aggressively pressured, the drop pass is much more difficult to make.

Defending the post
There are four basic ways to individually defend against a post player: defending on the high side, the low side, fronting the post and playing on the backside. The strategy used depends on the offensive player's strength. Obviously, each defender wants to force each post player to use the post player's least-effective moves. For example, if a post player has a good spin move to the right, the defender will play on that side, forcing the offensive player to catch a pass and spin less comfortably to the left.

Defending the high side places the defender on the side of the offensive player toward the free-throw line. Defending the low side places the defender on the side of the offensive player toward the endline. Fronting the post means the defender is directly in front of the post player, between the ball and the post player. Playing the backside means the defender is directly behind the post player and is not challenging the drop pass.

Rough post play is a point of emphasis.

OFFICIATING COVERAGE

To effectively officiate halfcourt offenses versus man-to-man defenses, the trail and lead must get good angles.

The trail
When on-ball, you must get off the sideline to get good angles on plays that are away from you (see "Trail movement off sideline," p. 92). Maintain proper spacing and avoid straightlining. Sometimes an inside-out look provides the best view of a play (see "Inside-out look," p. 91).

When off-ball, look weak side (see "Trail looks weak side," p. 98). When a shot is taken in your coverage area, watch the shooter for potential fouls until the shooter returns to the floor. Penetrate toward the endline for good rebounding angles (see "Trail movement on jump shot," p. 99).

The lead

When off-ball, you must watch players in the lane area. When anticipating a drop pass, move ball side (see "Lead must use ball side mechanics," p. 85). Move along the endline to get good angles.

When on-ball, maintain proper spacing off the endline and move toward the sideline, if necessary (see "Lead movement toward sideline," p. 87).

TROUBLE SPOTS

There are areas that need special attention from the officials.

Aggressive perimeter play

With defenders trying to beat offensive players to spots and dribblers penetrating toward the basket, contact is likely to occur. Did the defender establish legal guarding position? Did the dribbler push off? Watch for defenders handchecking and offensive players extending elbows.

Screens

Whether on-ball or off-ball, watch for illegal screens. Was the defender being screened afforded proper spacing? Did the screener extend an elbow or leg into the path of the defender? Did the defender push through the screen?

Low post play

Play in the low post can get very physical. Watch for defensive players pushing post players in the lower back, away from the low block. Also look for the defensive player's knee in the post player's backside. Watch for the post player pushing off the defender by extending an arm or elbow when receiving a drop pass. Also watch for the post player who has the ball to illegally hook the defender with an arm or elbow while spinning around the defender.

Double-teams

Double teams, especially on-ball, are usually aggressive. Watch for the backside defender fouling the player with the ball. Also watch for the offensive player splitting the defenders by pushing or hooking a defensive player.

Penetration toward the basket

Since dribbling is one way to beat a man-to-man defense, watch for dribbling-related violations, especially at the start of a play. Recognize an offensive player's pivot foot and watch for carrying the ball (illegal dribble) on cross-over moves.

After a dribbler beats a defender to the basket, look for the beaten defender to grab the dribbler from behind. Watch for other defenders stepping into the dribbler's path to help stop the dribbler. That's when you are most likely to see block/charge and pass/crash plays.

Notes

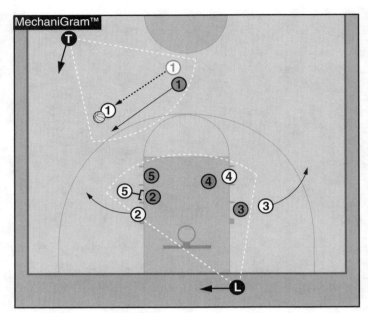

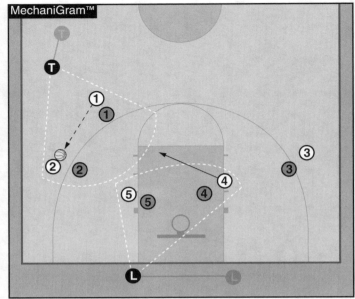

Action on the court:

① dribbles toward sideline. ⑤ screens ❷. ② breaks toward 3-point arc. ③ moves toward 3-point arc.

① passes to ②. ④ cuts toward free-throw line. ⑤ posts up on low block.

Lead Official Responsibilities

Primary: Off-ball. Watch players in lane area. Watch ⑤ screen ❷.
Anticipate play.
Begin moving ball-side to opposite lane line.

Primary: Off-ball. Watch players in lane area. Watch ⑤ post-up.

Trail Official Responsibilities

Primary: On-ball. Watch ① dribble toward sideline.
Anticipate play.
Adjust to sideline for proper angle.

Primary: On-ball. Watch ① pass to ②.

KEY

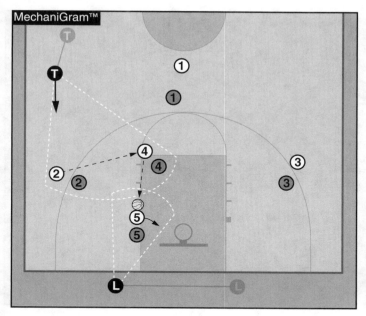

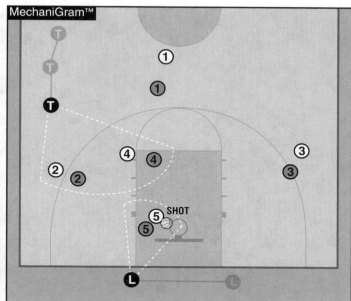

② passes to ④. ⑤ seals ❺ on low block. ④ passes to ⑤.	⑤ shoots.
Primary: Off-ball. Watch ⑤ seal ❺. Adjust angles to avoid being straightlined. **Primary: On-ball.** Watch ⑤ catch pass from ④.	**Primary: On-ball.** Watch ⑤ shoot. Observe strong-side rebounding.
Primary: On-ball. Watch ② pass to ④. Penetrate toward endline for angles. Watch ④ pass to ⑤.	Penetrate toward endline for angles. **Primary: Off-ball.** Watch players around free-throw line area. Observe weak-side rebounding.

① OFFENSE   🏀◄----① PASS   ⊢— SCREEN

❶ DEFENSE   🏀①◄·······① DRIBBLE

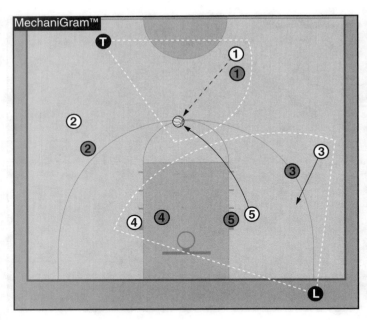

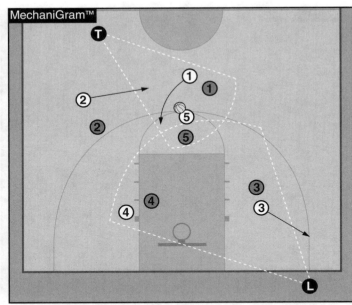

Action on the court:

⑤ moves to top of the key. ① passes to ⑤. ③ moves toward low block.

① rolls toward basket off of ⑤. ② moves toward top of the key. ③ moves toward three-point arc.

Lead Official Responsibilities

Start wide.
Primary: Off-ball. Watch players in lane area.
Watch ③ cut toward low block.

Primary: Off-ball. Watch players in lane area.

Trail Official Responsibilities

Primary: On-ball. Watch ① pass to ⑤.

Primary: On-ball. Watch ① cut off of ⑤.

KEY

 LEAD OFFICIAL
 TRAIL OFFICIAL

PRIMARY
COVERAGE
AREA

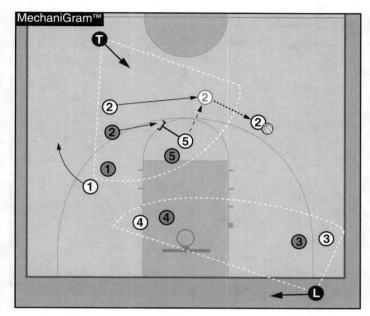

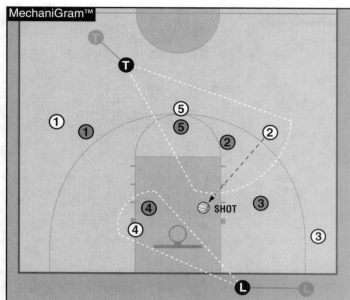

⑤ passes to ②. ⑤ screens ②. ② dribbles toward opposite free-throw line extended. ① moves toward three-point arc.	② shoots.
Anticipate play. Adjust toward nearest lane line for angles. **Primary: Off-ball.** Watch players in lane area.	**Primary: Off-ball.** Watch players in lane area. Observe strong-side rebounding.
Primary: On-ball. Watch ⑤ pass to ②. Watch ⑤ screen ②. Adjust toward center court for angles. Watch ② dribble to opposite free-throw line extended. **Secondary: Off-ball.** Watch players around free-throw line area.	**Primary: On-ball.** Watch ② shoot. Penetrate toward endline for angles. Observe weak-side rebounding.

 OFFENSE   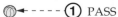 PASS   ⊢— SCREEN

 DEFENSE    DRIBBLE

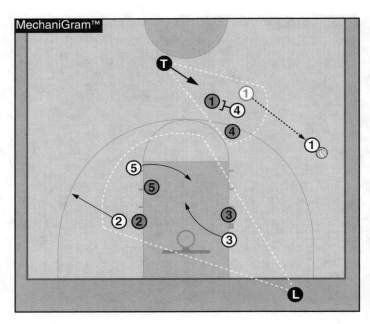 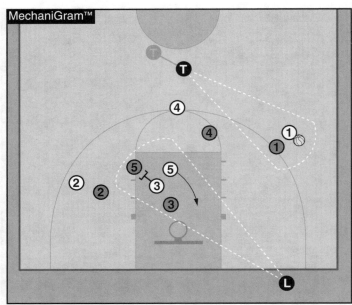

Action on the court:

④ screens ①. ① dribbles toward opposite free-throw line extended. ② move toward three-point arc. ③ moves into lane. ⑤ moves toward low block.

③ screens ⑤. ⑤ moves toward low block.

Lead Official Responsibilities

Start wide.
Primary: Off-ball. Watch players in lane area.
Watch ③ moves into lane.
Watch ⑤ cut toward low block.

Primary: Off-ball. Watch ③ screen ⑤.
Watch ⑤ cut toward low block.

Trail Official Responsibilities

Primary: On-ball. Watch ① dribble toward opposite free-throw line extended
Secondary: Off-ball. Watch ④ screen ①.
Adjust toward center court for angles.

Primary: On-ball. Watch ① with ball.

KEY · **L** LEAD OFFICIAL · **T** TRAIL OFFICIAL · PRIMARY COVERAGE AREA

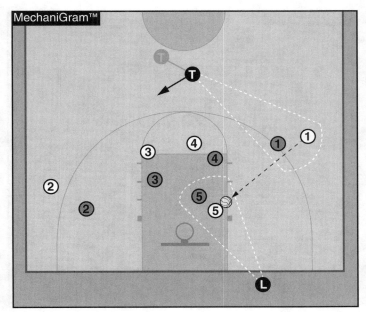

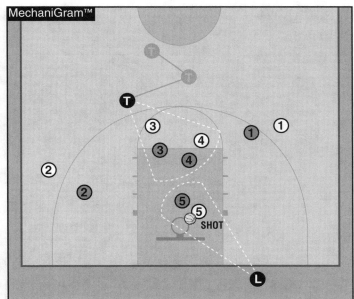

① passes to ⑤.	⑤ shoots.
Anticipate play. Adjust angles to avoid being straightlined. **Primary: On-ball.** Watch ⑤ catch pass.	**Primary: On-ball.** Watch ⑤ shoot.
Primary: On-ball. Watch ① pass to ⑤. Adjust to sideline for proper angle.	**Primary: Off-ball.** Watch players around free-throw line area. Penetrate toward endline for angles. Observe weak-side rebounding.

---

① OFFENSE PASS ⊢— SCREEN

① DEFENSE  DRIBBLE

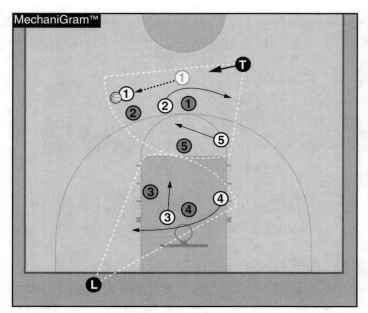

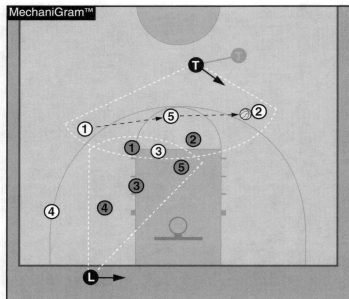

Action on the court:

① dribbles toward sideline. ② moves toward opposite sideline. ⑤ moves toward top of the key. ③ moves toward free-throw line. ④ swings toward three-point arc.

① passes to ⑤. ⑤ quickly passes to ②.

Lead Official Responsibilities

Primary: Off-ball. Watch players in the lane area.

Primary: Off-ball. Watch players in the lane area. As ball shifts beyond opposite lane line, move toward nearest lane line.

Trail Official Responsibilities

Primary: On-ball. Watch ① dribble toward opposite sideline.
Adjust toward center court for angles.
Secondary: Off-ball. Watch players around free-throw line area.

Primary: On-ball. Watch ① pass to ⑤.
Watch ⑤ pass to ②.
Penetrate toward center of court for inside-out angle.

KEY

L LEAD OFFICIAL

T TRAIL OFFICIAL

PRIMARY COVERAGE AREA

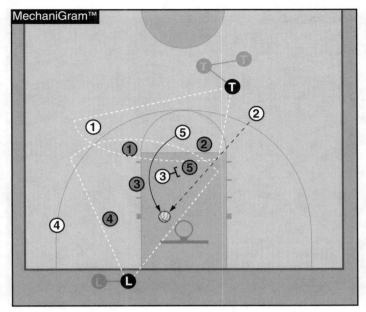

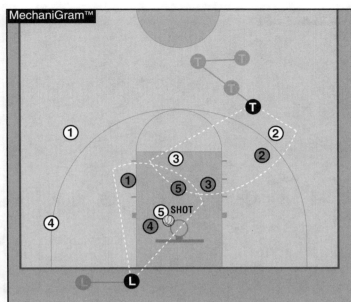

③ screens ⑤. ⑤ cuts toward basket. ② delivers lob pass.	⑤ catches lob pass and shoots.
Primary: Off-ball. Watch ③ screen ⑤. Watch ⑤ cut toward basket.	**Primary: On-ball.** Watch ⑤ catch lob pass and shoot. **Secondary: Off-ball.** Watch players in lane area.
Primary: On-ball. Watch ② pass to ⑤. **Then: Primary: Off-ball.** Watch players around free-throw line area. Penetrate toward endline for angles.	Penetrate toward endline for angles. **Primary: Off-ball.** Watch players around free-throw line area. Observe weak-side rebounding.

① OFFENSE   🏀◀----① PASS   ⊢— SCREEN

① DEFENSE   🏀①◀·······① DRIBBLE

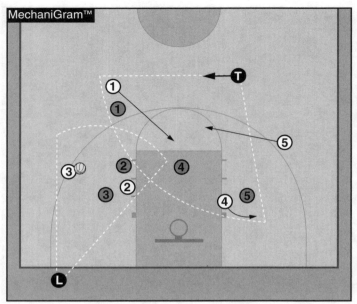

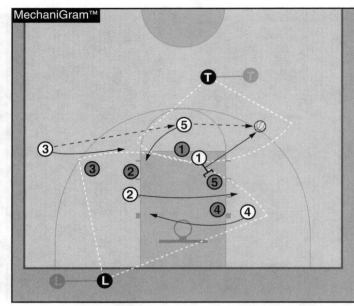

Action on the court:

③ holds the ball near the free-throw line extended opposite the trail. ① cuts toward free-throw line. ⑤ moves toward top of the key. ④ moves toward sideline.

① screens ⑤, then breaks toward free-throw line extended. ③ passes to ⑤, then cuts toward top of the key. ⑤ quickly passes to ①, then cuts toward free-throw line. ② moves to opposite lane line. ④ moves to opposite lane line.

Lead Official Responsibilities

Primary: On-ball. Watch ③ with ball.
Secondary: Off-ball. Watch players around nearest lane line.

Primary: On-ball. Watch ③ pass to ⑤.
Then: Primary: Off-ball. Watch players in lane area. As ball shifts beyond opposite lane line, move toward nearest lane line.

Trail Official Responsibilities

Adjust toward center court for angles.
Primary: Off-ball. Watch players around free-throw line area.

Primary: On-ball. Watch ⑤ catch pass from ③. Watch ① catch pass from ⑤.

KEY

L LEAD OFFICIAL

T TRAIL OFFICIAL

PRIMARY COVERAGE AREA

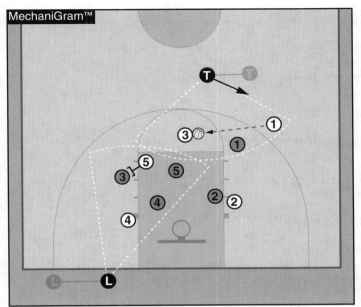

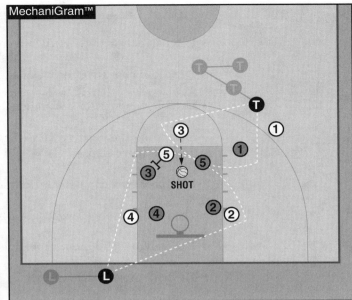

① passes to ③. ⑤ screens **③**.	⑤ screens **③**. ③ shoots.
Primary: Off-ball. Watch ⑤ screen **③**.	**Primary: Off-ball.** Watch ⑤ screen **③**. Observe strong-side rebounding.
Primary: On-ball. Watch ① pass to ③. Adjust to sideline for proper angle.	**Primary: On-ball.** Watch ③ shoot. Penetrate toward endline for angles. Observe weak-side rebounding.

 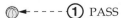 OFFENSE   ⊚◄----① PASS   ⊢— SCREEN

  DEFENSE   ⊚①◄·······① DRIBBLE

Halfcourt vs. Man-to-Man

• Offensive teams use many screens against man-to-man defenses.

• Backdoor cuts are effective against an over-aggressive defense.

• Dribble penetration is usually effective against man-to-man defenses.

• Defending the post is a necessary ingredient to stopping a team with a man-to-man defense.

• Low post play can get very physical.

• The trail must look weak side when the lead moves ball side.

• The trail must help on dribble penetration into the lane.

• The lead must watch off-ball for illegal screens.

• The lead must move toward the sideline if necessary.

Quiz

Without referring back, you should be able to answer the following true-false questions.

1. Double-teaming occurs when two defensive players defend against a single offensive player.

2. Defenders try to force opponents weak side.

3. Screens are only legal if they are on-ball screens.

4. The officials must watch for offensive players hooking defensive players at the start of dribble penetration.

1 - True, 2 - True, 3 - False, 4 - True

Chapter 19

Halfcourt vs. Zone

Halfcourt vs. zone

OFFENSIVE STRATEGY

There is far less dribble penetration against a zone defense than there is against a man-to-man. Passing beats zones. The passes go from player to player around the perimeter, over the top of the defense or from the perimeter to the low post, then back out. Offensive plays versus zone defenses include skip passes, high-low passes, post passes and perimeter shots.

Skip passes

Skip passes are usually thrown over a zone defense. It's called a skip pass because the pass skips a player in a normal passing sequence. For example, a player on the right wing has the ball beyond the three-point arc. A teammate is near the top of the key and another teammate is on the left wing. To get the ball from the right wing to the left wing in a normal passing sequence, the right wing player would pass to the player near the top of the key, who would then pass to the player on the left wing. With a skip pass, the right wing player throws the pass over the defense to the left wing, "skipping" the player near the top of the key. Years ago skip passes, then usually called cross-court passes, were taboo; but greater athleticism and modern offensive theory have embraced the tactic.

Skip passes are extremely effective against zones. Zone defenses tend to shift together slightly toward the ball. An offensive player who is well away from the ball can step into an open area (usually near the three-point arc) and be in a perfect position to catch a skip pass and immediately shoot.

One of the ways to break down a zone defense is to get it moving back and forth. Skip passes allow that to happen. Simply put, a passed ball tends to move much faster than a recovering defender. When the zone is moving back and forth, it's easier for offensive players to step into open areas.

High-low passes

The high-low pass is a pass from the free-throw line area to the low block, sometimes from one post player to another. It is an effective play because when an offensive player flashes to the area near the free-throw line, that low-block area is usually open. The post defenders don't want to wander up that high and leave the area under the basket unattended. A perimeter defensive player usually then has to guard two offensive players in the same area — likely a shooter on the wing or near the top of the key and the offensive player who flashed to the free-throw line area. It's very difficult to defend both.

After receiving a pass near the free-throw line, the offensive player turns and faces the basket in a triple-threat position. (The triple-threat means from that position the player could effectively shoot, penetrate toward the basket or pass.)

At about the same time, a low post player flashes into the lane area around the low block, sealing off the post defender. A post player seals off a player by stepping in front of a defender and using the post player's body to keep the defender away from the passing lane.

If the seal is effective, the post player is open. The player with the ball near the free-throw line delivers a pass to the open post player, who turns and shoots. The pass went from "high" to "low."

The high-low pass usually happens quickly. Why? Both players are usually in the lane, meaning they've got only three seconds to do something. Plus, a seal move is only effective for a very short period of time; any hesitation by the offense and the defender is usually able to get around the seal move and defend against the pass.

Post passes

Drop passes into the post usually occur from perimeter players (guards and small forwards) to post players (centers and power forwards). The counterpart to a drop pass is a post pass, which usually occurs after the post player has received a drop pass from the perimeter.

The post pass is a pass from a post player on the low block back out to a perimeter player. That often occurs after a drop pass when the perimeter player's defender turns to help defend against the post player with the ball, leaving the perimeter player open for a possible shot.

Post players with the ball also look to the opposite wing area for open teammates. Because angles are critical for offensive plays versus zones, looking opposite is an effective way to take advantage of an open passing lane and find an open teammate.

Perimeter shots

Good shooters salivate when they see zone defenses. It's much easier to get open jump shots against a zone than it is against a man-to-man. In fact, if a team has outstanding shooters they're more likely to see man-to-man defenses than zones.

The skip pass and the post pass from the low block offer perimeter players ample opportunities for open jump shots. Good perimeter players move to open spots against a zone and float there, improving passing lanes for teammates. They also step into open areas, ensuring they are within shooting range when receiving the pass.

At higher-level games, perimeter players tend to hover around the three-point arc. The reason is pretty logical: Why take a 17-foot jumper when you can back up a step and get three points?

DEFENSIVE STRATEGY

Zone defense is characterized by defensive players who guard areas rather than individual offensive players. The defenders do not follow assigned offensive players in the frontcourt, rather they remain in assigned areas and guard offensive players who enter that area.

Perimeter players are usually at the top of the defensive zone and post players at the bottom, closer to the basket. Common formations include 2-3, 1-2-2 and 2-1-2 zones. A 2-3 zone has two guards positioned near each end of the free-throw line. The center is positioned under the basket flanked by a forward on either side, positioned even with center but outside the lane. A 1-2-2 zone has a guard near the top of the key, two perimeter players near each end of the free-throw line and two post players near the low blocks. A 2-1-2 zone is similar to the 2-3, except the center is positioned near the middle of the lane instead of under the basket.

Defensive strategies for a zone include "packing it in," match-up zones, traps and gimmick defenses.

Packing it in

Teams often play zone when their opponent doesn't have good perimeter shooters. If an offensive team lacks a perimeter game, the defense will dare perimeter players to shoot by sitting back in the zone — packing it in — and not challenging the shots.

Teams also pack it in against a team with exceptional post players. By having many defenders around the post area, the offensive post player's movements are restricted, thus limiting scoring opportunities.

Match-up zones

Match-up zones combine parts of man-to-man and zone defenses. The defensive set is exactly the same as a regular 2-3 or 1-2-2 zone, with defensive players guarding areas. In a match-up zone, however, when an offensive player with the ball is in a defender's area, that defender aggressively guards the player with ball, similar to a man-to-man defense. When the ball leaves that area, the defender falls back into regular zone coverage.

The match-up zone is effective because offensive players don't get clean looks to the basket or unchallenged passing opportunities.

Traps

Aggressive zone defenses apply trapping principles. A trap is similar to a double-team. Double-teaming occurs when two defensive players work together against a single offensive player. Double-teams occur against specific players; traps double-team when a player with the ball enters a specific area. Defensive players in a zone trap entice offensive players into those specific undefended areas. When a player with the ball moves into that perceived open area, two (or even sometimes three) defenders swarm the ball, trapping the offensive player.

Traps tend to occur near sidelines. In effect, a trap near a sideline uses the sideline as an extra defender. Defensive players not involved in the trap anticipate passing lanes and attempt steals.

Traps are effective when trying to force turnovers. A good trapping team gambles and often wins.

Gimmick defenses

Once in a while zone schemes get a little funky. The most common gimmick defenses are the box-and-one and the triangle-and-two.

The box-and-one defense is designed to stop one offensive star player. Four players play zone defense — two players on each end of the free-throw line and two players on each low block. The remaining defensive player plays aggressive man-to-man defense against the offensive team's star player. That defender shadows the star player all over the court, never leaving that player to defend others. It is designed to keep the star player from getting the ball and eventually frustrate the player.

The triangle-and-two follows similar principles. One defender is positioned near the free-throw line and two players are on each low block, forming a triangle. The remaining two defenders play man-to-man shadow defense against two star players.

Gimmick defenses are rarely used but can be effective when a team has only one or two offensive players worth defending aggressively.

OFFICIATING COVERAGE

To effectively officiate halfcourt offenses versus zone defenses, the trail and lead must get good angles.

The trail
When on-ball, you must get off the sideline to get good angles on plays that are away from you (see "Trail movement off sideline," p. 92). Maintain proper spacing and avoid straightlining. Sometimes an inside-out look provides the best view of a play (see "Inside-out look," p. 91). Stay deep to avoid being in passing lanes.

When off-ball, look weak side (see "Trail looks weak side," p. 98) and give special attention to players in the top of the lane area and above the free-throw line.

When a shot is taken in your coverage area, watch the shooter for potential fouls until the shooter returns to the floor. Penetrate toward the endline for good rebounding angles (see "Trail movement on jump shot," p. 99).

The lead
When off-ball, you must watch players in the lane area. Move along and away from the endline to get good angles. Because the ball usually swings from side to side on the perimeter, there are fewer drop passes. That means there is usually less need to move ball side (see "Lead must use ball side mechanics," p. 85). However, when a drop pass does occur moving ball side still provides the best look. If the ball is passed out of the post area, simply move back toward the other side of the court to balance the floor. When moving along the endline, avoid getting caught in the "quicksand" when a shot is taken (see "Avoid quicksand," p. 23).

When on-ball, maintain proper spacing off the endline and move toward the sideline, if necessary (see "Lead movement toward sideline," p. 87).

TROUBLE SPOTS

There are areas that need special attention from the officials.

Perimeter shots
Since there are many jump shots against a zone, there are many related concerns for officials. Among them: the three-point arc and fouls by and against shooters. You must get a good angle — likely an inside-out look — to see if a player took a shot from behind the three-point arc. You must also avoid straightlining when a player takes a jump shot in front of you.

When a player takes a jump shot, watch the player return to the floor before turning your attention to rebounding action. That ensures you're watching the entire play, which may include a foul by a defender well after the shot is released.

High-low passes
The high-low pass presents challenges for the off-ball lead. The lead must watch the offensive player flash to the free-throw line and catch the pass. Since the area is near the free-throw line, that is likely a shared coverage; the trail must also look on-ball in that area. When a player catches a pass in that area, defenders converge quickly. Look for fouls from all angles against the player with the ball. Also look for the offensive player to push off the oncoming defenders.

The lead also needs to focus on the low block seal. Watch for the offensive player sealing off illegally with an elbow or backing into the defender. Make sure the defender doesn't push the post player from behind. Be especially wary of the "swim stroke." That move is used by offensive and defensive post players to get around an opponent. The player swings the inside arm overhead — similar to a swim stroke — and places the elbow in the opponent's chest while stepping around the opponent. It's common in the low post and it's illegal if the player pushes or holds the opponent; don't miss it.

Skip passes
With passes sailing over zone defenses, the trail must stay deep and move off the sideline to get proper angles and avoid passing lanes. The trail must hustle back and forth from the center of the court to the sideline when passes swing from side to side. The trail must also pick up the skip pass normally in the lead's coverage area when the lead has moved ball-side and doesn't have enough time to balance the floor (see "Trail must pick up shooter on skip pass," p. 94).

Traps

Traps are usually aggressive. Watch for the second defender fouling the player with the ball from the backside. Also watch for the offensive player splitting the defenders by pushing or hooking a defensive player.

When a trap occurs near a sideline, it usually occurs above the free-throw line extended. That means the trail must get well off the sideline and stay deep to get a good angle on the trap and cover the boundary lines (see "Boundary coverage," p. 76).

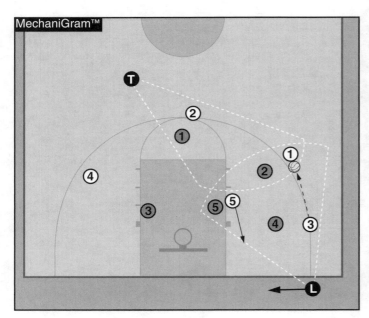 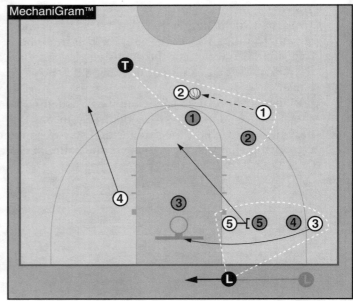

Action on the court:

③ passes to ①. ⑤ cuts to low block.

① passes to ②. ⑤ screens **5**, then moves toward the free-throw line. ③ cuts off screen through lane. ④ cuts to three-point arc.

Lead Official Responsibilities

Start wide.
Primary: On-ball. Watch ③ pass to ①.
Secondary: Off-ball. Watch players around nearest lane line.

Primary: Off-ball. Watch players around nearest lane line.
Watch ⑤ screen **5**.
Watch ③ cut through lane.
As ball shifts beyond opposite lane line, move toward nearest lane line.

Trail Official Responsibilities

Adjust toward center court for angles.
Primary: Off-ball. Watch players around free-throw line area.

Primary: On-ball. Watch ① pass to ②.

KEY

L LEAD OFFICIAL
T TRAIL OFFICIAL

PRIMARY COVERAGE AREA

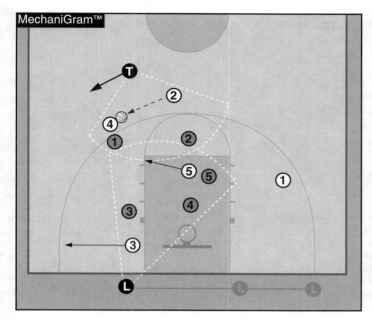

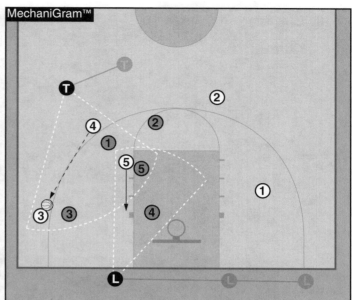

② passes to ④. ⑤ moves toward the free-throw line. ③ cuts toward three-point arc.	④ passes to ③. ⑤ moves to low block. Swing passes continue from side to side.
Anticipate swing pass. Move ball-side to opposite lane line. **Primary: Off-ball.** Watch players in lane area.	**Primary: Off-ball.** Watch players in lane area.
Primary: On-ball. Watch ② pass to ④. Anticipate swing pass. Adjust to sideline for proper angle.	**Primary: On-ball.** Watch ④ pass to ③. **Secondary: Off-ball.** Watch players around nearest lane line. Continue to swing from sideline to center of court when ball swings from side to side.

① OFFENSE   ◄----① PASS   ⊢— SCREEN

① DEFENSE   ◄·······① DRIBBLE

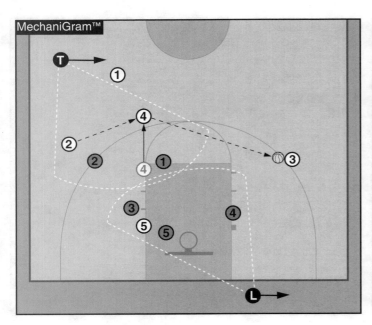

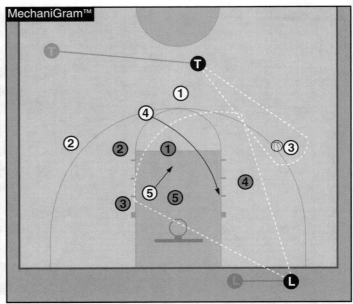

Action on the court:

④ breaks to top of the key. ② passes to ④. ④ quickly passes to ③.

④ cuts to opposite low block. ⑤ moves to free-throw line.

Lead Official Responsibilities

Primary: Off-ball. Watch players in lane area. As pass swings to ③, adjust to sideline for proper angle.

Primary: Off-ball. Watch players in lane area. Watch ④ and ⑤ move through lane.

Trail Official Responsibilities

Primary: On-ball. Watch ② pass to ④. Watch ④ pass to ③.

Adjust toward center court for angles. **Primary: On-ball.** Watch ③ with ball.

KEY   🅛 LEAD OFFICIAL   🆃 TRAIL OFFICIAL   PRIMARY COVERAGE AREA

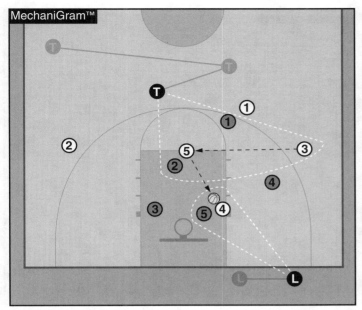

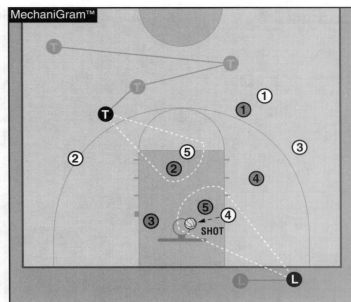

③ passes to ⑤. ④ seals off **⑤**. ⑤ quickly passes to ④.

④ shoots.

Primary: On-ball. Watch ④ post up and catch pass from ⑤.

Primary: On-ball. Watch ④ shoot.
Observe strong-side rebounding.

Primary: On-ball. Watch ③ pass to ⑤.
Adjust to sideline for proper angle.
Watch ⑤ pass to ④.

Primary: Off-ball. Watch players around free-throw line area.
Penetrate toward endline for angles.
Observe weak-side rebounding.

 OFFENSE 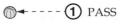 PASS ⊢— SCREEN

 DEFENSE  DRIBBLE

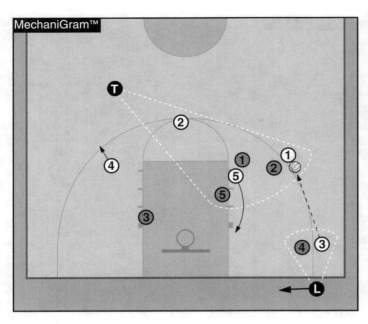

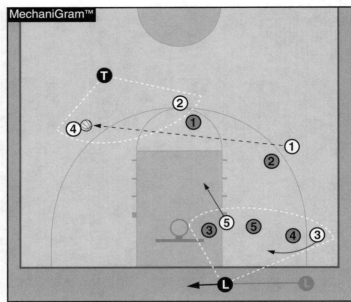

Action on the court:

③ passes to ①. ⑤ cuts to low block. ④ starts a run to the three-point line.

① passes to ④. ⑤ moves into lane. ③ cuts into lane.

Lead Official Responsibilities

Start wide.
Primary: On-ball. Watch ③ pass to ①.
As ball shifts toward top of the key, move toward nearest lane line.

Primary: Off-ball. Watch players in lane area.
Anticipate play.
Move ball-side to opposite lane line.

Trail Official Responsibilities

Primary: On-ball. Watch ① catch pass from ③.

Primary: On-ball. Watch ④ catch pass from ①.

KEY

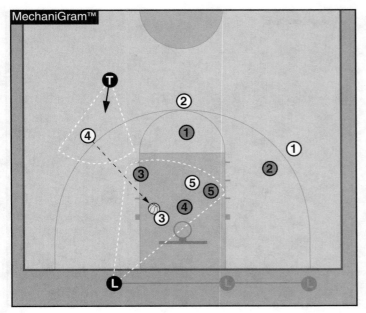

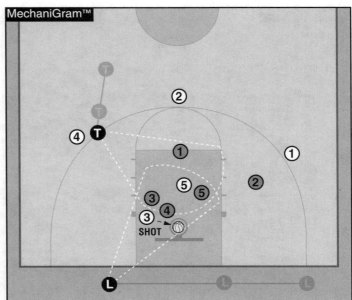

④ delivers drop pass to ③.	③ catches pass from ④. ③ shoots.
Primary: On-ball. Watch ③ catch pass from ④. **Secondary: Off-ball.** Watch players in lane area.	**Primary: On-ball.** Watch ③ shoot. **Secondary: Off-ball.** Watch players in lane area. Observe strong-side rebounding.
Primary: On-ball. Watch ④ pass to ③. Penetrate toward endline for angles.	**Primary: Off-ball.** Watch players in lane area. Penetrate toward endline for angles. Observe weak-side rebounding.

① OFFENSE   ⬤◄----① PASS   ⊢— SCREEN

① DEFENSE   ◎①◄·······① DRIBBLE

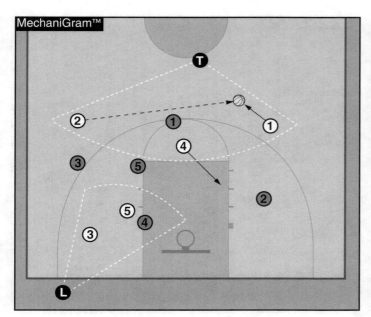

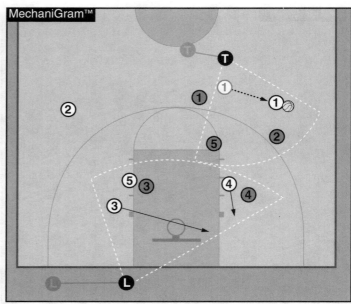

Action on the court:

① moves toward top of the key. ② passes to ①. ④ cuts toward low block.

① dribbles toward sideline. ③ cuts toward opposite free-throw lane line.

Lead Official Responsibilities

Primary: Off-ball. Watch players in lane area.

Primary: Off-ball. Watch ③ cut through lane. As ball shifts beyond opposite lane line, move toward nearest lane line.

Trail Official Responsibilities

Start toward center of court.
Primary: On-ball. Watch ② pass to ①.

Adjust to sideline for proper angle.
Primary: On-ball. Watch ① dribble toward sideline.

KEY

L LEAD OFFICIAL
T TRAIL OFFICIAL

PRIMARY COVERAGE AREA

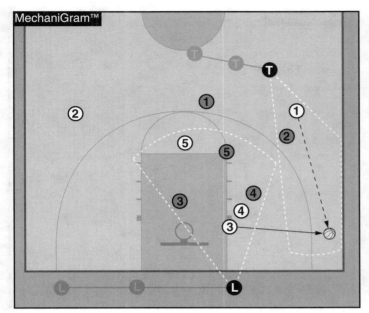

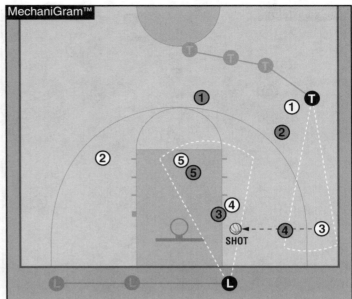

③ cuts toward three-point arc. ① passes to ③.	③ catches pass and shoots three-point shot.
Anticipate corner pass. Move ball-side to opposite lane line. **Primary: Off-ball.** Watch players in lane area.	**Primary: Off-ball.** Watch players in lane area. Observe strong-side rebounding.
Primary: On-ball. Watch ① pass to ③. Adjust to sideline for proper angle. Watch ③ catch pass from ①.	**Primary: On-ball.** Watch ③ shoot three-point shot. Penetrate toward endline for angles. Observe weak-side rebounding.

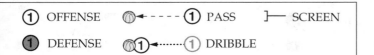

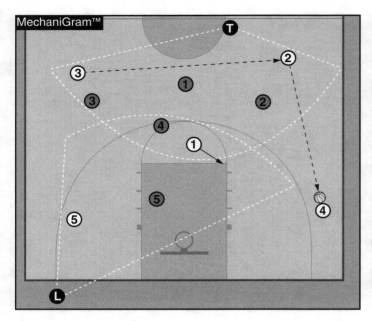

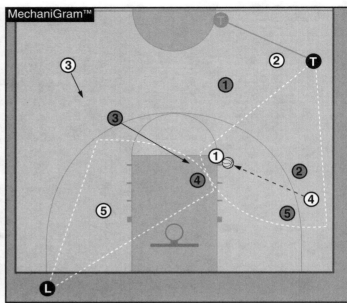

Action on the court:

③ passes to ②. ② passes to ④. ① moves toward ball-side free-throw lane line.

④ passes to ①. ③ moves to double team ①. ③ steps into three-point arc area.

Lead Official Responsibilities

Start wide.
Primary: Off-ball. Watch players in lane area.

Stay wide anticipating that the play will come back to you.
Primary: Off-ball. Watch players in lane area.

Trail Official Responsibilities

Start toward center of court.
Primary: On-ball. Watch ③ pass to ②.
Watch ② pass to ④.

Adjust to sideline for proper angle.
Primary: On-ball. Watch ④ pass to ①.
Watch ① catch pass from ④.

KEY

LEAD OFFICIAL
TRAIL OFFICIAL
PRIMARY COVERAGE AREA

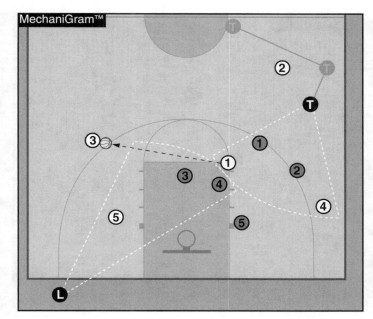

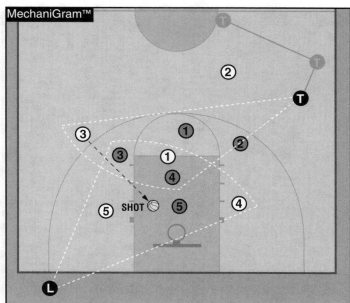

After ③ double-teams ① with the ball, ① passes to ③.	③ catches pass and shoots three-point shot.
Stay wide. **Primary: Off-ball.** Watch players in lane area.	**Primary: Off-ball.** Watch players in lane area. Observe strong-side rebounding.
Primary: On-ball. Watch ① pass to ③. Penetrate toward endline for angles.	**Primary: On-ball.** Watch ③ shoot three-point shot. Penetrate toward endline for angles. Observe weak-side rebounding.

① OFFENSE   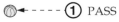 PASS   ⊢— SCREEN

① DEFENSE    DRIBBLE

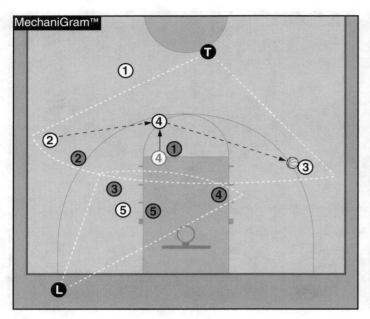

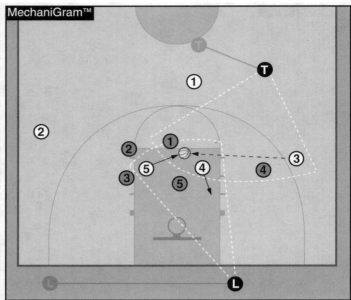

Action on the court:

④ cuts to top of the key. ② passes to ④. ④ passes to ③.

④ cuts toward low block. ⑤ cuts toward free-throw line. ③ passes to ⑤.

Lead Official Responsibilities

Start wide.
Primary: Off-ball. Watch players in lane area.

As ball shifts beyond opposite lane line, move ball-side to opposite lane line.
Primary: Off-ball. Watch players in lane area.
Secondary: On-ball. Watch ⑤ catch pass from ③.

Trail Official Responsibilities

Start toward center of court.
Primary: On-ball. Watch ② pass to ④.
Watch ④ pass to ③.

Adjust to sideline for proper angle.
Primary: On-ball. Watch ③ pass to ⑤.

KEY		
L LEAD OFFICIAL		PRIMARY COVERAGE AREA
T TRAIL OFFICIAL		

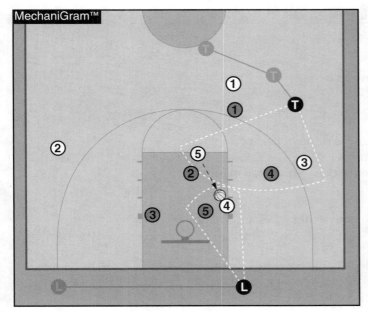

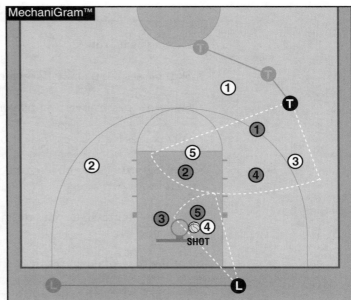

④ seals ⑤ on low block. ⑤ passes to ④.	④ catches pass and shoots layup.
Primary: Off-ball. Watch ④ post-up ⑤. **Then: Primary: On-ball.** Watch ④ catch pass from ⑤.	**Primary: On-ball.** Watch ④ shoot layup.
Penetrate toward endline for angles. **Primary: On-ball.** Watch ⑤ pass to ④.	**Primary: Off-ball.** Watch players around free-throw line area. Observe weak-side rebounding.

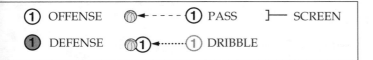

Review

Halfcourt vs. Zone

- Passing beats zones.

- Skip passes are usually thrown over a defense.

- High-low passes free post players.

- Post passes lead to post player offense or open perimeter shots.

- Match-up zones are effective because they have some man-to-man principles.

- Traps are aggressive zones designed to steal passes and frustrate opponents.

- For the trail, often an inside-out look is the best angle to officiate a zone.

- For the lead, there is usually less need to move ball side.

- There is usually little dribble penetration against a zone.

Quiz

Without referring back, you should be able to answer the following true-false questions.

1. The trail must stay deep to avoid passing lanes.

2. The trail doesn't have to worry about the three-point arc; that's the lead's responsibility.

3. The trail must hustle back and forth when swing passes move from one side of the court to the other.

4. The official must watch for players stepping through a trap and pushing with elbows.

5. The lead should move onto the court since there's little chance of dribble penetration.

Chapter 20

Three-point Offenses

Three-point offenses

OFFENSIVE STRATEGY

The three-point field goal has had significant impact at all levels. Many teams with strong perimeter shooting live or die by the three-point shot. Teams design three-point attempt plays versus zones and man-to-man defenses. Strategies include: double-screens, high picks, wing motion and corner passes.

Double-screens
Usually good shooters attract defensive pressure. Defenders try to disrupt a shooter's rhythm and get close to the shooter to alter the shot. Screens are effective when trying to free up a shooter. When one screen isn't doing the job, teams occasionally use double-screens. Double-screens are identical to a normal screen, only two offensive players screen instead of one. Why? It's harder for a defender to get around two offensive players than it is one.

Double-screens almost always occur off-ball. Down screens are often used against man-to-man defenses. Down screens occur when players move from the perimeter to the low block area to screen defenders. The offensive player near the low block cuts off the double-screen toward the perimeter beyond the three-point arc.

They work effectively against match-up zones or man-to-man defenses.

High pick
The high pick or screen is effective for a three-point shot attempt against a man-to-man or a zone with a single defensive player on the top of the zone (for example, a 1-2-2 or 1-3-1).

The high pick occurs near the top of the key. It is usually an on-ball screen. The screener picks the defender guarding the dribbler. The dribbler moves off the pick and is open for a potential shot.

The high pick is also used off-ball when a shooter near the top of the key is trying to get open to receive a swing or skip pass.

Wing motion
A wing motion offense moves shooters to different locations around the perimeter, usually against a zone. It is designed to let good shooters move to weak-spot defensive areas.

The wing motion offense is characterized by swing and skip passes plus perimeter players cutting through the zone. The swing and skip passes get the zone moving from side to side. The cutting players move to areas left open by the moving zone. That movement allows a good shooter to move often, making it more difficult for the defense to key on the player than if the good shooter stayed in one area.

Corner passes
Most three-point offenses run against zones. Swing and skip passes effectively get the zone moving from side to side, eventually leaving open spots. One offensive variation against a zone is a corner pass.

The area in the corner of the frontcourt (near the intersection of the sideline and endline) is sometimes left unguarded, especially when swing passes get the zone moving from side to side. Good shooters find the open corner, then wait for the pass.

The pass usually comes from the wing area on the same side of the shooter. Sometimes, a good corner pass is a skip pass from the opposite wing.

If a shooter receives the corner pass and does not shoot, the shooter often quickly looks to pass back out to the wing or pass to the high post. After passing the ball, the shooter might slide up toward the wing area or cut through the lane to the corner, looking for an open spot.

DEFENSIVE STRATEGY

Defensive strategies against three-point offenses include: aggressive man-to-man defense; match-up zones; packing it in; and traps.

Man-to-man
If a team is shooting well against a zone, an obvious remedy is to get out of the zone defense. Two things make shooting easier: space and time. If a shooter knows there's no defender in the immediate area, the shooter doesn't have to worry about getting the shot altered. That much open space means the shooter can take time to get balanced and in a good shooting rhythm.

Defenders must make shooting uncomfortable. One of the best ways to be in the shooter's area and lessen the amount of time the shooter has to shoot is an aggressive man-to-man defense. Shooters don't like to be followed around.

Match-up zones
Match-up zones combine parts of man-to-man and zone defenses. The defensive set is exactly the same as a

regular 2-3 or 1-2-2 zone with defensive players guarding areas. In a match-up zone, however, when an offensive player with the ball is in a defender's area, that defender aggressively guards the player with ball, similar to a man-to-man defense. When the ball leaves that area, the defender falls back into regular zone coverage.

The match-up zone is effective against three-point offenses because offensive players don't get clean looks to the basket or unchallenged passing opportunities.

Packing it in

When a team isn't shooting well from the perimeter, the obvious defensive strategy is to let them keep shooting. If an offensive team lacks a perimeter game, the defense dares perimeter players to shoot by sitting back in the zone — packing it in — and not challenging the shots.

Traps

Aggressive zone defenses apply trapping principles. A trap is similar to a double-team. Double-teaming occurs when two defensive players defend against a single offensive player. Double-teams occur against specific players; traps double-team when a player with the ball enters a specific area. Defensive players in a zone trap entice offensive players into those specific undefended areas. When a player with the ball moves into that perceived open area, two (or even sometimes three) defenders swarm the ball, trapping the offensive player.

Traps frustrate shooters and are effective against three-point offenses.

OFFICIATING COVERAGE

The three-point shot has made officials' jobs easier in some respects and more difficult in others.

Trail must get off sideline

In order to get a good look at three-point attempts, the trail must get off the sideline and move toward the center of the court (see "Trail movement off sideline," p. 92). Often, an inside-out look provides the best look on a three-point attempt and helps avoid straightlining (see "Inside-out look," p. 91).

Lead stays wide; trail stays deep

Since most three-point offenses are run against zones, the same officiating principles apply. In most situations, the lead must stay wide and move toward the near sideline to improve angles on potential shooters. The lead must also back off the sideline to provide proper perspective on plays, especially when the lead is on-ball.

The trail must stay deep, closer to the center restraining circle, to avoid being in passing lanes. Be aware of potential swing and skip passes and adjust accordingly to improve angles.

New lead helps on fast break

Many teams that use the three-point shot often take the shot on a fast break. A team in transition with good floor balance likely has the player with the ball dribbling in the middle of the floor and advancing to about the free-throw line. A wing player would make an angle cut toward the basket for a possible pass and layup. With the development of the three-point shot, the third player on the fast break — referred to as the "trailer" in hoop lingo — often spots up behind the three-point arc somewhere near the free-throw line extended, looking for a pass and a quick three-point attempt. A team with that type of fast break can try to get three points the "old fashioned way" — by passing to the cutting teammate, who drives the lane, scores the layup and gets fouled in the act of shooting — or three points the new way by simply hitting an outside jump shot.

The quick three-pointer off the break means a mental and physical adjustment for the covering official. An old school of thought said on any fast break the trail who becomes the new lead must *turn* and sprint downcourt. No longer. Turning often means dropping your head. Any time you drop your head or turn away from the action, you're missing something. In today's three-point crazy games, you're likely missing a quick three-point attempt.

As you are moving with the fast break, keep your head up, staying wide and looking over your shoulder as you are sprinting, to see the action and rule on three-point shots. In a fast-break situation, as the new lead you are responsible for judging *all* three-point attempts — even those that normally would not be in your area in a typical halfcourt setting — until your partner is in an area where he can assist and see the play. If the fast break shuts down and no shot is attempted, you're partner is now likely in the frontcourt and you return to normal court coverage (see "Transition: Lead helps on three-point attempt," p. 182).

Fewer double teams in the post

The three-point shot has cleaned up the lane area. If a team has good outside shooters, they are less likely to get double-teamed when the ball is passed to a post player. Why? If the player with the ball is double-teamed in the post, that leaves a perimeter player open. That player, if a talented shooter, will hover around the three-point arc, get a pass from the post and shoot.

Because there are fewer double teams, one part of the lead's job is easier; another part is tougher. There is less crowding in the post for a three-point shooting team, which means the lead can see action in the paint better. The further the defense moves out to cover the perimeter shooters, the fewer bodies in the middle and the clearer the view for the lead. That allows you to officiate post play better.

The downside is there are more block/charge judgments because of the three-point shot. Why? Again, the lane is less congested, meaning there's more cutting and wider passing lanes for the offense. That means more drives to the basket with defenders working to cut off the path to the hoop. If you go into a game knowing you'll see many three-point attempts, review legal guarding position and talk about the block/charge in your pregame. It will be a factor in your game.

Signaling

The on-ball official signals a three-point attempt upon release of the shot. The official signals the attempt by extending the arm that is closest to the division line at head level with three fingers extended. The on-ball official holds the attempt signal overhead until the shot is successful or clearly unsuccessful.

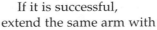

If the shot is successful, the on-ball official signals the successful field goal with both hands overhead (see PlayPic). If the shot is not successful, the on-ball official simply lowers the arm.

If the lead is on-ball and signals a successful three-point attempt, the trail mirrors by using the successful three-point field goal signal. Why? It's easier for the scorer to see the trail. The lead should never mirror a three-point successful signal from the trail.

Two-point attempt. A play that sometimes needs an extra bit of selling occurs when a

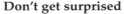

shooter is just barely on or inside the three-point arc, making the successful shot a two-pointer. Though not an approved mechanic, signaling that a try is a two-point attempt immediately after the try is released helps sell the call.

When a player is barely on the line and the shot is released, point down with two fingers (indicating two points) toward the spot nearest the shooter along the three-point arc. Use the signal as soon as the ball is released (in the same manner that you'd signal a three-point attempt). Hold the signal until the try is clearly successful or not successful.

If it is successful, extend the same arm with two fingers toward the scorer, ensuring the scorer knows the shot was worth two points and not three. If the shot is unsuccessful, simply lower your arm.

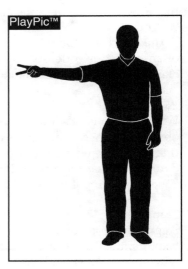

Signaling a close two-point attempt immediately shows that you saw the play correctly, which may help reduce arguments. Keep in mind, that signal is only used for close calls, not for all two-point attempts. It is not an approved signal but, if your governing bodies allow, use it to help sell the close ones.

Don't get surprised

Don't be surprised by the three-point shot and don't guess. If you're unsure whether a player was on, over or behind the three-point arc, rule it a two-point shot.

Discuss the problem areas on the floor in your pregame with your partner and you'll have a better chance of getting it right during the game.

TROUBLE SPOTS

There are areas that need special attention from the officials.

Watching the shooter

Getting a good angle to see if the shooter is behind the three-point arc is just the start of watching the shooter. The on-ball official must watch the shooter during the entire try. That includes the release point and the landing. Watch the shooter return to the floor to ensure there are no fouls before turning your attention to rebounding action.

Screens

Whether on-ball or off-ball, watch for illegal screens. Was the defender afforded proper spacing? Did the screener extend an elbow or leg into the path of the defender? Did the defender push through the screen?

Players cutting through the lane

In a motion three-point offense, players will cut through the lane area to move to an open spot. Defenders sometimes try to stop an offensive player from moving to that spot. Watch for defenders holding or pushing the cutting offensive players in the lane area. Be especially aware of defenders using an extended arm or elbow into the path of the cutting player.

Changing the call

The area along the three-point arc near the free-throw line extended furthest from the trail is a trouble spot for the officials. That's generally the break in coverage between trail and lead. Sometimes, for a brief period both officials are watching the player with the ball.

If one official signals a successful three-point field goal attempt and the other official is certain that the shooter was on or inside the three-point arc, there's a specific procedure for getting the call right.

The correcting official should stop the clock, signal a two-point attempt (point to the spot of the shot with arm and two fingers extended, then signal two points at about head height to the scorer) and simultaneously verbalize that the shooter's foot was on or over the three-point arc.

There's no need to huddle together with your partner to confer. If you clearly saw the play, there's nothing to talk about. Getting together adds confusion. Stopping the clock and signaling immediately gets the game going on quickly and smoothly.

Discuss changing successful three-point field goals in your pregame conference with your partner.

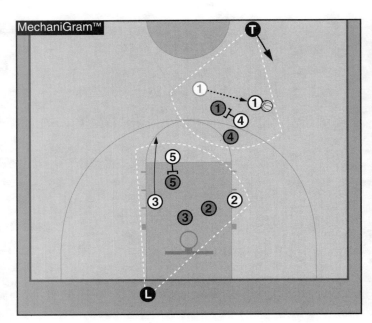

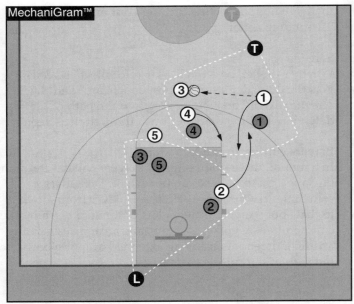

Action on the court:

④ screens ①. ① dribbles toward sideline. ⑤ screens ⑤. ③ cuts toward top of the key.

① passes to ③. ① cuts toward low block. ④ cuts toward low block. ② moves toward three-point arc.

Lead Official Responsibilities

Primary: Off-ball. Watch players in lane area. Watch ⑤ screen ⑤.

As ball shifts beyond opposite lane line, move toward nearest lane line.

Primary: Off-ball. Watch players in lane area.

Trail Official Responsibilities

Primary: On-ball. Watch ① dribble toward near sideline.
Secondary: Off-ball. Watch ④ screen ①.
Adjust to sideline for proper angle.

Primary: On-ball. Watch ① pass to ③.
Secondary: Off-ball. Watch ④ and ① cut toward low block.

KEY

LEAD OFFICIAL

TRAIL OFFICIAL

PRIMARY COVERAGE AREA

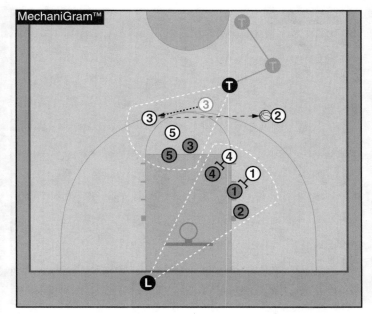

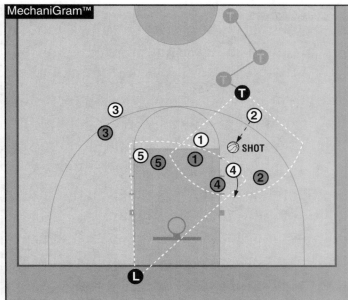

③ dribbles toward lane line, then passes to ②. ④ screens ④. ① screens ①.	② shoots.
Watch players in lane area. **Primary: Off-ball.** Watch ④ screen ④. Watch ① screen ①.	**Primary: Off-ball.** Watch players in lane area. Observe strong-side rebounding.
Primary: On-ball. Watch ③ dribble toward opposite sideline. Adjust toward center court for angles. Watch ③ pass ball to ②.	Move field of vision for inside-out look. **Primary: On-ball.** Watch ② shoot. Penetrate toward endline for angles. Observe weak-side rebounding.

  OFFENSE   PASS   ⊢— SCREEN

 DEFENSE    DRIBBLE

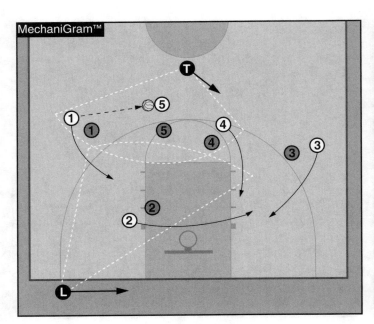 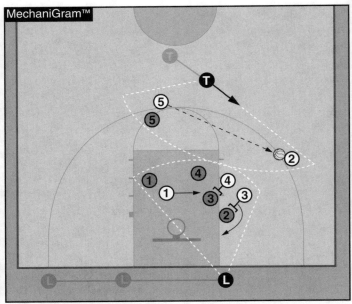

Action on the court:

① passes to ⑤, then cuts toward lane. ④ cuts toward low block. ③ cuts toward low block. ② swings toward opposite sideline to three-point arc.

⑤ passes to ②. ④ screens ❸. ③ screens ❷, then ③ cuts into lane. ① moves toward lane line.

Lead Official Responsibilities

Primary: Off-ball. Watch players in lane area. As ball shifts toward opposite lane line, move toward nearest lane line.

As ⑤ passes to ②, move ball-side to opposite lane line.
Primary: Off-ball. Watch players in lane area.
Watch ④ screen ❸.
Watch ③ screen ❷.

Trail Official Responsibilities

Primary: On-ball. Watch ① pass to ⑤. Adjust to sideline for proper angle.

Primary: On-ball. Watch ⑤ pass to ②. Adjust to sideline for inside-out angle.

KEY — **L** LEAD OFFICIAL   **T** TRAIL OFFICIAL   PRIMARY COVERAGE AREA

MechaniGram™

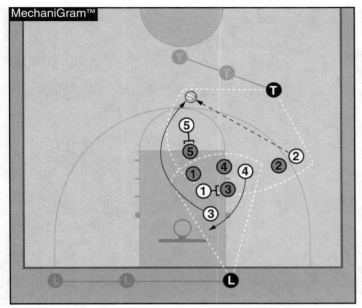

MechaniGram™

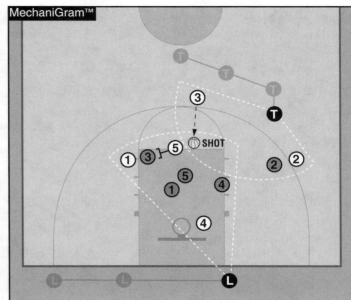

① screens ❸. ③ moves toward top of key and catches pass from ②. ④ rolls toward basket.	⑤ screens ❸. ③ shoots.
Primary: Off-ball. Watch players in lane area. Watch ① screen ❸.	**Primary: Off-ball.** Watch players in lane area. Observe strong-side rebounding.
Primary: On-ball. Watch ② pass to ③. Watch ⑤ screen ❺.	**Primary: On-ball.** Watch ③ shoot. Penetrate toward endline for angles. Observe weak-side rebounding.

 ① OFFENSE ◄----① PASS ⊢— SCREEN

① DEFENSE  DRIBBLE

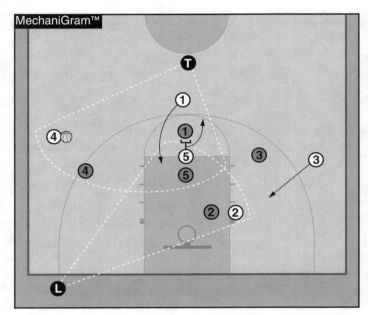

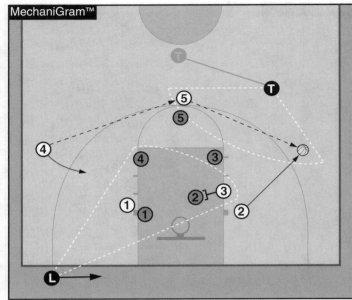

Action on the court:

① cuts toward low block. ⑤ screens ❶ then rolls to top of the key. ③ cuts toward low block.

④ passes to ⑤. ② breaks toward three-point arc. ⑤ passes to ②. ③ screens ❷. ④ cuts toward lane.

Lead Official Responsibilities

Primary: Off-ball. Watch players in lane area.

Primary: Off-ball. Watch players in lane area. As ball shifts toward opposite lane line, move toward nearest lane line.
Watch ③ screen ❷.

Trail Official Responsibilities

Adjust toward center court for angles.
Primary: On-ball. Watch ④ with ball.
Secondary: Off-ball. Watch ⑤ screen ❶.

Primary: On-ball. Watch ④ pass to ⑤.
Watch ⑤ pass to ②.
Adjust to sideline for proper angle.

KEY

 LEAD OFFICIAL
 TRAIL OFFICIAL

PRIMARY
COVERAGE
AREA

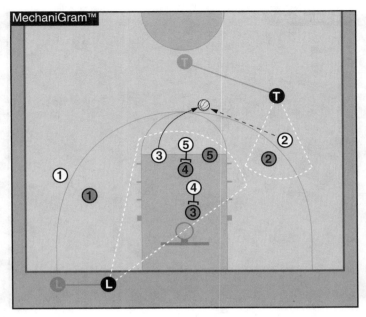

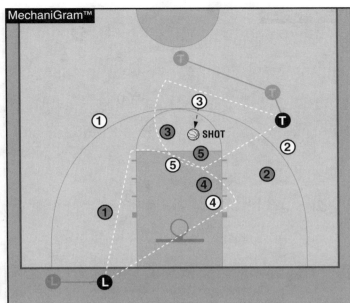

④ screens ③. ⑤ screens ④. ③ rolls to the top of the key. ② passes to ③.	③ shoots.
Primary: Off-ball. Watch players in lane area. Watch ⑤ screen ④. Watch ④ screen ③.	**Primary: Off-ball.** Watch players in lane area. Observe strong-side rebounding.
Primary: On-ball. Watch ② pass to ③.	**Primary: On-ball.** Watch ③ shoot. Penetrate toward endline for angles. Observe weak-side rebounding.

 OFFENSE PASS ⊢— SCREEN

 DEFENSE  DRIBBLE

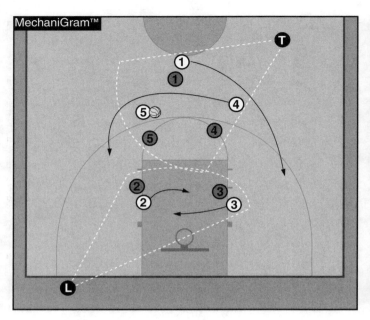

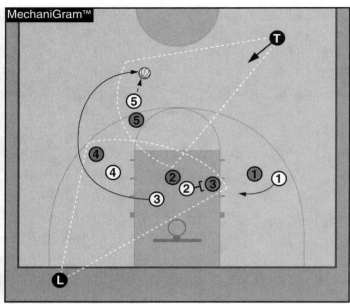

Action on the court:

① cuts toward three-point arc. ④ wheels around ⑤ toward opposite lane line. ② cuts into lane. ③ cuts into lane.

② screens ③. ③ rolls to the midcourt area. ⑤ passes to ③. ① cuts toward lane.

Lead Official Responsibilities

Primary: Off-ball. Watch players in lane area.

Primary: Off-ball. Watch players in lane area. Watch ② screen ③.

Trail Official Responsibilities

Primary: On-ball. Watch ⑤ with ball.
Secondary: Off-ball. Watch cutters ① and ④ move around key.

Primary: On-ball. Watch ⑤ pass to ③. Adjust toward center court for angles.

KEY

L LEAD OFFICIAL
T TRAIL OFFICIAL

PRIMARY
COVERAGE
AREA

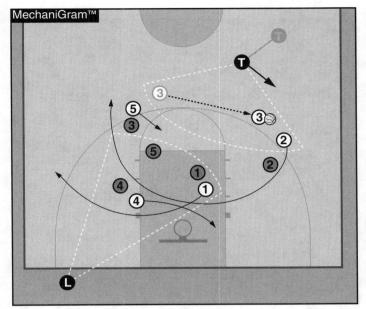

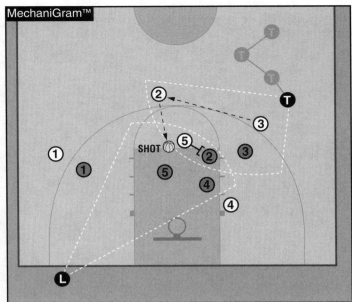

③ dribbles toward sideline. ⑤ moves toward free-throw line. ④ moves to opposite low block. ① moves toward three-point arc. ② moves through lane to top of the key.	⑤ screens **②**. ② catches pass from ③ at top of the key. ② shoots.
Primary: Off-ball. Watch players in lane area.	**Primary: Off-ball.** Watch players in lane area. Observe strong-side rebounding.
Primary: On-ball. Watch ③ dribble. Adjust to sideline for proper angle.	**Primary: On-ball.** Watch ③ pass to ②. Watch ⑤ screen **②**. Watch ② shoot. Penetrate toward endline for angles. Observe weak-side rebounding.

① OFFENSE ←- - - -① PASS ⊣— SCREEN

① DEFENSE ←·······① DRIBBLE

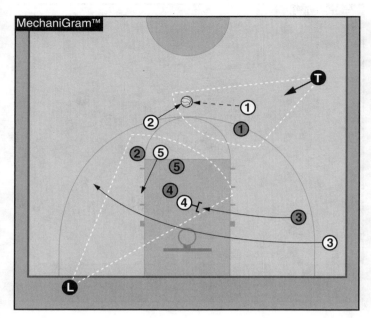 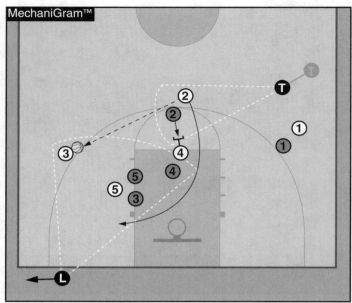

Action on the court:

② moves to top of the key. ① passes to ②. ⑤ cuts to middle of lane line. ③ swings to opposite three-point arc. ④ screens ③.

② passes to ③. ④ screens ②. ② cuts through lane to three-point arc.

Lead Official Responsibilities

Primary: Off-ball. Watch players in lane area. Watch ④ screen ③.

Primary: On-ball. Watch ③ catch pass from ②. Adjust to sideline for proper angle.
Secondary: Off-ball. Watch players in lane area.

Trail Official Responsibilities

Primary: On-ball. Watch ① pass to ②. Adjust toward center court for angles.

Primary: On-ball. Watch ② pass to ③. Watch ④ screen ②.

KEY

L LEAD OFFICIAL

T TRAIL OFFICIAL

PRIMARY COVERAGE AREA

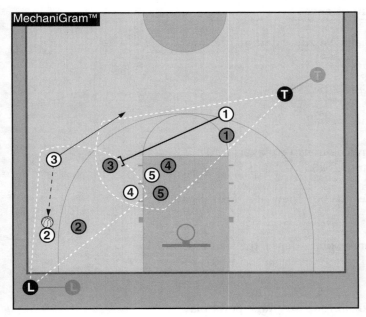

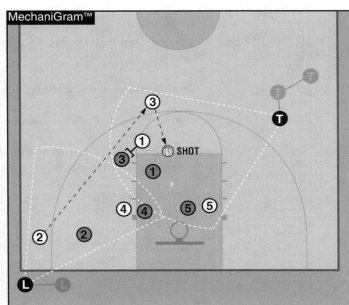

③ passes to ②. ① screens ❸. ③ moves toward top of the key.	① screens ❸. ② passes to ③. ③ shoots.
Primary: On-ball. Watch ③ pass to ②. **Secondary: Off-ball.** Watch players in lane area.	**Primary: On-ball.** Watch ② pass to ③. **Then: Primary: Off-ball.** Watch players around nearest lane line. Observe strong-side rebounding.
Primary: Off-ball. Extend field of vision through opposite lane line. Watch ① screen ❸.	**Primary: On-ball.** Watch ③ catch pass from ②. Watch ② screen ❸. Watch ③ shoot. Penetrate toward endline for angles. Observe weak-side rebounding.

① OFFENSE   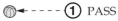----① PASS   ⊢— SCREEN

❶ DEFENSE   ----① DRIBBLE

Three-point offenses

• Teams design three-point offenses against zones and man-to-man defenses.

• Good shooters usually attract defensive pressure.

• Double-screens almost always occur off-ball.

• Defensive players in a zone trap entice offensive players into a perceived open area and then swarm the ball.

• An inside-out look usually provides the best view of a three-point attempt.

• Since many passes occur with a three-point offense, the lead must stay wide and close down only on rare drives to the basket or after a shot has been released.

• Effective signals are critical when dealing with a three-point play.

Quiz

Without referring back, you should be able to answer the following true-false questions.

1. The official signaling a three-point attempt uses both arms overhead, simulating a touchdown signal.

2. The on-ball official holds the attempt signal overhead until the shot is successful or clearly unsuccessful.

3. The on-ball official should immediately turn toward rebounding action as soon as a shot is released by an airborne shooter.

4. The officials should always mirror three-point attempt signals.

5. The officials should always huddle together when there's a discrepancy on a three-point attempt.

Chapter 21

Defensive Traps and Presses

Traps and presses

OFFENSIVE STRATEGY

Defensive team traps and presses are designed to entice the player with the ball in a specific area of the court, where dribbling or passing is difficult because of defensive pressure. Obviously, offensive players want to stay out of those trapping areas.

Teams usually beat traps and presses with passing, not dribbling. To do that, offensive teams use swing passes, skip passes, baseball passes, midcourt passes and "in-and-out" dribbling.

Swing passes

To beat a trap or press, the offense must get the defense moving from side to side. Swing passes are effective. Swing passes usually involve three offensive players: one on the right wing, one on the left wing and one in the middle. The players pass the ball from side to side, effectively moving the zone side to side. It works because the passed ball generally moves much faster than any defensive player, creating open space to advance the ball upcourt.

Skip passes

Skip passes are usually thrown over a trapping defense. It's called a skip pass because the pass skips a player in a normal swing passing sequence. For example, with a skip pass, the right wing player throws the pass over the defense to the left wing player, "skipping" the player in the middle of the court.

Skip passes can be effective against traps if they are timed correctly and thrown accurately. Non-trapping defensive players want that pass to occur because they're sitting in the passing lanes for a potential steal. Still, thrown correctly a good skip pass can help beat a press.

Baseball passes

Baseball passes are thrown completely over traps and presses. Thrown like a baseball, it is a long pass that usually travels half the court or more.

A baseball pass is effective when a pressing team is gambling often in the backcourt and forgetting about offensive players in the frontcourt.

Midcourt passes

Traps are effective when pushing offensive players toward the sideline, using the sideline as an extra

defender. Offensive players want to avoid the sidelines and keep the ball in the middle of the court.

A midcourt pass against a press usually comes from a wing player to a teammate who flashes into the middle, usually near the center restraining circle. That player receives the pass and immediately turns and looks downcourt for teammates breaking into the frontcourt. The midcourt player must get rid of the ball quickly because backcourt defenders converge quickly on the ball.

In-and-out dribbling

Traps and presses want an offensive player to dribble through a press. Dribbling through a trap or press is difficult to do and easier to defend against than a passing offense.

One effective dribbling strategy, however, is the in-and-out dribble. Trapping teams want players to dribble into certain areas. When the player with the ball enters that area, the defenders trap the player there. The in-and-out dribble uses the defensive team's aggressive trapping against them.

The dribbler moves toward the area intentionally left open by the defense for trapping. Then, when the defenders begin to trap, the dribbler backs out of that area and quickly passes to an open area. That in-and-out movement makes the defense commit to the dribbler then counters that by moving the ball quickly to another area.

That dribbling movement usually occurs against halfcourt traps near the division line. The pass usually is a midcourt pass to an open teammate.

DEFENSIVE STRATEGY

Defensive traps and presses are aggressive. They are designed to force an up-tempo style of play by creating turnovers. Traps can occur anywhere on the court, but usually occur near the midcourt area. Presses are always fullcourt.

Traps

A trap is similar to a double-team. Double-teaming occurs when two defensive players defend against a single offensive player. Double-teams occur against specific players; traps double-team when a player with the ball enters a specific area. Defensive players in a zone trap entice offensive players into those specific undefended areas. When a player with the ball moves into that perceived open area, two (or even sometimes three) defenders swarm the ball, trapping the offensive player.

Traps tend to occur near sidelines. In effect, a trap near a sideline uses the sideline as an extra defender. Defensive players not involved in the trap anticipate passing lanes and attempt steals.

Traps are effective when trying to force turnovers. A good trapping team gambles and often wins.

Presses

Presses can be either man-to-man or zone (usually a 1-2-2 or 1-3-1). Most presses are aggressive and apply trapping and double-teaming principles.

Some presses are not as aggressive (sometimes referred to as "token pressure"). Token pressure is generally designed to either tire a specific dribbler or take time off the game clock by making the dribbler work a little harder than normal to bring the ball up the court. Token pressure is not designed to steal the ball.

Some aggressive full court presses have a defender pressure the inbounds passer. Others entice the throw-in to a specific area (usually a corner), then double-team the player with the ball.

Non-trapping defenders anticipate passes and position themselves in passing lanes to attempt steals. A good pressing team gambles and often wins.

Usually, a post player is positioned in the frontcourt lane area as the last line of defense. If the offensive team breaks the press, the frontcourt defender staves off the offensive players until the other defenders can recover and help.

OFFICIATING COVERAGE

The trail

When on-ball, you must get off the sideline to get good angles on plays that are away from you (see "Trail movement off sideline," p. 92). Maintain proper spacing and avoid straightlining. Sometimes an inside-out look provides the best view of a play (see "Inside-out look," p. 91). Stay deep to avoid being in passing lanes.

Stay deep. Avoid moving straight toward the play because you could negatively impact the play by being in a passing lane. Take an angle toward the backcourt endline to decrease your chances of interfering with the play.

When off-ball, look weak side (see "Trail looks weak side," p. 98) and give special attention to players in the top of the lane area and above the free-throw line.

By moving off the sideline and angling toward the play, you're in a much better position to see the play.

The lead

When play moves from one endline toward the other, the trail has primary responsibility in the backcourt. However, when there's defensive pressure in the backcourt the lead must help.

There is a general rule to determine when the lead helps the trail in the backcourt. If there are four or fewer players in the backcourt, the trail works alone; more than four players, the lead helps.

When there are more than four players in the backcourt, the lead is positioned near the division line. If all the players are in the backcourt, the lead may move closer to the backcourt endline for better angles. If some players are in the frontcourt, however, the division-line area is the best position.

When near the division line, the lead must stay wide and constantly glance from backcourt to frontcourt. That "swivel" glance allows the lead to help the trail with backcourt traffic plus watch players in the frontcourt.

TROUBLE SPOTS

There are areas that need special attention from the officials.

Skip and swing passes

With passes sailing over traps and presses, the trail must stay deep and move off the sideline to get proper angles and avoid passing lanes. The trail must hustle back and forth from the center of the court to the sideline when passes swing from side to side.

Midcourt passes

Traps are usually aggressive, especially when a player has the ball near the division line. Watch for defenders converging on and fouling the player with the ball from all sides. Also watch for the offensive player splitting the defenders by pushing or hooking a defensive player.

Traps near sideline and division line

Halfcourt traps usually occur near a sideline and the division line. That means the trail must get well off the sideline and stay deep to get a good angle on the trap. The lead must stay positioned on the sideline to offer help (see "Lead helps in backcourt," p. 180). Watch for the defender converging on and fouling the player with the ball. Also watch for the offensive player

splitting the defenders by pushing or hooking a
defensive player.

Pass/crash near midcourt

One problem for officials is the pass/crash when a team
in transition beats a press and starts a break up the
court. Many times you'll see players leave their feet to
make a pass, then crash into defenders in the midcourt
area. Block? Charge? No-call?

During a press or trap, the new lead must be ready to
help out on pass/crash plays near midcourt.

Fastbreak off beaten press

When a trap or press gets beat, a fastbreak play often
ensues. The new lead must hustle to the endline to get a
good angle on a fastbreak play. Buttonhooking is usually
not an option because players are scattered all over the
court, leaving no room for the new lead to safely move
onto the court.

Since most presses have a post player in the
frontcourt lane area as a last line of defense, two-on-one
fastbreaks are the norm. That means the pass/crash play
in the lane is a real possibility.

In normal, halfcourt pass/crash plays, the trail must
help (see "Pass/crash in lane," p. 75). However, when a
fastbreak develops off of a press the trail rarely has
enough time to get into the frontcourt and help. That
means the new lead has the play alone. Move along the
endline to get good angles on the play.

Notes

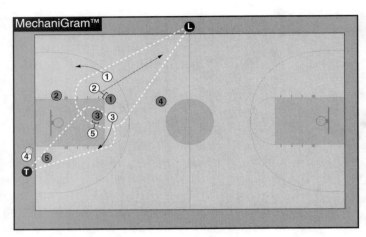

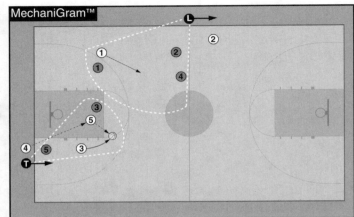

Action on the court:

④ has the ball for inbounds pass. ⑤ screens ❸. ③ cuts to low block. ② screens ❶ then ② runs to division line. ① moves toward endline.

④ passes to ⑤. ③ breaks downcourt. ⑤ passes to ③. ① cuts toward center restraining circle.

Lead Official Responsibilities

Stay wide near intersection of division line and sideline.
Primary: Off-ball. Watch backcourt players.
Watch ② screen ❶.

As the play moves upcourt, begin movement toward endline.
Primary: Off-ball. Watch backcourt players.

Trail Official Responsibilities

Administer throw-in using boxing-in method.
Primary: On-ball. Step away from thrower unless you bounce pass the ball; watch thrower.
Secondary: Off-ball. Watch ⑤ screen ❸.

Primary: On-ball. Watch ④ pass to ⑤.
Move onto the court.
Watch ⑤ pass to ③.
Watch ③ catch ball and dribble toward basket.

KEY

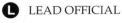

LEAD OFFICIAL

TRAIL OFFICIAL

PRIMARY COVERAGE AREA

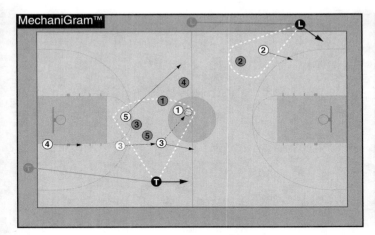

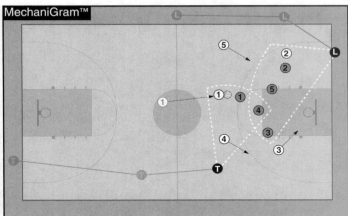

③ dribbles near division line then passes to ①. ⑤ circles around the play to division line. ③ cuts toward basket. ② cuts toward basket.	③ cuts toward basket. ④ moves toward three-point arc. ⑤ moves toward low block. ① dribbles to top of the key to start a play.
Primary: Off-ball. Watch ② fill the lane toward the basket. Move quickly downcourt for possible two-on-one action.	Obtain endline position. **Primary: Off-ball.** Watch players fill the lanes toward the basket.
Move quickly up court to division line. **Primary: On-ball.** Watch ③ pass to ①.	Move into frontcourt. **Primary: On-ball.** Watch ① dribble toward top of the key.

 OFFENSE   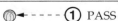 PASS   ⊢— SCREEN

① DEFENSE    DRIBBLE

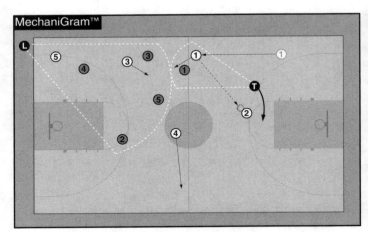

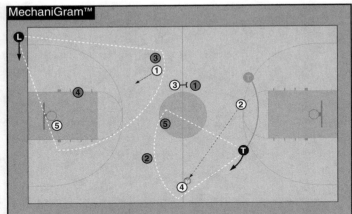

Action on the court:

① dribbles to division line. ① passes to backcourt ②. ④ breaks toward sideline. ③ breaks toward center circle.

② passes ball to ④. ③ screens ①. ① breaks toward top of the key.

Lead Official Responsibilities

Stay wide near intersection of endline and sideline. **Primary: Off-ball.** Watch frontcourt players.

As the play develops toward opposite sideline, begin movement toward basket. **Primary: Off-ball.** Watch frontcourt players.

Trail Official Responsibilities

Move beyond center of court. **Primary: On-ball.** Watch ① dribble toward halfcourt trap. Stay deep to avoid backward pass to ②. Watch ① pass to ②.

Swing back toward sideline opposite lead. **Primary: On-ball.** Watch ② pass to ④.

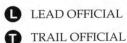

KEY

L LEAD OFFICIAL

T TRAIL OFFICIAL

PRIMARY COVERAGE AREA

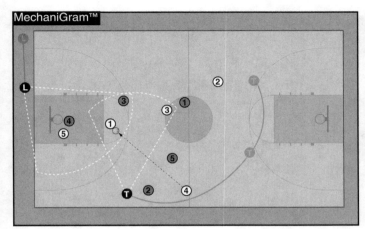

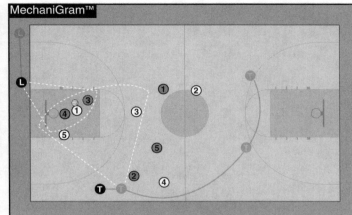

④ passes to ①.	① dribbles toward basket: two-on-one action around the basket.
Primary: On-ball. Watch ① catch pass and dribble toward basket. Adjust position for two-on-one action.	**Primary: On-ball.** Watch ① dribble toward basket. Adjust angles to avoid being straightlined.
Primary: On-ball. Watch ④ pass to ①. Penetrate toward endline for angles. Watch ① catch pass and dribble toward basket.	Penetrate toward endline for angles. **Primary: On-ball.** Watch ① dribble toward basket.

① OFFENSE   ← ------ ① PASS]—— SCREEN

① DEFENSE 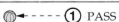 ← ········ ① DRIBBLE

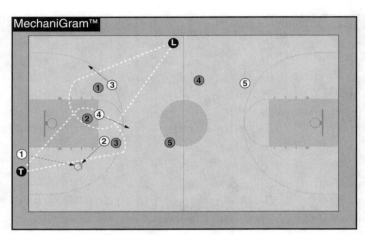

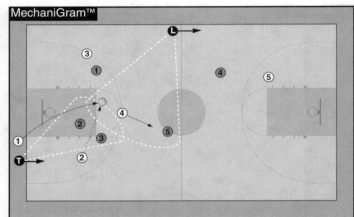

Action on the court:

① has the ball for inbounds pass. ② breaks toward near corner. ① passes to ②. ④ moves to top of the key. ③ breaks toward opposite corner.

① cuts toward free-throw line. ② passes to ①. ④ moves toward division line.

Lead Official Responsibilities

Stay wide near intersection of division line and sideline.
Primary: Off-ball. Watch backcourt players.
Secondary: Off-ball. Glance occasionally at frontcourt players.

As the play moves upcourt, begin movement toward endline.
Primary: Off-ball. Watch backcourt players.
Then: Primary: On-ball. Watch ① catch pass.
Secondary: Off-ball. Glance occasionally at frontcourt players.

Trail Official Responsibilities

Administer throw-in using boxing-in method.
Primary: On-ball. Step away from thrower unless you bounce pass the ball; watch thrower.
Watch ① pass to ②.
Watch ② catch pass.
Secondary: Off-ball. Watch players in lane area.

Primary: On-ball. Watch ② pass to ①.
Move onto the court.

KEY

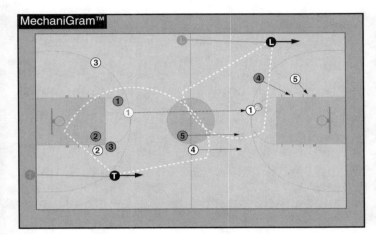

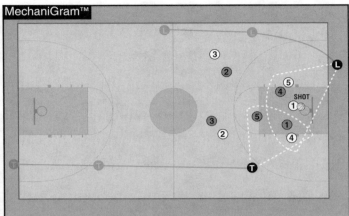

① dribbles toward top of the key. ⑤ cuts toward basket. ④ cuts toward basket.	① drives in for a layup.
Primary: On-ball. Watch ① dribble toward the basket. Move quickly downcourt for possible fastbreak action.	Obtain endline position. **Primary: On-ball.** Watch ① dribble toward the basket and shoot.
Move quickly up court to division line. **Primary: On-ball.** Watch ① dribble upcourt.	Move into frontcourt. Penetrate toward endline for angles. **Primary: Off-ball.** Watch players around nearest lane line. Observe weak-side rebounding.

 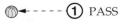

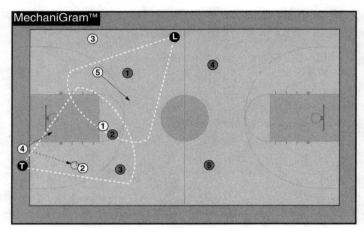

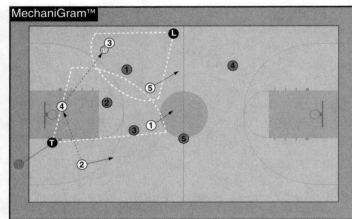

Action on the court:

④ inbounds to ②. ④ moves to center of backcourt lane. ⑤ moves toward center restraining circle.

② passes to ④. ④ passes to ③. ⑤ cuts toward division line. ① breaks into center restraining circle.

Lead Official Responsibilities

Stay wide near intersection of division line and sideline.
Primary: Off-ball. Watch backcourt players.

Primary: On-ball. Watch ③ catch pass. Remain near division line.

Trail Official Responsibilities

Administer throw-in using boxing-in method.
Primary: On-ball. Step away from thrower unless you bounce pass the ball; watch thrower.
Watch ④ pass to ②.
Watch ② catch pass.
Secondary: Off-ball. Watch players in lane area.

Primary: On-ball. Watch ② pass to ④.
Move onto the court.
Watch ④ pass to ③.

KEY

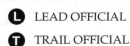

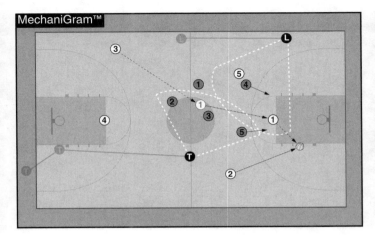

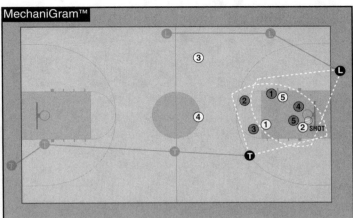

③ passes to ①. ① dribbles to frontcourt free-throw line. ② breaks to basket. ① passes to ②.

② drives in for a layup.

Primary: On-ball. Watch ③ pass to ①.
As the play moves upcourt, begin movement toward endline.
Move quickly downcourt for possible fastbreak action.
Watch ① dribble to free-throw line.

Obtain endline position.
Primary: On-ball. Watch ② dribble toward the basket and shoot.
Observe strong-side rebounding.

Move quickly up court to division line.
Primary: On-ball. Watch ① catch pass and dribble upcourt.

Move into frontcourt.
Penetrate toward endline for angles.
Primary: On-ball. Watch ② dribble in for layup and shoot.
Secondary: Off-ball. Watch players in lane area.
Observe weak-side rebounding.

 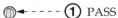 ① OFFENSE   PASS   ⊢— SCREEN

   DEFENSE   DRIBBLE

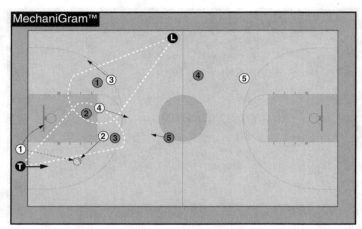

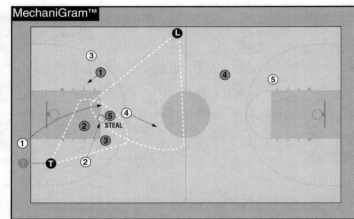

Action on the court:

① inbounds to ②. ① moves to center of backcourt free-throw lane. ④ moves toward top of the key. ⑤ moves toward passing lane.

④ moves toward center restraining circle. ② passes toward ①. ⑤ steals pass. ① breaks toward basket.

Lead Official Responsibilities

Stay wide near intersection of division line and sideline.
Primary: Off-ball. Watch backcourt players.
Secondary: Off-ball. Glance occasionally at frontcourt players.

Primary: On-ball. Watch ⑤ step into passing lane and intercept pass.

Trail Official Responsibilities

Administer throw-in using boxing-in method.
Primary: On-ball. Step away from thrower unless you bounce pass the ball; watch thrower.
Watch ① pass to ②.
Watch ② catch pass.

Move onto the court.
Primary: On-ball. Watch ② pass to ①.
Watch ⑤ intercept pass.

KEY

L LEAD OFFICIAL
T TRAIL OFFICIAL

PRIMARY
COVERAGE
AREA

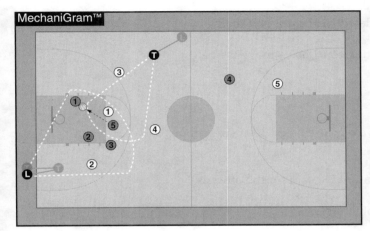

MechaniGram™

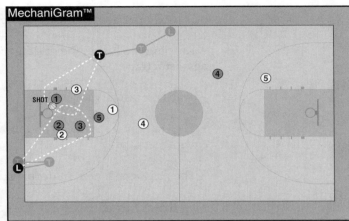

MechaniGram™

---

⑤ passes to ①.

① drives in for a layup.

Become new trail.
Penetrate toward endline for angles.
Primary: On-ball. Watch ⑤ pass to ①.

Penetrate toward endline for angles.
Primary: On-ball. Watch ① dribble toward the basket and shoot.
Observe weak-side rebounding.

Become new lead.
Move back to endline.
Primary: On-ball. Watch ① catch pass and dribble to basket.
Secondary: Off-ball. Watch players in lane area.

Primary: On-ball. Watch ① dribble in for layup and shoot.
Secondary: Off-ball. Watch players in lane area.
Observe strong-side rebounding.

 OFFENSE   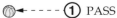 PASS   ⊢— SCREEN

 DEFENSE   DRIBBLE

 **Review**

Traps and Presses

• Teams usually beat traps and presses with passing, not dribbling.

• Baseball passes are thrown completely over traps and presses.

• Keeping the ball in the middle of the court helps move the ball against a trap.

• Traps are usually aggressive.

• The trail must stay deep and move off the sideline to ensure proper coverage.

• The pass/crash near midcourt is a trouble spot for the officials.

• Fastbreaks usually occur off a beaten press.

Quiz

Without referring back, you should be able to answer the following true-false questions.

1. Pass/crash plays are always handled by the lead.

2. "Token pressure" does not try to steal the ball.

3. The new lead should glance to help the trail with backcourt pressure.

Chapter 22

Delay/Spread Offense

The delay offense

OFFENSIVE STRATEGY

The delay (or "spread") offense positions offensive players out to all corners of the frontcourt. There are two uses for the spread offense: to create dribbling lanes to the basket or to run the clock down at the end of a period while avoiding double-teams. The spread offense uses swing passes, skip passes, backdoor cuts and dribble penetration.

Swing passes

If the defense is pressuring the spread offense and attempting steals, the offense must get the defense moving from side to side. Swing passes are effective. Swing passes usually involve three offensive players: one on the right wing, one on the left wing and one in the middle near the center circle. The players pass the ball from side to side, effectively moving the defense side to side. It works because the passed ball generally moves much faster than any defensive player, creating open space to advance the ball upcourt.

Skip passes

Skip passes are usually thrown over an aggressive defense. It's called a skip pass because the pass skips a player in a normal swing passing sequence. For example, with a skip pass, the right wing player throws the pass over the defense to the left wing player, "skipping" the player in the middle of the court.

Skip passes can be effective against traps and double-teams if they are timed correctly and thrown accurately. Non-trapping defensive players want that pass to occur because they're sitting in the passing lanes for a potential steal. Still, thrown correctly, a good skip pass can help beat a defense.

Backdoor cuts

Another common strategy: backdoor cuts, which are designed to take advantage of an over-aggressive defensive player. Backdoor cuts always move toward the basket and usually start well away from the basket. The offensive player reads the over-playing defender's movements and, instead of moving further away from the basket to catch a pass, cuts toward the basket. The offensive player with the ball reads the cut and delivers a pass to the streaking teammate, who catches the ball and beats the defender to the basket.

Dribble penetration

If the defense aggressively defends the spread offense, there's ample room for dribble penetration. Good penetrators are usually adept at handling the ball with both hands and have a quick first step toward the basket. Since most players are right-handed and — especially at the lower levels — aren't that good at dribbling with their left hands, dribblers tend to use their right hands. After a dribbler beats a defender, the dribbler usually looks to score or pass to an open teammate when another defender moves to help stop the dribbler.

DEFENSIVE STRATEGY

A defense has two choices against a spread offense: Sit back and let the offense take time off the clock or aggressively pressure the offense to try and force a turnover. When attacking a spread offense, the defense will try to force dribblers weak side, double-team and, if trying to stop the clock, foul.

Forcing weak side

Defensive players want to stop offensive players from going where they want to go. That's especially true with dribblers. For example, if a dribbler is right-handed and is attempting to go right, a good defensive player will force the dribbler left to thwart the offensive move. The defender attempts to beat the dribbler to a spot and establish legal guarding position. If the strategy works, the dribbler either is called for a player-control foul or the offensive team's play is disrupted because the dribbler can't go where the dribbler wants to go.

Double-teaming

Double-teaming occurs when two defensive players defend against a single offensive player. One common on-ball double team occurs when an offensive player is dribbling facing away from the basket and looking over a shoulder. One defensive player "bodies up" the dribbler, effectively cutting off the dribbler's path. Another defender, usually from behind the dribbler, moves toward the dribbler to either attempt a steal from behind or force a bad pass.

Fouling

If the defensive team can't steal the ball and must stop the clock near the end of the game, the defensive team will foul, likely forcing the offensive team to win the game at the free-throw line.

OFFICIATING COVERAGE

The spread offense presents unique challenges for two-person crews.

The trail
When a team goes into a spread offense, the trail must referee from the center of the court positioned in the backcourt. That way the players have enough room to maneuver without using the trail as a screen and the trail is out of the passing lanes. The trail's angle is an inside-out look (see "Inside-out look," p. 91). If near the end of a period, be aware of clock ramifications (see "Last-second shot," p. 264).

The lead
The lead must start and stay wide, near the intersection of the sideline and endline. If play dictates, the lead may creep up the sideline a bit to improve angles and help the trail in the area near the top of the key. Normal on-ball, off-ball (see "Court coverage," p. 73) and sideline responsibilities (see "Boundary coverage," p. 76) are the same.

TROUBLE SPOTS

There are areas that need special attention from the officials.

Skip and swing passes
With passes sailing over an aggressive defense, the trail must stay deep and stay in the center of the court to get proper angles and avoid passing lanes.

Penetration toward the basket
Since dribbling is one way to beat an aggressive defense, watch for dribbling-related violations, especially at the start of a play. Recognize an offensive player's pivot foot and watch for carrying the ball (illegal dribble) on cross-over moves.

After a dribbler beats a defender to the basket, many things can occur. Look for the beaten defender to grab the dribbler from behind. Watch for other defenders stepping into the dribbler's path to help stop the dribbler. That's when you are most likely to see block/charge and pass/crash plays.

Pass/crash in the lane
When a dribbler beats a defender in a spread offense, other defenders will step into the dribbler's path to stop the movement toward the basket. The situation is ripe for a block/charge decision.

Another common occurrence is the pass/crash in the lane (see "Pass/crash in the lane," p. 75). A player driving the lane, passing off to a teammate, then crashing into a defender can be one of the most difficult plays to officiate. Why? There's a lot going on in a small area in a short period of time.

If the trail can get from the center of the court to the sideline near the free-throw line extended, the trail must help. By aggressively penetrating toward the endline when players drive the lane, the trail can take some of the pressure off the lead by being in great position to judge the play.

The common phrase that sums up responsibilities is, "Lead takes the pass, trail takes the crash." That's generally accurate. The trail should watch the dribbler penetrate. Watch for the dribbler being fouled on the drive or being fouled while passing.

Also, the trail watches for the dribbler crashing into a defender after releasing a pass. Referee the defense to see if the defender obtained legal guarding position. Be especially wary of dribblers who leave their feet to make a pass. Don't bail out an out-of-control player by making a no-call.

With the trail watching that action, the lead can concentrate primarily on the pass and the player receiving it. Don't fall into the trap, however, of leaving all crashes to the trail. For the lead, the pass is primary, but the crash is secondary. You would rather have a call on the crash from the lead than a no-call that lets a foul get away.

Because the trail is moving a long way from the center of the court toward the endline, the trail is probably not going to have enough time to get into proper position. That means the lead must take the play alone.

Whatever call is made and whoever makes it, sell it! It's a real "bang-bang" play that can have major implications. For example, if the dribbler went airborne to make the pass, the player filling the lane caught the pass and is about to lay it in, then the airborne player crashes into a defender, that foul wipes away the basket. The calling official must have the intestinal fortitude to make that call.

Fouls designed to stop the clock
Fouls at the end of the game can be difficult to judge. Was the foul intentional or common? Most of the time, common fouls are correctly called, even though they are clearly "intentionally" committed to stop the clock (see "End-of-game fouling," p. 266).

One way to avoid controversy is to call the *first* foul. Most of the time the player being fouled is the one with the ball. Defenders are usually frantically trying to get to the player. They reach in and try to slap at the ball and/or the player. Call the foul immediately, at the first hint of contact. Why? Because that stops the action and prevents more and harder fouling. If you let the first minor slap go, the defender is going to foul harder next time. The harder the foul, the more you'll hear, "Intentional!" and the more players will get angry. Though you might ignore that minor slap in the middle of the second quarter, now is the time to get it right away. Don't make the defender push the offensive player into the third row to get a whistle.

However, don't be afraid to call an intentional foul if play warrants. A 2003-04 Point of Emphasis on intentional fouls addresses just that. A foul committed by players who are not clearly playing the ball and have the sole purpose of stopping the clock should be called intentional. Though it may not be a popular call, intentional fouls should be called when players' safety is put in jeopardy. Common sense will often be your best guide in whether to call a foul intentional or common and rules are written to back your call.

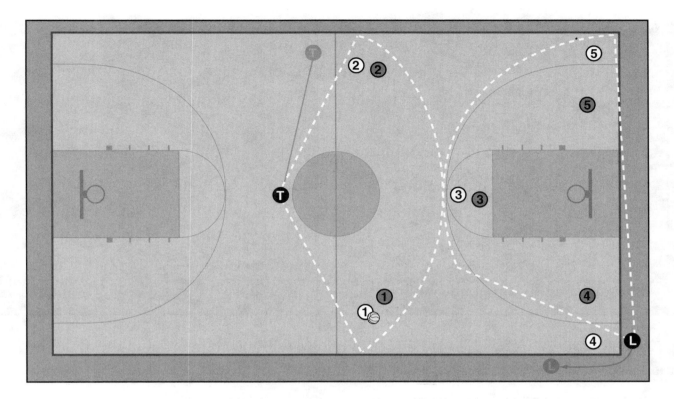

Officiating the delay offense

The delay (sometimes referred to as the "spread") offense presents unique challenges for two-person crews. The delay offense spreads players out to all corners of the frontcourt and is designed to run the clock down while avoiding double-teams.

When a team goes into a delay offense, the trail must referee from the center of the court, normally positioned in the backcourt. That way the players have enough room to maneuver without using the trail as a screen and the trail is out of the passing lanes. The trail's angle is an inside-out look (see "Inside-out look," p. 91).

The lead must start and stay wide, near the intersection of the sideline and endline. If play dictates, the lead may creep up the sideline a bit to improve angles and help the trail in the area near the top of the key. If the play moves toward the endline, the lead must "close down" along the endline toward the basket to obtain good angles. Be ready to close down on dribble penetration and backdoor cuts toward the basket.

Normal on-ball, off-ball (see "Court coverage," p. 73) and sideline responsibilities (see "Boundary coverage," p. 76) are the same.

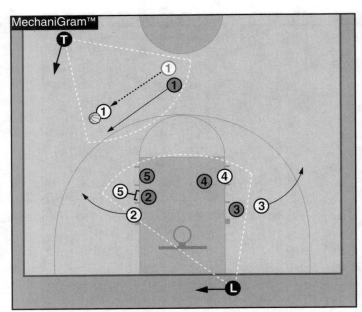

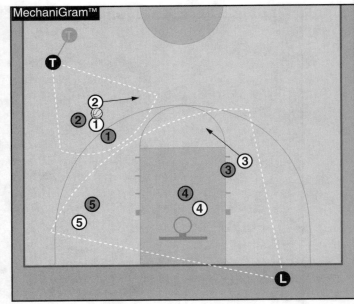

Action on the court:

① dribbles toward sideline. ② moves toward top of the key.

① hands off to ②. ③ moves to top of the key.

Lead Official Responsibilities

Primary: Off-ball. Watch players in lane area.

Primary: Off-ball. Watch players in lane area. Watch ③ move to the top of the key.

Trail Official Responsibilities

Start wide and deep.
Primary: On-ball. Watch ① dribble toward sideline.

Adjust angles to avoid being straightlined.
Primary: On-ball. Watch ① hand off to ②.

KEY
L LEAD OFFICIAL
T TRAIL OFFICIAL
PRIMARY COVERAGE AREA

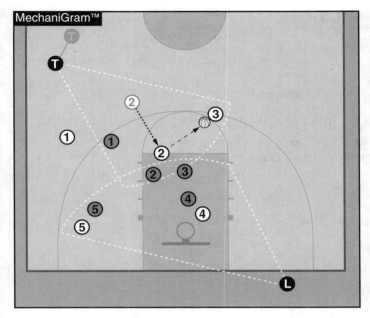

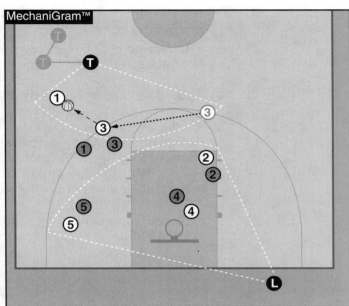

② dribbles to free throw line. ② passes to ③.	③ dribbles past opposite lane line extended. ③ passes to ①. Delay offense continues.
Primary: Off-ball. Watch players in lane area.	**Primary: Off-ball.** Watch players in lane area.
Primary: On-ball. Watch ② dribble to free-throw line. Watch ② pass to ③.	**Primary: On-ball.** Watch ③ dribble to near lane line extended. Adjust angles to avoid being straightlined. Watch ③ pass to ①.

 OFFENSE   PASS   ⊢— SCREEN

 DEFENSE    DRIBBLE

Review

Delay/Spread Offense

• The spread positions offensive players out to all corners of the frontcourt.

• Backdoor cuts are effectively used to beat defenses.

• If the defensive team can't steal the ball and must stop the clock near the end of the game, the defensive team will likely foul, forcing the offensive team to win the game at the free-throw line.

• The trail must work from the center of the court.

• The lead must move out toward the sideline and maybe even up the sideline a bit.

Quiz

Without referring back, you should be able to answer the following true-false questions.

1. All fouls in the last minute are intentional fouls.

2. The trail should stay on the sideline to avoid the passing lanes.

3. Normal on-ball, off-ball coverages apply.

Chapter 23

Last-second Shot

Last-second shot

OFFENSIVE STRATEGY

A last-second shot occurs near the end of a period. Specific plays are designed to make sure a shot is attempted before the period-ending horn sounds. When that occurs near the end of a game, the shot is usually a game-tying or game-winning shot, which creates many challenges for officials.

Last-second-shot plays often start with a throw-in, especially at the end of the game. That's because most teams call a timeout to stop the clock and discuss strategy before attempting the final shot. The throw-in may be from anywhere along any boundary line, but most last-second-shot-throw-in plays start along the backcourt endline or near the division line.

Last-second shots at any other time other than the end of the game are usually not related to throw-ins because teams rarely call timeouts to set up plays in those situations. For example, it doesn't make much sense to call a timeout at the end of the first period when a team can save a timeout in case the situation comes up again at the end of the game.

When a throw-in does not start the play, usually either a long pass or individual dribble penetration precedes the last-second shot.

Last-second-shot plays include screens, lob passes, dribble penetration and attempts to draw a foul.

Screens

On-ball screens free the dribbler to penetrate toward the basket or give the dribbler enough room to make passes. The screener will occasionally roll toward the basket looking for a pass from the dribbler — if the screener's defensive player moved to cut off the dribbler (commonly referred to as the "pick and roll").

Off-ball screens free players to catch passes. They are almost always used in last-second shot plays, especially when the play starts with a throw-in.

There are two types of off-ball screens: down screens and cross screens. Down screens occur when players move from the perimeter to the low block area to screen defenders. The offensive player near the low block cuts off the screen toward the perimeter, sometimes beyond the three-point arc. Down screens usually start with perimeter players (guards and small forwards) near the low block and post players (centers and power forwards) near the perimeter. The post players screen for the perimeter players.

Occasionally, a post player will cross screen for another post player. A cross screen occurs when a post player cuts across the lane to screen for another post player on the other side of the lane. The cross screen frees the post player, who moves into the open area and looks for a pass from the perimeter.

Lob and baseball passes

Lob and baseball passes are common with last-second shot plays. Both passes are high-aching passes which allow offensive players to leap to catch the pass and either immediately shoot or land and quickly shoot. Lob passes occur in a halfcourt setting while baseball passes travel the length of the court. Baseball passes are thrown completely over traps and presses. A baseball pass is effective when a pressing team is gambling in the backcourt or there's little time to advance the ball upcourt.

The lob and baseball passes are thrown to strong post players, good-leaping perimeter players or quality shooters freed by screens.

Dribble penetration

Occasionally individual penetration plays lead to a last-second shot. Though dribbling is slower than passing, dribble penetration occurs when a team is out of timeouts and can't stop the clock to set up a play. It also occurs if the defense is doing its job by cutting off passing lanes; the player with the ball has no choice but to create a shot.

Good penetrators are usually adept at handling the ball with both hands and have a quick first step. Since most players are right-handed and — especially at the lower levels — aren't that good at dribbling with their left hand, offenses tend run to the offensive player's right. After a dribbler beats a defender, the dribbler usually looks to score or pass to an open teammate as another defender moves to help stop the dribbler.

Drawing a foul

A last-second shot is often a desperation attempt. Teams with little time on the clock realize that advancing the ball up the court, successfully running a play and making the shot is against the odds.

To help their cause, offensive players will try to draw fouls and get to the free-throw line to try and tie or win the game. Drawing a foul means an offensive player tries to get a defender to foul. It can occur on-ball or off-ball.

DEFENSIVE STRATEGY

Forcing weak side

Defensive players want to stop offensive players from going where they want to go. That's especially true with dribblers in the waning seconds of a game. For example, if a dribbler is right-handed and is attempting to go right, a good defensive player will force the dribbler left to thwart the offensive move. The defender attempts to beat the dribbler to a spot and establish legal guarding position. If the strategy works, the dribbler either is called for a player-control foul or the offensive team's play is disrupted because the dribbler can't go where the dribbler wants to go.

Double-teaming

Double-teaming occurs when two defensive players defend against a single offensive player. That can occur on-ball or off-ball. In end-of-game situations, defenders will sometimes double-team a dribbler, ensuring more time runs off the clock than if the defender was unguarded. Also, double-teaming the dribbler makes it more difficult for the dribbler to get a good look at the basket when shooting or to clearly see passing lanes when passing.

Defenders will also double-team off-ball. Last-second off-ball double teams are designed to stop the offensive player most capable of making a last-second shot from receiving a pass. That leaves one offensive player open, but the defense is willing to gamble that that player can't make a last-second shot.

Pressuring the passer

Since good passes are essential in most last-second plays, defenders want to make passing difficult.

Pressuring the passer is a good defensive strategy against last-second shots, especially on throw-ins. Simply, if the passer has a clean look to make a lob or baseball pass, it's an easier pass to make. If the passer is aggressively pressured, the pass is much more difficult to make.

Traps

A trap is similar to a double-team. But while double-teams occur against specific players, traps double-team when any player with the ball enters a specific area. Defensive players in a zone trap entice offensive players into those specific "undefended" areas. When a player with the ball moves into that perceived open area, two (or even sometimes three) players swarm the ball, trapping the offensive player.

Traps tend to occur near sidelines. In effect, a trap near a sideline uses the sideline as an extra defender. Defensive players not involved in the trap anticipate passing lanes and attempt steals.

Traps are effective when trying to force turnovers. A good trapping team gambles and often wins.

Presses

Presses can be either man-to-man or zone (usually a 1-2-2 or 1-3-1). Presses near the end of a game are aggressive and apply trapping and double-teaming principles — but not too aggressive (defenders do not want to foul and possibly put the other team at the free-throw line to tie or win the game).

Sometimes end-of-game presses are not as aggressive (sometimes referred to as "token pressure"). Token pressure in last-second shot situations is designed to take time off the game clock by making the dribbler work harder than normal to bring the ball up the court. Token pressure is not necessarily designed to steal the ball.

Usually, a post player is positioned in the frontcourt lane area as the last line of defense. If the offensive team breaks the press, the frontcourt defenders stave off the offensive players until the other defenders can recover and help. Defenders don't want to get beat deep with a baseball pass in last-second shot situations.

OFFICIATING COVERAGE

The trail

When on-ball, you must get off the sideline to get good angles on plays that are away from you (see "Trail movement off sideline," p. 92). Maintain proper spacing and avoid straightlining. Sometimes an inside-out look provides the best view of a play (see "Inside-out look," p. 91).

When off-ball, look weak side (see "Trail looks weak side," p. 98). When a shot is taken in your coverage area, watch the shooter for potential fouls until the shooter returns to the floor. Penetrate toward the endline for good rebounding angles (see "Trail movement on jump shot," p. 99).

The lead

When off-ball in a halfcourt setting, you must watch players in the lane area. When anticipating a lob pass, move ball side if necessary (see "Lead must use ball side mechanics," p. 85). Move along the endline to get good angles.

When off-ball in a fullcourt setting, position yourself between the division line and the midcourt area above the top of the key in the frontcourt. That spot gives you a great look at midcourt area cuts and screens, and allows you enough time to get back to the endline for baseball and lob passes if necessary.

When on-ball, maintain proper spacing off the endline and move toward the sideline, if necessary (see "Lead movement toward sideline," p. 87).

End-of-game procedures

When the clock is winding down at the end of a game and the score is close, emotions rise. Fans, coaches and players all get a bit more excited. You can't afford to do the same. There are some techniques you can use to ensure you'll remain level-headed when most others around you are losing their composure.

Talk with your partner during a timeout

Almost inevitably, there will be a timeout by one of the teams. That's a great time to get together with your partner to discuss the situation and how you're going to handle it. Review such things as court coverage, who has the call on a last-second shot and how many timeouts remain for each team. By going through the final seconds mentally before they happen, you're more likely to react dispassionately when they do.

Talk with the table personnel

If you're the referee, take the time to review procedures with the personnel at the scorer's table. Remind the timer to watch the official responsible for starting the clock and start it only when that official signals. Also remind the timer to watch for the officials stopping the clock after a last-second shot is taken. Timers are often from the home school and can get caught up in the emotions, especially if their team just made a last-second shot. The timer must focus on the officials and not celebrate, because the other team may quickly request and be granted a timeout with little time left. It's extremely frustrating when you signal for the clock to stop before the horn sounds and the timer isn't paying attention. Remedy that by reminding the timer to continually watch the officials.

If there are scorers from each team, make sure the scorebooks add up correctly. That's the time to fix scorebook problems, not after a last-second shot is attempted.

Inform the scorer that the official responsible for judging whether a shot attempt is before or after the final horn will make eye contact with the scorer. That way, there's no confusion if the goal counts or not.

By talking to the table personnel about procedures, etc., you'll ensure they don't get caught up in the emotion.

Talk to yourself

Relax by taking a few deep breaths. At the same time, mentally review the potential play scenarios. That way, you'll be ready when things do happen.

End-of-game fouling

If the team with the ball near the end of the game is leading, the defensive team must get the ball back in a hurry and try to score often. When the defensive team can't steal the ball, defenders often foul to stop the clock.

End-of-game fouling situations present unique dilemmas for officials. The hard part is that officials know darn well the team behind on the scoreboard is fouling intentionally to stop the clock and force the other team to make free throws. But are the losers fouling *intentionally*?

The NFHS definition for intentional foul reads, "An intentional foul is a personal or technical foul designed to stop or keep the clock from starting, to neutralize an opponent's obvious advantageous position, contact away from the ball or when not playing the ball. It may or may not be premeditated and is not based on the severity of the act. A foul shall also be ruled intentional if, while playing the ball, a player causes excessive contact with an opponent."

If you read that verbatim, it sounds like most end-of-game fouls should be ruled intentional. Easy to say, much harder to do. Why? Because that's not what is accepted. The reality is, if a winning-team dribbler gets his arm slapped by a losing-team player who is just trying to stop the clock and you call it an intentional foul, you're in trouble.

With that said, don't cop out from calling a foul intentional either. Intentional fouls are again a point of emphasis with special regard to fouling away from the ball. When a player fouls and the opponent is clearly not playing the ball, an intentional foul must be called.

There are some little things you can do to make sure end-of-game fouling situations don't get out of hand.

Call the *first* foul

Most of the time, the player being fouled is the one with the ball. Defenders are usually frantically trying to get to the player. They reach in and try to slap at the ball and the player. Call the foul immediately at the first hint of contact. Why? Because that stops the action — and prevents more and harder fouling. If you let the first minor slap go, the defender is going to foul harder next time. The harder the foul, the more you'll hear, "Intentional!" and the more angry players will get. Though you might ignore that minor slap, say, in the middle of the second quarter, now's the time to get it right away. Don't make the defender push the offensive player into the third row to get a whistle.

Talk to both teams
Usually teams are coming out of post-timeout huddles near the end of close games. That's a great time to talk to both teams. Tell the team that's behind to "play the ball," "don't commit a hard foul," and "make it look like a normal foul." By planting those seeds in their head, they know you're looking to call the first foul and they don't have to do anything extreme. Tell the leading team to expect fouls. Remind them that the other team is merely trying to stop the clock and not trying to hurt them. Assure them that you'll protect them. That lets them know you know they're about to be fouled and don't need to overreact and earn a stupid retaliatory foul.

Call the hard foul intentional
Violent contact must be ruled intentional. Look for two-handed pushes from behind and jersey grabs, especially on airborne players. Call them intentional and send the message they won't be tolerated.

Keep calling them
It's not fun to shoot lots of free throws in the last few minutes, but some games just go that way. Stay with it. You've got to keep calling the quick foul. Trouble starts and fights erupt when officials ignore fouls with seconds left, hoping the horn will sound to end the game. Yes, you'll be there an extra few minutes, but the alternative — a bench-clearing brawl as time expires — is worse.

Clock responsibilities
In all halfcourt and most fullcourt situations, the trail is responsible for the clock and judging whether a try occurred before or after the final horn. *Unless alternate coverage was discussed at the end of the game during a timeout, the trail is solely responsible.*

There are some possible fullcourt exceptions. Those exceptions should only occur, however, if governing bodies allow and both officials have had a chance to talk about it in their pregame conference and had a chance to remind each other either during a timeout.

One possible fullcourt exception occurs when there's a length-of-the-court baseball pass throw-in and very little time left — roughly two seconds or less. With the new lead positioned near the midcourt area, it's much easier for the new lead to see the release of shot clearly. The new trail simply doesn't have enough time to move from near the throw-in spot to near midcourt to get a good look at the shot. A general rule: When the new lead is positioned near midcourt and the new trail is positioned on the backcourt endline, shots taken from the backcourt (three-quarter court heaves, etc.) are the trail's responsibility; shots taken from the frontcourt are the lead's responsibility. Again, that alternate coverage applies only if the two officials discussed it in the pregame and have had a chance to remind each other on the court.

Another possible exception occurs when the new lead is trailing a fastbreak toward the basket and the new trail started the play on the endline. That can occur via a baseball pass or a quick steal near midcourt that turns into a last-second-shot attempt going the other direction. A general rule: When a transition play occurs and the new lead is trailing the play, the new lead is responsible for judging whether or not the shot beat the clock. Why? The new lead has a much better view of the shot. The new trail doesn't have enough time to move from the backcourt endline to near midcourt to get a good look at the shot. Plus, the new lead is much closer to the play, meaning the ruling has a much better chance of being accepted than if the new trail made the call from half the court away. Perception is important. Again, that alternate coverage applies only if the two officials discussed it in the pregame. If it's a steal play that quickly goes the other direction, there's obviously no time to discuss the alternate coverage. That's why talking about these plays in your pregame is critical.

Make sure both officials know who is responsible for the clock. There's nothing worse than having neither official make the call or having two officials make different calls.

Signal immediately

If a shot attempt is after time expired, signal emphatically *immediately* as the horn sounds and the ball is still in the player's hands. Use the "goal does not count" signal (see PlayPic A). Wave the shot off a few times for extra selling; consider blowing your whistle a few times with short, loud blasts while waving. You may want to move slightly toward the scorer's table, making eye contact with the scorer so there's not doubt the shot did not count. If the player follows through with the shot and it's no good, there's nothing to argue about. If the player follows through with the shot and it enters the basket, you've already signaled that it didn't count, which helps sell it and shows everyone you are confident in the call. Waiting to wave it off until after the ball enters the basket creates confusion and chaos.

If the shot is released in time, hold your hand with three fingers extended at a 45-degree upward angle (or two fingers if it's a two-point try) to indicate the try will count if it is successful. If it's no good, there's no signal to make. If the shot is good, emphatically use the "count the goal" signal (see PlayPic B). You may want to move slightly toward the scorer's table, making eye contact with the scorer so there's no doubt the shot did count.

Get off the court

If you've done everything correctly in the last-second-shot situation (checked the scorebook during the last timeout, made eye contact with the scorer and emphatically signaled your ruling, etc.), there's nothing more for you to do but get off the court. Do not go over to the scorer's table unless absolutely necessary. Emotions run high at the end of close games and you want to avoid upset coaches, players and fans. There shouldn't be anything left for you to do at the scorer's table. (You shouldn't have to get your warm-up jackets because you should have brought them into your locker room at halftime and left them there. You shouldn't have to sign the scorebook now because you should've signed it before the game. If you've got to fill out a pay sheet, etc., either do it before the game or have table personnel bring you the paperwork in the locker room.)

Once you've made your ruling and you're confident the scorer saw your signal correctly, jog off the court.

Because end-of-game situations are highly emotional, think of your own safety. Fans sometimes rush the floor, usually in celebration. Unfortunately, sometimes fans rush the floor to get at the officials. Immediately after the horn sounds and the game is over, remove your whistle from around your neck. That way no one can grab your lanyard to stop you from running away and it won't get accidentally caught on someone else's hand or clothing.

If you are closer to the locker room than your partner when the game ends, wait to make sure your partner gets off the court safely. Jog together. Ideally, game management or security personnel are waiting for you just off the court to make sure you get to the locker room safely. Use common sense and avoid trouble when leaving the court.

TROUBLE SPOTS

Perimeter shots
Since there are many desperation jump shots in end-of-game situations, there are many related concerns for officials. Among them: the three-point arc and fouls by and against shooters. You must get a good angle and avoid straightlining when a player take a jump shot in front of you.

When a player takes a jump shot, watch the player return back to the floor before turning your attention to rebounding action. That ensures you're watching the entire play, which may include a foul by a defender well after the shot is released.

Aggressive perimeter play
With defenders trying beat offensive players to spots, and dribblers penetrating toward the basket and trying to draw fouls, contact is likely to occur. Did the defender establish legal guarding position? Did the dribbler push off? Watch for defenders handchecking and offensive players extending elbows.

Screens
Whether on-ball or off-ball, watch for illegal screens. Was the defender afforded proper spacing? Did the screener extend an elbow or leg into the path of the defender? Did the defender push through the screen?

Low post play
Play in the low post can get very physical, especially when battling for the position to receive a lob or baseball pass. Watch for defensive players pushing post players in the lower back. Also look for the defensive player's knee in the post player's backside. Watch for the post player pushing off the defender by extending an arm or elbow when receiving the pass. Also watch for the post player who has the ball to illegally hook the defender with an arm or elbow while spinning around the defender.

Rough post play is a point of emphasis. However, you should have cleaned it up in the first three quarters rather than continue to deal with it in the final seconds of the game.

Double teams
Double teams, especially on-ball, are usually aggressive. Watch for the backside defender fouling the player with the ball. Also watch for the offensive player splitting the defenders by pushing or hooking a defensive player.

Penetration toward the basket
Since dribbling is one way to beat a defense, watch for dribbling-related violations, especially at the start of a play. Know the offensive player's pivot foot and watch for carrying the ball (illegal dribble) on cross-over moves.

After a dribbler beats a defender to the basket, many things can occur. Look for the beaten defender to grab the dribbler from behind. Watch for other defenders stepping into the dribbler's path to help stop the dribbler. That's when your most likely to see block/charge and pass/crash plays. ·

Players drawing fouls
Players who fake contact create problems for officials. Watch for dribblers leaning into defenders; watch for shooters jumping into defenders. A player leaning a shoulder in either case is a pretty good clue.

Offensive players are not the only ones that try to draw fouls. Sometimes defenders "flop" after mild contact trying to draw fouls. A general rule on flops: If the defender flies backward and the offensive player's momentum does not go forward toward the defender (for example, the offensive player doesn't even step toward the defender during the fall), the defender likely flopped. If the offensive player's momentum carries into the defender, a legitimate foul may have occurred. Don't react to the flopper's fall; see the entire play and no-call it if appropriate.

One play related to the flop is the "pull down." Similar to the flop, the flopper waits for mild contact from the opponent and, while flopping backward, grabs the opponent's arm, leg or jersey to pull opponent on top of the flopper. That turns mild contact into apparently severe contact, often drawing the foul in the flopper's favor. Don't fall for it.

Offensive rebounding
If time allows, the offensive team will take a shot with a few seconds remaining, leaving enough time for an offensive rebound and shot or tap. Watch for offensive players crashing the boards and pushing defenders from behind on a missed shot. The offensive rebounder has little to lose and will gamble that the officials will resist calling fouls near the end of the game. Don't swallow the whistle on that one. If an offensive rebounder crashes through a defender to get the ball, call the foul.

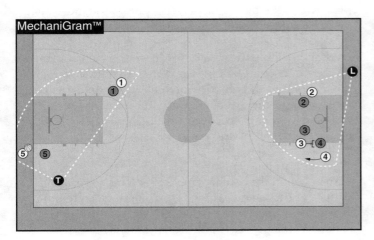

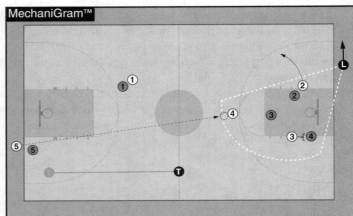

Action on the court:

⑤ has ball on the endline for fullcourt throw-in play. ③ screens ④. ④ rolls to top of the key.

③ screens ④. ⑤ passes to ④. ② moves to three-point arc.

Lead Official Responsibilities

Primary: Off-ball. Watch players in lane area. Watch ③ screen ④.

As ④ catches pass and ② swings to three-point arc, adjust to sideline for proper angle.
Primary: On-ball. Watch ④ catch pass from ⑤.
Secondary: Off-ball. Watch players in lane area.

Trail Official Responsibilities

Administer bounce pass throw-in using boxing-in method.
Primary: On-ball. Step away from thrower; watch thrower.

Advance quickly toward division line after throw-in is released.

KEY

L LEAD OFFICIAL

T TRAIL OFFICIAL

PRIMARY COVERAGE AREA

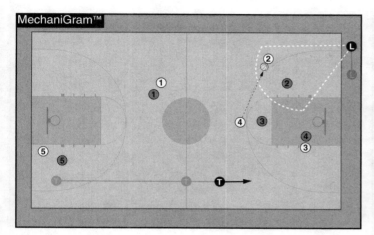

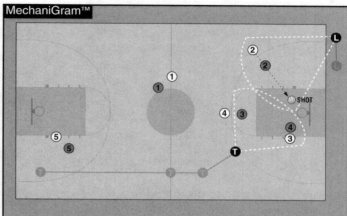

④ passes to ②.	② shoots.
Primary: On-ball. Watch ④ pass to ②.	**Primary: On-ball.** Watch ② shoot. Determine two- or three-point try.
Advance quickly toward top of the key.	**Primary: On-ball.** Watch ② shoot for clock judgment purposes. Give the three-point attempt if released with time remaining on the clock. Give the no-score signal if the horn sounded before the release. **Secondary: Off-ball.** Watch players in lane area. Observe weak-side rebounding.

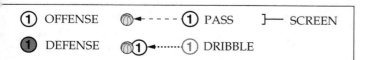

① OFFENSE   ◉◂----① PASS   ⊣— SCREEN

① DEFENSE   ◎①◂·······① DRIBBLE

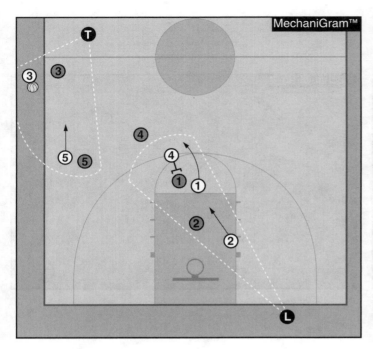

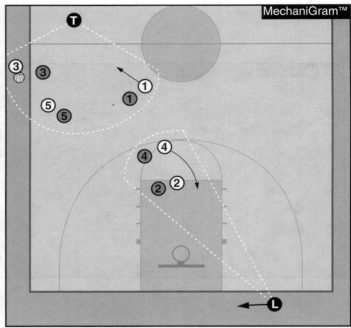

Action on the court:

③ has ball for throw-in near division line. ⑤ breaks toward ③. ④ screens ❶. ① rolls toward jump circle. ② moves toward free throw line.

① moves toward ③. ④ rolls toward basket.

Lead Official Responsibilities

Start wide.
Primary: Off-ball. Watch ④ screen ❶.

Primary: Off-ball. Watch ④ roll toward basket.
Anticipate lob pass.
Move toward nearest lane line.

Trail Official Responsibilities

Administer bounce pass throw-in using boxing-in method.
Primary: On-ball. Step away from thrower; watch thrower.

Primary: On-ball. Watch thrower.
Secondary: Off-ball. Watch players above top of the key.

KEY

L LEAD OFFICIAL

T TRAIL OFFICIAL

PRIMARY
COVERAGE
• AREA

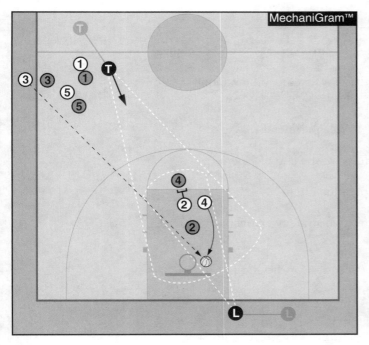 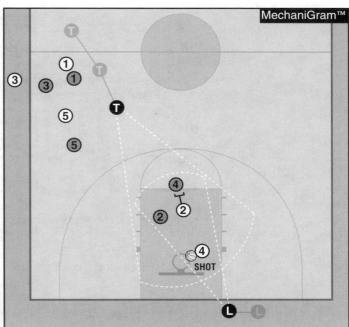

② screens ④. ③ throws lob pass to ④.	④ catches lob pass and shoots.
Primary: Off-ball. Watch ② screen ④.	**Primary: On-ball.** Watch ④ catch and shoot. **Secondary: Off-ball.** Watch players in lane area.
Primary: On-ball. Watch ③ pass to ④. Penetrate toward endline for angles.	Penetrate toward endline for angles. **Primary: On-ball.** Watch ④ shoot for clock judgment purposes. **Secondary: Off-ball.** Watch players above top of the key. Observe weak-side rebounding.

 **Review**

Last-second Shot

• Many last-second shots are related to throw-ins at the end of games.

• When a throw-in does not start the play, usually either a long pass or individual dribble penetration precedes the last-second shot.

• Off-ball screens are used heavily to free perimeter players.

• Lob and baseball passes are common at the end of a period.

• A last-second shot is often a desperation attempt.

• Pressure the passer is a good defensive strategy against last-second shots.

• Talk with your partner during a timeout near the end to check responsibilities.

• Review procedures with table personnel.

• Relax.

• Communicate with the players.

• Call the first foul and get the ball in play quickly.

• The trail is usually responsible for the clock.

Quiz

Without referring back, you should be able to answer the following true-false questions.

1. The trail is never responsible for the clock.

2. Every foul under the one-minute mark should be ruled intentional.

3. You should signal the goal (or no goal) immediately.

Chapter 24

Odds and Ends

Odds and Ends

The following items will help you in your games.

GLANCE AT THE CLOCK

Each time a whistle blows to stop the clock, quickly glance at the clock to see the time. Before glancing, however, make sure players' actions are under control; you don't want to look away from the players if there's a potential problem among them.

Both officials should glance. In fact, the off-ball official may have a better chance to glance more quickly since that official is not involved with action around the ball.

In addition, glance at the clock just before allowing the ball to become live. Obviously, the time that was on the clock when the ball became dead should be the same as the time when the ball next becomes live.

By gathering clock information, you are fully prepared if the clock malfunctions or if time is run off the clock — accidentally or intentionally. It takes some discipline to develop this good habit, but once accomplished, glancing at the clock becomes second-nature. Your efforts will pay off the first time you confidently — and correctly — handle a clock problem.

HANDLING THE LOOSE-BALL SCRAMBLE

Bad things happen when basketball players act like wrestlers. That's what happens when the ball squirts along the floor and players dive for it. A loose ball scramble is among the most dangerous plays for players and officials. It also leads to cheap shots, trash talking and fighting.

The scrambles are going to happen in just about every game; it's the results of the scrambles that dictate whether your game goes well or not. There are some things officials can and should do to ensure loose ball plays don't lead to problems.

Understand player tendencies

Before you're even faced with a loose ball situation, think about what the players are likely to do. When the ball goes down to the floor, so do the players. Their aggressiveness picks up as they dive for the ball. Often, opposing players arrive simultaneously. Other players also dive in to join the fray. Once the ball is in player possession, opponents try to pry the ball away. The player with the ball swings elbows to assert control. Rarely does a loose ball play involve only two players.

You must judge each situation as it pertains to the entire loose ball scenario. By thinking about what the players are likely to do, you'll be better prepared to respond when they do it.

Understand the rules and philosophies

Review all the rules that pertain to loose ball situations. For example, what's the call when a player dives for the ball, controls it while sliding and slides a few feet? "Nothing yet" is the right answer, despite what you'll hear from coaches, players and fans. If the player rolls over to gain an advantage you've got a traveling violation. Go over play rulings to ensure you know what to do when it happens.

Contact foul philosophies should not change when a ball is loose, yet they often do. A ball on the floor does not give a player the right to push, hold or charge into another player. Illegal contact happens most often when players not directly involved in the play dive in a moment later to get their money's worth. Call the foul.

Blow your whistle quickly

Whether you've got a violation, a held ball or a foul, once you've got something blow your whistle quickly to prevent further action. That doesn't mean you invent a held ball simply because bodies are on the floor. Sounding your whistle does help prevent problems, for example, when two players are wrestling for the ball. When you blow the held ball quickly in that situation, the players tend to stop pulling at the ball and swinging their elbows.

The covering official penetrates

Advance toward the play when a loose ball scramble occurs in your area, closer than you normally would on most plays. Why? When players are wrestling on the floor, tempers flair. You want a striped shirt to be the first thing a player sees when the player is in a pile. The player is less likely to throw that extra elbow or say something derogatory when the player knows an official is right there on top of the play.

Consider dropping to a knee and placing your hands *gently* on the players, letting them know you are there. Talk to them firmly, using positive statements, like, "Good hustle! Now relax." For liability reasons, do not push players to the ground or hold them down. If you're going to touch them, do so gently and for communication purposes only. If you push a player in the back too hard while the player is looking elsewhere, the player will probably think it's an opponent, not an official, and react negatively with words or, worse, with an elbow or punch. Just like dealing with a football running back who is at the bottom of a pile, urge that player to remain calm while others roll off. If the player at the bottom is pushing to get out, problems escalate quickly.

SAFETY NOTES: Do not move in on the play too quickly. If only two players are involved in the loose ball, more players will be joining in soon. If you get in too quickly you could have players diving for the ball and contacting you instead. Your anterior cruciate ligament won't be happy when a player slams into the side of your knee. Also remember the tendency for players to swing elbows once they possess the ball. Don't get too close and catch one accidentally. When moving in to break up the pile (after the whistle), be sure your whistle is out of your mouth so the lanyard doesn't get caught or tugged and loosen your teeth.

The non-covering official stays wide
When you're not the official immediately involved in the play, it is imperative you stay back to keep the entire scene and all players within your field of vision. With your partner going into the trenches, you're responsible for watching all that happens around your partner, including players that are immediately behind your partner. If both officials go diving into the fray, that leaves players unwatched and trouble brews quickly. Plus, by staying wide you can better see the action of the extra players diving in and make judgments on fouls. Keep an eye on the bench, too, when a scramble occurs in front of a team area. The last thing you need is a player on the bench kicking or holding an opponent.

Get play started again quickly
The non-covering official likely has a better view of the possession arrow and can point the proper direction quickly while talking to the partner. Sometimes the official involved in the scramble gets disoriented and loses track of which team is going in what direction. That's why the non-covering official must communicate clearly.

Give the ball to the thrower-in as soon as possible. The quicker the ball is in play, the less time there is for the players to mingle, stare down and trash talk opponents. They've got to get back on defense!

Anticipate a cheap shot on the ensuing play
If you followed the other points above, you've done a great job preventing a physical situation from developing into a problem. The new problem is that certain players have long memories. For example, the player at the bottom of the pile may not have been able to deliver that extra elbow during the scramble because the covering official moved in quickly. The player may then try to get even on the next play down the floor. You're obviously looking for problem players all the time, but pay special attention to the players involved for the first few plays after a scramble. If the cheap shot is going to happen, the delivering player will likely take a chance early.

Talk about it during your pregame
Review the loose ball scramble as part of your thorough pregame conference with your partner. You'll handle the situation better when it happens.

KEEPING TRACK OF ALTERNATING-POSSESSION

Keeping track of the alternating possession arrow in your mind can be a difficult task. Once in a while the arrow ends up pointing in the wrong direction — sometimes intentionally.

There's an easy way to keep track of the arrow while on the floor. Carry a spare whistle or air needle (used to take air out of the game ball, if necessary) in your pocket. Keep the whistle or needle in the pocket that points the correct direction of the alternating-possession arrow when you are standing facing the scorer's table. When facing the table and the whistle or needle is in your right pocket, you know the team going to your right gets the ball, and vice versa. When the arrow correctly changes, simply switch the whistle or needle to the other pocket. You'll always know who is supposed to get the throw-in even if there's a "mistake" at the scorer's table.

ADVANCING ON THE FOUL

"Advancing on the foul" means moving toward the area where the foul occurred. There are two main reasons you should advance on the foul: Acceptance of the call and preventive officiating.

Acceptance of the call
When you call a foul, the farther you are away from the foul, the less likely the call will be accepted without comment from the offended coach or player. Perception is important. If you are in the vicinity of the foul, your ruling has a better chance of being accepted.

In most situations, if you already have proper spacing on the play you only need to advance on the foul a step or two. That's especially true for the lead in a halfcourt setting since most fouls the lead calls will be in the lane area.

The trail, on occasion, must advance on the foul a greater distance, especially when the trail is off the sideline and watching the area above the free-throw line extended in a halfcourt setting. A general rule: As a trail advance on the foul no less than half the distance from where you are to the spot of the foul. If you're already in good position and have maintained proper spacing, you may only need to advance on the foul a step or two. Do not advance too closely to the fouler. Advancing up to the fouler appears aggressive and confrontational.

When you see the foul, hold your fist raised above your head and simultaneously blow the whistle. When advancing on a foul, move toward the spot of the foul with your fist raised above your head only. In NFHS games, do *not* move toward the spot using the fist up and opposite hand pointed to the fouler's hip (see "Signals chart," p. 39); use that signal only for clarification of who the foul is on and after you've reached a comfortable spot closer to that player.

The speed with which you advance depends on the distance you must travel and the need to sell the call. If you're a great distance away and must sell the call, sprint when advancing on the foul. If you're already nearby and are only advancing a few feet, a walk or slight jog is all that's necessary. If you run at the foul all the time you'll be overhustling and appear confrontational and aggressive. Again, do not advance all the way to the fouler.

As the lead in a halfcourt setting (especially if you're a short official), you may want to advance from the out-of-bounds area and onto the court when signaling a foul. That ensures players, coaches, fans and table personnel will see what you've called and not lose you in the crowded lane area.

Preventive officiating

The only time it's acceptable to advance all the way to the spot of the foul is when you're trying to prevent something negative from happening. The best example is the hard foul. When a player is fouled hard (especially an airborne player), tempers tend to flare. That's especially true when a player (or players) is knocked to the floor.

When a hard foul occurs or when players get knocked to the floor, anticipate a negative reaction from the fouled player. The fouled player may say something derogatory or attempt to retaliate.

When you sense possible retaliation, advance all the way to the spot of the foul and position yourself between the combating players. Use your voice to help calm the situation, saying things like, "I've got the foul," or, "That's enough." If the fouled player sees you're in the immediate area and hears that you've taken care of business by calling the foul, the fouled player is less likely to retaliate. Your proximity alone may prevent a fight.

Stay near the trouble area for an extra second or two to ensure players are calm before heading to the table. Before leaving the spot, make sure your partner is performing good dead-ball officiating by closely watching the players.

WHISTLE CONTROL

Think of the whistle as a communication tool. It's really just an extension of your voice and your signals. Blowing the whistle loudly has the same impact as screaming; blowing the whistle softly equates to whispering. A "normal" whistle blow is as if you were talking in a normal tone of voice.

When stopping the clock (using either the open-hand or closed fist overhead signals), simultaneously use a sharp, strong whistle blast. There's no need to blow the whistle many times with short blasts; that doesn't communicate anything of substance and draws unnecessary attention to the call. Officials who blow the whistle many times while making a single call are generally showboating. It's not needed.

SUBSTITUTIONS

Blowing the whistle while beckoning in a substitute is debatable. Some supervisors want officials to blow their whistle when beckoning all substitutes. Why? The whistle gets the attention of the substitute and the official's partner, letting both know the substitution is taking place.

Other supervisors don't want officials blowing the whistle when beckoning in substitutes. Why? Blowing the whistle is demonstrative and draws attention to the official. Plus, with good signals and eye contact, the whistle isn't needed.

Here might be the most obvious *Referee* recommendation in this book: Do what your supervisor wants. If there is no supervisor or no decision on what method to use, *Referee* recommends blowing the whistle only when there is some confusion as to when the substitute shall enter or when the substitute can't hear your voice or see your signals. On most substitutions, it's not necessary to blow the whistle.

TIMEOUTS

When a team requests and is granted a timeout, use a slightly longer whistle while signaling the timeout. That longer whistle distinguishes a timeout from a normal whistle blast that stops the clock.

DOUBLE-WHISTLES

Some play movements have both officials briefly watching the same player(s). That's especially true with on-ball coverage in a halfcourt setting in the lane area. Sometimes both officials blow the whistle at the same time. By following the correct procedure, you'll avoid the embarrassment and confusion of having one official signaling one thing and the other signaling something else at the same time.

There's a general rule for double-whistles: If the play is moving toward you, you have the call. If the play is moving away from you, you give the call up to your partner.

Following correct signal procedures is critical with double-whistles. If you don't, you'll probably have an unwanted double call. It's important to take the time to use the correct signal to stop the clock (either open hand or fist overhead, depending on the call) and simultaneously blow your whistle. If you hear your partner's whistle, quickly make eye contact before signaling anything else. You and your partner will likely need to penetrate on the play and quickly tell each other what you've got. Again, in most cases, the official who the play is moving toward likely takes the call.

An exception is if the official who has the play moving away has a foul or violation that occurred before the partner's whistle. Here's an example that occurs often in a halfcourt setting: A1 drives the lane. B2 attempts to gain legal-guarding position and take a charge. A1 jump stops just before B2, but significant contact is made. B2 did not establish legal guarding position. The lead judges the blocking foul and signals to stop the clock with a closed fist overhead and a whistle.

At the same time, the trail also watched A1 drive the lane. The trail saw A1 commit a traveling violation while trying to jump stop *before* the contact with B2. The trail judges the travel and signals to stop the clock with an open hand overhead and a whistle.

Both officials hear their partner's whistle. Before either of them makes another signal, they move closer together to talk about the play. The lead, who normally would take the call because the play is moving toward the lead, says "I've got a block." The trail says, "I've got a travel *before* the block." The lead's arm lowers and the trail takes the call because the travel happened before the block. The trail then signals (and sells) the traveling violation.

Imagine the confusion if the officials didn't use proper signals or make eye contact! You would have had the lead signaling a block at the same time the trail was signaling traveling. Nothing good comes out of that.

Understand that most double whistles occur in the lane area. When you make a call in that area, expect that there might be a double whistle and quickly glance at your partner before signaling the type of foul or violation. Knowing where double whistles tend to occur helps when you can't hear your partner's whistle because of crowd noise or the noise of your own whistle.

Disciplined signals, good eye contact and verbal communication eliminate double calls on double whistles.

THE WHISTLE IS A TOOL

Use your whistle as a tool to your advantage. Think of it as an extension of your voice. Blow it louder than normal when you really need to sell something. Use a strong, short blast in most situations. Avoid blowing a soft whistle. Just like soft signals that aren't crisp and clear, soft whistles convey that you're not sure about what you've called. Make sure your whistle blasts exude confidence and control without going overboard.

GET THE BALL IN PLAY QUICKLY

One of the great aspects of basketball is that the action is nearly non-stop. You can take advantage of that and help the game move along smoothly by getting the ball in play quickly after a stoppage.

When the ball is dead and little is happening on the court, it's prime-time for trouble. Players stop worrying about offensive plays and defensive schemes and start focusing on other players or the officials. The same is true for coaches. When the ball is dead they've got little to worry about and begin unnecessary conversations with opponents and officials.

When the ball is dead, get the ball back in play as quickly as possible without rushing or sacrificing duties. The faster the ball gets back in play, the more likely players and coaches return their focus to the game.

Here's an example: You've just whistled a violation after the dribbler stepped on the endline. The dribbler is unhappy because the dribbler thought there was a push before the violation. The dribbler begins complaining to the covering official. Then, the coach chimes in. What's the quickest way to end the conversations? Get the ball back in play as soon as possible. When you put the ball back in play, the dribbler must now get back on defense. The dribbler and the coach still may not like your call, but they'll have less chance to talk to you about it. That keeps you out of trouble and keeps the game moving.

HELP ON OUT-OF-BOUNDS CALLS

Sometimes you know the ball went out-of-bounds, but you don't know who touched it (or was touched by it) last. You can look to your partner for help, but there's a specific procedure that should be followed.

When needing help
When you see the ball is out-of-bounds, stop the clock using the open-hand above head signal. Do not point a direction. Immediately make eye contact with your partner. Keep holding your hand up.

When helping
When you see your partner still has an open hand raised overhead, hasn't pointed a direction yet and is making eye contact with you, your partner didn't see the play and is looking for help. If you know the correct direction, immediately give a strong directional point. Do *not* give a sneaky, small hand signal with your thumb extended against your body in front of your torso or a head nod indicating direction. There's nothing to hide: Your partner didn't see the play clearly and needs your help. Using sneaky signals make it look like you're trying to get away with something instead of simply getting the play right.

When no one knows
If your partner looks to you for help and you didn't see it clearly either, tell your partner that and make no signal. The calling official then immediately gives the jump ball signal and gives a directional-point signal favoring the team with the alternating-possession arrow, which is awarded a throw-in.

Helping on an out-of-bounds call is a quick process. Do not hesitate when asking for help or when helping. In most cases, there's no need to get together with your partner and discuss it. Make the call and get the ball back in play as quickly as possible.

CHANGING CALLS

Referee could write another entire book on the philosophy of changing your partner's call. There are definitely debatable pros and cons.

The first step in correctly changing a call is having the right attitude. Lose the word "overrule" from your vocabulary. You are not overruling your partner; you are helping your partner get the call right. That's a subtle yet critical attitude difference. Officials who have an overruling attitude tend to makes calls out their area and try to dominate the game. Officials who help their partners do so only in very rare instances. Maintaining the proper attitude will help alleviate over-officiating.

Procedures
When an incorrect call is made, the *calling* official makes the change, not the helping official.

Following correct procedure, the helping official blows the whistle and simultaneously uses the stop the clock signal with open hand overhead. The helping official then runs toward the calling official. That's an obvious indicator to the calling official that something may be amiss.

The helping official then asks the calling official, "Did you get a good look at the play?" That initiates a quick conversation about what happened. The helping official then tells the calling official what the helping official saw. The *calling official* makes the decision on how to handle it. If the calling official changes the call, only the calling official makes the new signal.

The helping official should never make the call, especially from the area where the helping official started the play and without talking to the calling official.

Here's an out-of-bounds play example: The ball bounces out-of-bounds in front of the lead and the lead signals it's team A's ball for a throw-in. The call is clearly wrong because the ball bounced off of A2's leg before going out-of-bounds. The trail saw the entire play correctly.

Using the correct procedure, the trail blows the whistle, signals to stop the clock (even though the clock is already stopped) and runs toward the lead. The trail asks the lead if the lead got a good look at the play. A quick discussion ensues and both officials state what they saw. If a change is to be made, the lead makes the correct signal. The trail helped the lead get the play right.

In that play, the trail should never just stand in the trail's spot, blow the whistle and signal team B's ball. The discussion is necessary because there's always a chance the trail didn't see the end of the play correctly. The decision is the calling official's only.

Here are some general guidelines for changing calls. Each play, however, must be judged on the impact that a change has on the game.

ONLY OBVIOUS MISTAKES SHOULD BE CORRECTED

We're only talking about a call that everyone in the building knows is wrong. The helping official must be 100 percent certain the calling official is wrong before offering up the suggested change. "I think it went off of 24," is not acceptable. "I clearly saw the ball go off of 24," is acceptable. The helping official must see the entire play clearly to offer an opinion. If you're 99 percent sure, that's not good enough.

Overall, you should only have to help an official change a call a few times a season. Any more than that and either you're over-officiating or your partner's not doing a very good job.

The change must have a positive impact on the game
Do not change things just to change them. Think about the long-term ramifications of changing the call. Is it good for the game or will every judgment by either official from that moment forward be questioned by players and coaches who want an "overrule?"

In almost all cases, only change out-of-bounds calls
Judgment on fouls and floor violations should almost never be changed. You don't want to have a debate about a block/charge out on the court. Let the official who made the foul or violation call live or die with it, then talk about it after the game.

Out-of-bounds calls are generally the easiest to change because sometimes the calling official doesn't have a great look at a ball flying out-of-bounds, especially through the lane to the endline. Help is expected and commonly accepted. Still, changing the call happens rarely.

Incorrect rule applications should be changed
Rules applications are different from judgment calls. If you know your partner is getting a rule wrong (like administering an intentional foul throw-in at the division line instead of at the spot of the foul), step in immediately and get it right.

Whether or not a change is made, get the ball back in play quickly.

CALLING OUT OF YOUR AREA

Calling things out of your normal coverage area is a controversial practice. Officials who try to dominate the game by making calls over the whole court, regardless of coverage area responsibilities, are bad for the game. They over-officiate and are not always watching what they're supposed to be watching. They certainly are not fun to work with.

In rare instances, however, it's OK to call something that's not in your normal coverage area. There are two key factors: The play has got to be blatantly obvious and the call has to be "good for the game." What does that mean? If the foul or violation went uncalled, game control would suffer immensely.

Sometimes your partner's view is blocked on a play; sometimes, your partner just freezes for whatever reason and doesn't react to a play. Be ready to make a call out of your area if it's obvious and good for the game. You must, however, have seen the entire play clearly to make a call. That should rarely happen if you're doing what you're supposed to: watching off-ball areas, etc.

Making a call out of your area should happen only a few times a season. If it happens more than that, you're either over-officiating or your partner's not doing a very good job. If you do make that call, sell it and get the ball back in play as quickly as possible.

MEET WITH YOUR PARTNER AFTER TECHNICAL FOULS

Technical foul situations can sometimes get emotional. If you're the calling official, you can occasionally get confused when figuring out which team shoots at which basket. It's embarrassing when you begin walking to one end of the court then halfway there figure out you're about to shoot at the wrong end. Beyond embarrassing, you look like you don't know what you're doing.

Alleviate that problem by meeting briefly with your partner near midcourt before walking in either direction. That meeting should take place after the technical foul is reported to the scorer. The non-calling official, after making sure all players are calm and there is no continuing action after the technical foul, walks up to the calling official and tells the calling official which basket to walk toward.

Why meet? The non-calling official is less emotional and can think about which direction to move while the calling official handles the problem and reports. The brief meeting ensures you're moving in the right direction.

GET BOTH COACHES TOGETHER

Sometimes a coach calls a timeout just to talk to you or your partner about the officiating. Once in a while it's a legitimate rule question. Most of the time, however, the coach is either complaining about your officiating or about the tactics of the other team's players. Other times the coach is trying to "schmooze" you by talking nice to you.

Coaches will sometimes try to bait you into a conversation by starting it out as a legitimate rule question, then turning it into a complaint about the other team. It's all a part of that coaching fantasy game they call "working the officials." One way to eliminate that conversation: Once you read the conversation is not going in a good direction and it's turned into complaining about the other team, stop the conversation and tell the coach that you're going to go get the opponent's coach to come over and hear the conversation. In almost all cases, the complainer will stop because the coach doesn't want the other coach to know what was said. The "working" stops.

Use the technique carefully: Bringing two coaches who hate each other together at an emotional time in the game may not be good for the game. In the right situations, however, it works well.

Also, get the coaches together when something strange happens and both deserve an explanation (usually a bizarre rule or after a fight situation). Make sure your partner is also listening to the conversation so you've got a witness to what was said if you need one later.

REPORTING DISQUALIFICATIONS

In a 2003-05 mechanics change, the NFHS now wants the non-calling official to report the disqualification. The non-calling official, after being informed of the disqualification, tells the coach first and then the player.

Coaches have 30 seconds to replace disqualified players and many times they'll use the entire time to give instructions to their players. Sometimes they'll use the entire time to slowly make the change in some sort of protest, thinking that the slow change upsets you. On occasion, they'll use the 30 seconds to voice their displeasure.

You must make sure they are given only 30 seconds. Immediately after informing the coach of the disqualification, make eye contact with the timer and tell the timer to start the 30-second clock (you may even want to point at the timer so you're seen on videotape starting the 30-second clock). Then, move away from the area. As soon as the substitute reports to the scorer, get the game moving again. Don't let the coach use any remaining time to instruct players. Get the ball back in play as soon as possible.

Chapter 25

Postgame Review

Postgame review

After the game, it's a good idea to review what happened during the game. The postgame review is another important part of the learning process.

The first order of business immediately after the game is to relax. Officiating can be stressful and postgame relaxation helps get you back to normal.

At a reasonable time after the game, review the game with your partner. Some like to review before taking a shower and relaxing. Others like to wait until the postgame dinner. Do whatever is convenient and comfortable for you and your partner.

When reviewing the game, talk about:

Points of emphasis

Were the pregame points of emphasis handled effectively. Many times, rough play is emphasized. Did you control the game effectively? Were off-ball fouls called appropriately? If the points of emphasis were not handled properly, discuss remedies for your next game.

Tempo

Did you let the game come to you or did you assert yourself when you didn't need to? Did the game develop a flow? If not, is there anything you could have done to keep the game moving? Did you get the ball back in play quickly without rushing?

Bench decorum

How did you handle the benches? Did you let the coaches go too far? Were you approachable?

Strange plays, rulings

Discuss and review any strange plays or rulings. If necessary, confirm your ruling with the rulebook and casebook. Make sure you've got the rule down so you can apply it correctly if it happens again.

Solicit constructive criticism

One of the ways to improve is to get opinions and advice from others. Your partner is a great source. Always ask if there's anything you could have done differently or better.

After asking, accept the constructive criticism. Don't be one of those referees that asks, "How'd I do?" expecting a shower of praise. If you don't want to know the truth, don't ask. Take the criticism offered, analyze the comments and apply the changes if you feel it's appropriate.

Be ready to offer a critique when asked. It's frustrating for an official who wants to learn to invite criticism only to hear, "You did a good job." There must be something that needs improving! You ought to be able to give your partner at least three things to think about after every game.

Write a journal

Consider keeping a journal during your season. Write down strange plays, your feelings about your performance, notes about your partner, things you did well and things you can improve on. The journal is a great way to look back during and after the season to see if there are patterns. If the same things keep appearing in your journal, you know there are things that need to be addressed.

Reviewing the journal is also a great way to start thinking about officiating before next season.

IF YOU LIKE THIS BOOK, YOU'LL LOVE THIS MAGAZINE!

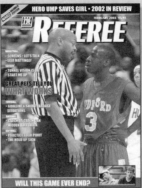

The only magazine exclusively for sports officials

Rulings, caseplays, mechanics – in-depth

Solid coverage of the sport(s) you work

Important, late-breaking news stories

Thought-provoking interviews and features

Opinions/editorials on vital topics